# FAMILY SCRIPTS

# FAMILY SCRIPTS

*Edited by*
**Joan D. Atwood, Ph.D.**
*Coordinator, Graduate Programs in Marriage and
Family Therapy
Hofstra University, Hempstead, New York*

**ACCELERATED DEVELOPMENT**
*A member of the Taylor & Francis Group*

| USA | Publishing Office: | ACCELERATED DEVELOPMENT<br>*A member of the Taylor & Francis Group*<br>1101 Vermont Avenue, N.W., Suite 200<br>Washington, DC 20005-3521<br>Tel: (202) 289-2174<br>Fax: (202) 289-3665 |
|---|---|---|
| | Distribution Center: | ACCELERATED DEVELOPMENT<br>*A member of the Taylor & Francis Group*<br>1900 Frost Road, Suite 101<br>Bristol, PA 19007-1598<br>Tel: (215) 785-5800<br>Fax: (215) 785-5515 |
| UK | | Taylor & Francis, Ltd.<br>1 Gunpowder Square<br>London EC4A 3DE<br>Tel: 0171 583 0490<br>Fax: 0171 583 0581 |

**FAMILY SCRIPTS**

1 2 3 4 5 6 7 8 9 0   B R B R   9 8 7 6

This book was set in Times Roman by Harlowe Typography, Inc. Technical development and editing by Cynthia Long. Cover design by Michelle Fleitz. Printing and binding by Braun-Brumfield, Inc.

A CIP catalog record for this book is available from the British Library.

♾ The paper in this publication meets the requirements of the ANSI Standard Z39.48-1984 (Permanence of Paper)

**Library of Congress Cataloging-in-Publication Data**

Family scripts/Joan D. Atwood, editor.
   p.  cm.
   Includes bibliographical references and index.
   1. Family psychotherapy.  2. Schemas (Psychology)
 3. Constructivism (Psychology)  4. Family—Psychological aspects.
 I. Atwood, Joan D.
 RC488.5.F33354  1996
 616.89′156—dc20
                                         96-1037
                                            CIP

ISBN 1-56032-411-2 (case)
ISBN 1-56032-401-5 (paper)

Dedicated to John H. Gagnon, Ph.D.

# TABLE OF CONTENTS

# LIST OF FIGURES

# INTRODUCTION

## SOCIAL CONSTRUCTION

When we consider knowledge is rooted in our way of seeing the world, when we accept a given item as known, we also are accepting the validity of many rules for establishing the reality of truth as something that exists outside of ourselves. Generally, we are unaware of these rules, or the particular "world" in which they belong. And generally we do not think about the means by which these worlds become established and how they can be challenged and overturned. The examination of such social constructions—definitions of reality under which individuals and their families operate—is one purpose of this analysis. A second purpose is to analyze various current socially constructed family scripts and relate them to the social worlds in which they are anchored.

Berger and Luckmann (1966), in their classic work *The Social Construction of Reality*, described the human origin of social realities very simply as a process by which individuals who repeatedly confront a task or situation relevant to their lives develop habitual ways of dealing with it. A situation once typified this way, leads to the development of roles, or functions, which cooperating partners or family members perform in connection with the task involved. The dialectical relationship between personal realities and social constructions is a recurring focus of this book. Often the individual brings his or her personal reality into line with the social constructions. The personal reality becomes a basis for seeing, accepting, attacking, or rejecting these social constructions.

## SOCIAL SCRIPTS

The notion of scripts first was introduced by Gagnon and Simon (1973) in reference to sexuality theory. In a series of articles, Gagnon and Simon challenged Freudian theory that posed the reduction of sexuality to a biological explanation. They believed instead that individuals are like actors with parts in scripts, which exist for the sexual life as they do for other areas of life. By scripts they meant a repertoire of acts and statuses that are recognized by a social group, together with the rules, expectations, and sanctions governing these acts and statuses.

It is this notion of social scripts that forms one of the basic tenets of the theoretical formulations proposed in this book. Human beings expect their lives to follow certain scripts, and they make efforts to follow these scripts. Human beings try to make their experiences congruent with these scripts, sometimes even reinterpreting their reality so as to make it fit them better. These scripts are usually recognizable to us: "the good mother," "the good husband," "the happy marriage." While there are perhaps gaps, such as when we are in between scripts (i.e., identity transition during divorce), scripts provide us with a general idea of how we are supposed to behave and what is supposed to happen.

## SOCIAL CONSTRUCTION OF FAMILY SCRIPTS

Social constructions include not only the routines and the scripts for educating or socializing youngsters in the system, but also the means for maintaining the definitions of reality on which scripts are based and the subjective loyalty of the family members. In applying the idea of social constructions to the area of family, a major assumption is that family behavior is scripted. "Family scripts" refers to the repertoire of acts and statuses that are recognized by the social group, along with the rules, expectations, and sanctions governing these acts and statuses. Theses are the dominant scripts that define family lives in this society. Constructions and scripts that compete with the dominant ones are on the periphery of each person's life, barely visible. Generally, alternative scripts are not as salient and are denigrated or denied. This denigration and denial has the function of maintaining the dominant constructions and scripts and preventing others from appearing as options. Therapy that flows from this view involves assisting families in bringing to light and developing these barely visible alternative constructions and scripts.

# COVERAGE

This book is more that an introduction to issues in family therapy. It focuses on the most current theoretical issues in the field and presents practical techniques and information for family therapy. Each chapter follows a basic constructionist epistemological therapeutic stance and integrates this new second order epistemology into practical, understandable techniques. The topics that are included were selected because of their frequent appearance in therapists' offices.

Although this book is comprehensive in its treatment of the subject areas identified in the table of contents, all topics in the field of family scripts are not included. The topics selected were those that we believed most students and colleagues experience in their professional lives. They are included because of their high frequency in the family therapy situation. The chapter format identifies the integrating theoretical theme and indicates that the approach is both theoretical, practical, and applied. The goal was to give both students and seasoned family therapist a new view of what they might need should they be confronted with a variety of clients presenting any one of the problems identified in this book. The intended audience for the book is marriage and family therapists, psychiatrists, psychologists, psychiatric nurses, social workers, and graduate students in these disciplines. Thus, the book can be utilized by any mental health and human service professional. The format is unique in that it presents a new model dealing with specific family issues in therapy using specific case study examples.

The model developed and presented in this book is based on many years of experience. The issues and problems presented are viewed as part of the family's struggle to learn and grow. The treatment strategies and interviewing techniques described are those that therapists could use while working with families who are having these types of problems. All case material is real but disguised, originating from the authors' clinical practices. thus, because the book represents a combining of the two disciplines of social construction theory and family therapy, it is a book appropriate for those who are learning about or beginning family therapy as well as those who have many years of experience wit family issues in therapy.

*Family Scripts* not only teaches the most current theoretical knowledge base in family therapy but also presents the theoretical framework while considering the most current research. In addition, therapeutic practice issues are presented and illustrated by case material. The book bridges the gap between family therapy techniques on the one hand and very current social psychological theory on the other. the family therapy view alone provides a practical, concrete approach to family problems that in many ways helps to foster rapid change. However, it sometimes lacks a view of the development and maintenance of the family's meaning system process. This deeper understanding of the family process is provided by the social construction/scripting approach.

An instructor could use several different approaches to teach the course. For example, an instructor could decide to teach an applied course in family counseling rather than taking a theoretical approach. In this case, the instructor would focus on various strategies that are used with families facing various problem situations rather than focus on the differences between the major theoretical approaches. Each chapter in this book contains a strong section on the practical application of theoretical principles. Another approach is to teach the theoretical foundations of family therapy. In this sense the professor would focus on the specific family scripts and meaning systems typically operating in each problem. another approach to teaching the course is to focus on similarities and differences among the different theoretical approaches. For example, an instructor could emphasize the more traditional structural or strategic assumptions, approaches, and interventions versus social psychological orientation. An instructor could focus on the specific family issues rather than on the family relationship or vice versa. The strength of the book, however, lies in its integration of the two fields. Each chapter in this book contains a strong theoretical section, along with a current review of the relevant research in the area.

In my opinion, the main criteria that instructors use in selecting a text are: Is the book comprehensive? Does it cover what the instructor feels it should cover? Is the text a good supplement to the lectures? Does it provide students with recent coverage of the issues and research in the field? Is the level of analysis sophisticated enough for the students who will be attending the class? The main problems that instructors would face in teaching such a course would be the selection of material they wish to present to the students in order to provide them with a good basic background in family therapy.

The other audience who would use the text, mental health professionals, will welcome such a text for similar reasons: it offers them a model that integrates meaning systems, family scripts, and family therapy; it offers a very current up-to-date literature and research review and presents the review with helpful practice techniques illustrated by in-depth case presentation. Often, professionals in the filed were trained in disciplines other than family therapy. Their original training was in psychology, sociology, or social work. Many times they have private practices that mandate a family oriented approach. These professionals, understanding their lack of systemic training (which only is offered in the relatively new marriage and family therapy programs), often find themselves floundering, trying to learn how to deal with families in an effective way. This text will be very helpful to them in that it will explain many of the theoretical principles underlying constructionism and systems theory (the bases of marriage and family counseling) that were lacking in their own training (primarily because they did not exist at the time) and would illustrate through case material various ways of intervening. More importantly, though, this text represents a truly integrative approach in that, for the first time, the two fields are combined in a comprehensive framework.

*Family Scripts* represents an expansion in the family therapy field in that, via presenting very practical therapeutic techniques, it also present a social constructionist theoretical stance in dealing with family issues.

## PURPOSE

Another goal of the book as being a teaching and learning aid is to teach students to deal with families who are experiencing problems in living from leading edge social constructionist theory standpoint. Yet another goal is to provide students with a general overview of social constructionist theory and to explore the social scripts that flow from this theory. This represents a unique contribution to the field. This will assist students in understanding and appreciating the importance of the social environment in the shaping of each individual's family script.

# APPROACH

The approach to the book is both theoretical and applied. This approach represents another one of its strong points. After an introduction to the theoretical knowledge base, each chapter presents the topical area, discusses the theoretical implications of the specific type of family issue, and presents a thorough discussion of the literature. In man cases, a case history is presented explaining the theoretical application in a clinical setting. And finally, there is a thorough discussion of therapy techniques and intervention strategies.

# SUMMARY

The field of family therapy has grown into a new developmental stage of life (perhaps adolescence), where it is questioning existing assumptions and realities of the traditional family therapy theory models. In so doing, it has embraced the social construction theory of Kenneth Gergen (1991), emphasizing the importance of language and the social environment. Theorists only recently have applied this theory to therapeutic situations. To this I add the notion of scripts. No one has applied it to family therapy situations. If we are to go forward as a field, we must expand our theories in a practical sense to assist people with problems in living. The present proposal addresses this significant problem.

# REFERENCES

Berger, P., & Luckmann, T. (1966). *The social construction of reality.* New York: Irvington.

Gagnon, J.H., & Simon, W. (1973). *Sexual conduct.* Chicago: Aldine.

Gergen, K.J. (1991). *The saturated self: Dilemmas of identity in contemporary life.* New York: Basic Books.

# Chapter 1

# SOCIAL CONSTRUCTION THEORY AND THERAPY ASSUMPTIONS

*Joan D. Atwood*

You live in a universe; and within you, you form pictures of the universe as it appears to you. And you know nothing of that universe and can know nothing except for the pictures. But the pictures within you of the universe are not the universe.
A.E. van Vogt (*Omni*, February, 1986, p. 31)

In all societies, there is a worldview (a story) according to which all is understood and evaluated. This worldview shapes our attitudes, incorporates new knowledge, dictates the form of our methodologies, and acts as the context through which we process all knowledge. It determines which measuring techniques we will invent to better understand the concepts we have invented about our behavior. When we consider knowledge as being embedded in our way of seeing the world, when we accept any given item or event as known, we are also accepting the notion that there is a reality of truth—something that exists outside of ourselves. In general, we are unaware of these rules, or the particular "world" in which they belong. We do not think about the means by which these worlds become established; nor do we think about the ways they can be challenged and overturned. Worldviews become questioned when faced with alternative views. Recently, an alternative view has emerged in the field of marriage and family therapy. This chapter explores the historical development of the new worldview, describes social construction theory and presents a model for psychotherapy.

# PSYCHOTHERAPY

## Pathology Models

Up until approximately the 1800s, most theoreticians believed, based on Newtonian physics, that there was an objective reality—a world "out there" waiting to be discovered. In the early pathology models, behavior was seen as the external manifestation of internal characteristics, traits, and conflicts (i.e., the delusions of a paranoid schizophrenic were deemed to result from the projection of his or her own unacceptable sexual and aggressive drives) (Masterson, 1976). Later, the field of psychotherapy evolved to a problem focused (behavioral, systemic) or a problem-solving stance. Here behavior was explained within a causal or functional system. "I did x because he did y" or "He does x in order to protect his parents from arguing."

Traditional psychological approaches adhere to first order cybernetics such that objectivity is assumed; there is a singular truth and if we dig deeply enough we can discover it; there is a search for "scientific" predictable essences and structures; the therapist is a rational, objective expert who discovers "facts" and prescribes corrective measures, and if the client does not agree with the therapist's view, he or she is in denial or being resistant. (If this occurs, the therapist is then justified in confronting the client or in imposing ideas or assignments on the client.) In this view, in order that the therapist can best know how to deal with the problem or the problematic person, the therapist gathers assessment information, assuming that detailed information about the problem, its cause, its history, its frequency, will lead to ideas about solutions. This view further assumes that psychological qualities or emotional qualities exist as measurable entities and that there is a standard or normative criteria for determining mental health. Therapists operating from these assumptions take the position of experts, gathering information as a basis for planning interventions and for identifying deficits, weaknesses or wounds. Therapy in this worldview then attempts to change, remediate, or heal. For the traditional therapist, truth is knowable, normality is identifiable, and both are able to be discovered (Gergen, 1985, 1988, 1992).

**New Epistemologies**

With Einstein's (Capra, 1983; Zukav, 1989) notions of relativity and Heisenberg's (1958) uncertainty principle, the predictable, reductionistic universe was pulled out from under us. The finding that human observations at the quantum level could actually change what was being observed moved us into a new way of understanding and "seeing." The resulting paradigmatic shift (Kuhn, 1970) infiltrated the social sciences in the sixties and now, supported by Maturana's (1980) research and Gergen's (1985) theory, has made its way into the family therapy literature as constructivism and social constructionism, the new epistemology or second order cybernetics, holding profound implications not only for family therapy theory but also for family therapy practice.

Constructivism is not new and may be traced back to philosophers Kant (Atwood, 1992), Hume (1934), Wittgenstein (Atwood, 1992), and Husserl (Nathanson, 1963). Piaget (1951) and Kelly (1969) represent the proponents from psychology. Biologists, Maturana (1980, 1987, 1988) and Varela (1979, 1981); cybernetician and biophysicist, von Foerster (1981a, 1981b, 1984); physicists, Heisenberg (1958) and Prigogine and Stengers (1984); constructivist, von Glaserfeld (1984); anthropologist, Bateson (1972, 1978, 1980, 1991); and finally the social psychologists, Cooley (1902), Mead (1934), Berger and Luckmann (1966), Reiss (1981), and Gergen and Gergen (1983, 1988), who, taking into account the larger sociocultural environment, also contributed to the notion that our knowledge about the world is constructed by the observer. In family therapy, the proponents of the new epistemology include Dell (1982), Keeney (1983), Keeney and Ross (1985), Tomm (1987), Anderson and Goolishian (1988), and Hoffman (1987, 1990). Constructivism and social constructionism represent the new epistemological explanations of how we know what we know.

Both constructivists and social constructionists believe that how we know what we know is *not* through an exact pictorial duplication of the world, "the map is not the territory." Rather, reality is seen experientially, in terms of how we subjectively interpret the constructions (von Glaserfeld, 1984). In this sense, we are responsible for what we believe, feel, and see. What this means is that our story of the world and how it works is *not* the world, although we behave as though it is. Our experiencing of the world is limited to our description of it. von Foerster (1981a, 1981b, 1984a, 1984b) stated, "If you desire to see, learn how to act [take action]." Using language (languaging) is action, and it is through languaging that persons define and experience reality. It is, therefore, through languaging in therapy that an environment conducive to change is created.

**Solution Focused Approach.**   In response to the deficit approach to problems based on first order cybernetics and in response to the developing postmodernist milieu, the solution focused therapies (deShazer, 1991; Dolan, 1991; Lipchik & deShazer, 1986; O'Hanlon & Weiner-Davis, 1989; Walter & Peller, 1992) then appeared. Postmodernism is philosophically rooted in Nietzsche's views that there are no facts, only "interpretations," that each perspective originates from a "lust to rule," and that claims to "truth" mask the workings of the "will to power." The postmodernists of the quantum world assume that our relations with the world do not always correspond with the world, the way we explain the world arises from active cooperation of persons in relationship, whether or not knowledge is maintained depends on social exchanges, and constructed meanings are social activities and are not separate from the rest of our social life (Gergen, 1988).

Solution focused therapists adhere to postmodernist assumptions, address and focus on the competencies and strengths of the clients, and thereby replace the deficit story with one of success. In this model, active participation in the solution by the client is required as the more positive aspects of the client's life become foreground—via finding exceptions—and the trauma or the problem fades into the background. See Figure 1.1 for a comparison of traditional/modernist and solution focused/postmodernist therapy assumptions.

de Shazer (1985) was one of the first theorists responsible for solution focused therapy. His work led him away from a focus on the problem in therapy to a focus on solution, which clients defined as more helpful. He stated that often the solution that clients constructed had very little to do with the problems that they presented but that it "fit" with the client's definition of the problem. Consequently, the therapy moved in a direction away from the therapist trying to understand the client's problem, and therefore trying to design a solution to it, to a focus on questioning the client about their own goals and exploring themselves as potential resources for problem solving. While doing this, Molnar and deShazer (1987) noticed that there were "exceptions" to the client's story—times when the problem was not happening. These therapists then focused on what that experience was like, when the problem was not happening, and developed the solution focused therapy model. This view, instead of focusing on the trauma/problem and its effects as do the traditional psychotherapies or the function of

| Traditional Approaches | Solution Focused Therapy |
|---|---|
| • Therapist is an expert—has special knowledge regarding the problem to which the client needs to submit (Colonialization/Missionary Model) | • Client and therapist both have particular areas of expertise (Collaborative Model) |
| • Client is viewed as damaged by the abuse (Deficit Model) | • Client is viewed as influenced but not determined by abuse history, having strengths and abilities (Resource Model) |
| • Remembering abuse and the expression of repressed affect (catharsis) are treatment | • Goals are individualized for each client, but do not necessarily involve goals of catharsis or remembering |
| • Interpretation | • Acknowledgment, valuing, and opening possibilities |
| • Past oriented | • Present/Future oriented |
| • Problem/pathology oriented | • Solution focused |
| • Must be long—term treatment | • Variable/individualized length of treatment |
| • Invites conversations for insight and working through | • Invites conversations for accountability and action and declines invitations to blame and invalidation |

**Figure 1.1.**   Comparison of problem/deficit models of therapy with solution focused models. From S. McNamee and K. Gergen, *Therapy as Social Construction*, p. 140, copyright © 1992 by Sage. Reprinted by permission of Sage Publications, Inc.

the problem as do the early systemic therapies, focuses on the competencies and strengths of clients.

Both these views, though, have in common an adherence to an either/ or perspective in that they tend to leave out the other half of the picture. In an attempt to correct this omission, the narrative therapies developed, with the goal to assist clients in *expanding* their reality rather than assisting them in *replacing* their reality. The newer models emphasized "in addition to" rather than "instead of."

**Narrative Therapies.**   Two strands of narrative therapies exist: one represented by a problem determined or collaborative language systems approach (Anderson, 1987; Anderson & Goolishian, 1988; Hoffman, 1990), and the other by the externalization approach (Epston, 1989; Tomm, 1987; White, 1989). White (1986, 1989), building on Bateson's (1972) notions of restraints, proposed a similar model of "alternate descriptions." As defined by Bateson (1972), restraints are the limitations that people hold—the beliefs, the values, that make it less likely for them to notice other aspects of their problem saturated lives. White termed these other aspects "subjugated knowledge." In so doing, he developed a narrative therapy through which people explore their ongoing story. Therapy in this sense involves assisting individuals in *reauthoring* their lives. Following White's tradition, one of this purposes of the book is to explore the processes by which individuals tell themselves stories, give themselves meanings, and interpret their behaviors.

# SOCIAL CONSTRUCTION THEORY

Although narrative therapy is used throughout this book, the approach to therapy used is more socially based, taking the socially defined meanings and scripts as the target for restorying. However, it is necessary to first explore the theoretical underpinnings of social construction theory, socially constructed meaning systems, and socially constructed scripts. Berger and Luckmann (1966) described social constructions as the consensual recognition of the realness and rightness of a constructed reality, plus the socialization process by which people acquire this reality. A social construction includes not only the routines and the mechanisms for socializing the children of the system, but also the means for maintaining the definition of reality on which it is based.

**Development of a Worldview: Social Routines**

As stated earlier, many of the insights into the nature of social constructions are derived from the work of Berger and Luckmann (1966). They described the origin of social realities very simply as a process by which individuals who repeatedly confront a task or situation relevant to their lives develop habitual ways of dealing with it. People recognize a situation as one that recurs, which then leads to the development of roles or functions that cooperating individuals perform in connection with the task involved.

If social arrangements are examined in detail, it is easy to see that each individual interaction involves processes of reciprocal accommodation and negotiations, with individuals making frequent attempts to disclose their own subjective reality and grasp each other's realities. At this small scale level, before the routines are institutionalized, the interactions between individuals appear to be fluid and flexible. They are adopted because they seem to work, and changing them requires no more than did the setting up of them—merely more communication.

Though one could define these arrangements as forms of social structure, the implication is not that they will last; nor do we have any indication of how long they will survive. At this rudimentary stage of social organization, social routines are heuristic devices; however, routinization is a small step away from the establishment of a problem-solving process in which all possibilities are considered. A routine is a solution to a problem that is available and on call. With continued usage of routines, over time, other elements of institutionalization develop. When speaking of full-fledged social constructions, the implication is that they contain all the stages of institutionalization: the consensual recognition of the realness and rightness of the constructed reality and the specification of the socialization processes by which people acquire the definition of the reality.

Just as routines are one step from spontaneous problem solving, the establishment of roles is one step away from ways of relating to total persons. For example, roles focus attention on some highlighted function or attribute of persons. To a degree, once roles are established, persons become interchangeable once they can fulfill the role expectations. Their identity is based according to their functions in the division of labor, rather than on them as total persons. If they perform these functions effectively, the need for communication, accommodation, and negotiation is reduced.

## Development of a Worldview: Social Constructions

Social constructions that have survived over time and have become standard are called institutions. Institutions have a history—they arise under specific material and historical conditions (for example, a war)—to which they are exactly the kind of heuristic solutions on which we have been focusing. They are products of individual agencies, not impersonal forces. Once they are reified, members of society lose sight of their origins and the related possibility that they may change. Members of society also forget that responses to problems can vary and carelessly slip into thinking that the form that they observe as a social institution is a response's only normal and/or natural form. This is similar to the assumption that often is made that the nuclear family, with father as breadwinner and wife and children as economic dependents, is the normal and best way of life. All other family forms are suspect. If problems appear to be associated with aspects of family life, the solution proposed is often to reinforce the dominant nuclear family form, rather than exploring new forms that might be more effective, in light of recent social and economic changes.

## Socialization: Getting Others to Share the Worldview

As previously stated, at a small scale level of analysis, individuals' interactions appear to be fluid and flexible. However, if individuals attempt to extend these social constructions, whether by including more individuals or by bringing in a new generation, much of the flexibility is lost. A new person who is to take part in the system must be taught the routines the others have worked out. The rules must be made explicit. Often in these situations, the system becomes frozen in its assumptions, and the new members perceive its features as absolutes, i.e., "This is the way things are." It is this understanding that is brought in by families entering therapy: they are "stuck" in their story and see no alternative ways of behaving. As Berger and Luckmann (1966) pointed out, the social structure they have inherited is "opaque" (p. 55). The ways in which it is constructed are invisible to individuals, as are the elements that compose it, and so they do not see the possibilities for combining these elements in new and different ways. Individuals seem to be unaware of the existence and characteristics of the social environment. Although social arrangements are developed with conscious intent, that intent is neither perceived nor questioned by those in future generations. They are accepted as ends in themselves rather than as means to ends.

**Socialization of Subjective Reality.** Socialization is the group of processes by which subjective realities and social constructions are brought into congruence. The social world we are born into is experienced by the child as the sole reality. Rules of the world into which we are born are nonproblematic, they require no explanation, and they are neither challenged nor doubted. However, as Foucault (1980) pointed out, the most powerful knowledge is often the most taken for granted. Through socialization, the socially constructed meanings are internalized; they are filtered and understood through meaningful symbols. Though socialization continues throughout the life cycle, it is primary (early) socialization to which we must ascribe the greatest impact (Berger & Luckmann, 1966).

**Socialization of Identity.** Through socialization, social constructions are internalized, and as experience is filtered and understood through meaningful symbols, the essence of individual identity is formed. Identity is built upon the foundation of family identity. The construction is the same as the construction of all identity: young children learn to use verbal labels for themselves and their behavior, as well as for others and their behavior. These labels then come to have the same meaning for the learners as they do for the "old hands." Social constructions thus embodied in the language shared within a group come to be embedded in the foundation of individual identities by means of language. Individuals observe their own behavior, judge it, and judge the behavior of others. In making these judgments, they use the scripts (the social plans of action) provided by society. The meanings of behaviors and the judgments that individuals attach to them are part of these scripts.

The evolution of identity thus involves individuals' attempts to match their experience with the available scripts. They learn not only the language that is applied to feelings and events, but also society's expectations for persons of their ages and genders. They learn reciprocal behaviors, attitudes, and postures expected of the opposite sex as well. In this way they learn and prepare to enact the scripts that are deemed appropriate by their culture.

A child is born into a social world that has the experienced characteristic of being the sole reality. To the young child, the family is the world. His or her mother is not simply a mother (i.e., one of many, one of a class), she is "Mother" (Berger & Luckmann, 1966, p. 124). The routines and the social arrangements are nonproblematic for the young child; they require no explanation, and they are neither challenged nor doubted. This suspension of questioning and doubt is not only functional for the society, but it simplifies daily life for those individuals involved. Any challenge to the individual's reality of the dominant social constructions serves to complicate the individual's life and ultimately society. Thus there are various social mechanisms in place in order to maintain the subjective credibility of the dominant realities.

The perceived absoluteness of subjective reality resulting from primary socialization appears to be a function of two factors: the cognitive immaturity of the young child and the effective quality of the teaching and learning that take place at this developmental stage. These early socializing agents (most often the parents) have control over important outcomes for the child, and the child's reliance on these early caretakers is total. They determine what and when the child's physical needs will be taken care of, which realities the child will be exposed to, and what conceptual tools the child will be given for solving problems. From the viewpoint of the child, he or she is physically, psychologically, and informationally dependent. This viewpoint affects the child's feelings of dependence and contribute to the perceived power of socializing agents and the probability of internalization (Jones & Gerard, 1967). Those individuals and events involved in subsequent socialization (teachers, peers, and/or media) have less power relative to the agents of primary socialization, and less monopolistic power simply because the child is not so completely dependent on them.

The other factor in the intensity of primary socialization is the emotional investment of caretakers in the child and in what they are teaching the child. This affective quality of primary socialization generally is not found in subsequent socialization, including formal academic education. The latter tends to be (at least in Western Cultures) deliberately affect free, objective, and impersonal. The reality claimed by such learning is "fugitive" and more easily bracketed (Berger & Luckmann, 1966, p. 131). An individual's reality is maintained by developing a personal sense of self that is congruent with the social constructions. Thus, based on early interactions and ongoing socialization, individuals construct realities around meanings that include a preferred way of relating to others. This then becomes the basis for how they view others and how they expect others to view them. In many ways, these perceptual sets determine predictable ways of interacting with others. The self is experienced as the most vividly real aspect of reality (Berger & Luckmann, 1966), and "reality" for the individual usually is perceived as unitary (Berger & Luckmann, 1966, p. 124). "Reality" is maintained by the kinds of social arrangements listed above and by a developing personal identity that is congruent with those social constructions.

**Meaning Systems**

Not only do social constructions contain routines and structures, they contain meaning systems as well. *Meaning systems* refer to the complex and unique definitions in each individual that can influence behavior. Meanings are components of interpersonal interaction. They originate in childhood and are maintained by ongoing interpersonal interactions. The meanings that events and behaviors have for individuals are determined by their social position and cultural indoctrination. Meanings can be individual (subjective), interpersonal (shared), and cultural (social). They are frames of reference for understanding—for making sense. The culture or subculture thus equips individuals with ways of understanding and judging many aspects of behavior, ranging from the biological functions of their bodies to moral systems. These ways of making sense of experiences are embedded in a worldview that is accepted as reality by all those around him or her and in the scripts that are part of the worldview.

Take for example the following vignettes:

**Account Number 1**

She awakened from a deep sleep, only to realize she was 15 minutes behind schedule. Skipping breakfast, she rushed to her car and drove to school. If she didn't hit any traffic, she would be on time for her class. Luckily the roads seemed empty and she didn't hit any traffic lights. She pulled into the university parking lot, noticing how empty it was. She then commented to herself on how many students had come down with the flu this year.

It was only when she walked into her empty classroom that she realized it was Saturday and she didn't have to go to class.

**Account Number 2**

She drove off the parkway because her car was making an awful sound and shaking all over. It appeared to be bumping down the street. She commented to herself how she must stop procrastinating and take the car for its needed tune-up. She was convinced that the dirty oil was clogging up the engine, causing it to bump.

It was only when the person in the next car gestured to the rear of her car that she realized she had a flat tire.

These kinds of interpretations presented in Accounts 1 and 2 occur every day, all day. Individuals attempt to make sense out of everyday life. Persons in the above accounts were fitting their experiences into their meaning systems, attempting to make sense out of experiences that appeared to be nonsensical. This making sense is an ever changing and ever emerging process. Processes we utilize in making sense out of our everyday life are socially constructed, are learned from and embedded in the larger socio-cultural environment, and operate at the social, interpersonal, and intra-personal levels.

**Maintaining Meaning Systems.**    A further developed social construction includes not only the routines and the mechanisms for educating or socializing the youngsters in the system, but also means for maintaining the definitions of reality on which it is based and the subjective loyalty of individuals. A community and a language that the community reaffirms as its dominant reality and the discrediting of competing social constructions are the two basic mechanisms that function to maintain the subjective reality of social constructions. Therefore, contact with both the community and its language must be consistent (Berger & Luckmann, 1966, pp. 117, 127). There must be face-to-face contact that repeatedly reinforces the desired definitions of individuals within the context of the social constructions in order for the subjective reality to be maintained. Moreover, competing constructions, even the awareness of them, must be kept at the periphery of each individual's life and identity. These alternative or shadow constructions tend to be denigrated or denied. This has the function of maintaining the dominance of the dominant or institutionalized constructions and preventing others from appearing as viable options. This has profound implications for application to family definitions. It is important to keep in mind that social constructionists believe that our explanations are not only created by individuals in society but are modifiable in the same way.

## Scripts

From these socially constructed meaning systems flow socially constructed scripts. Individuals' meaning systems determine the content of their scripts. A person attempts to match his or her own experience with the available meanings and scripts. In this way, the person learns the language and the appropriate behavior for his or her gender, age, and culture. Here too, as Reiss (1989) pointed out, scripts are intrapsychic, interpersonal, and cultural.

The concept of scripts was first discussed by Gagnon and Simon in 1973 when they introduced the idea of sexual scripts. In a series of articles, they challenged Freudian theory and the reduction of sexuality to biological explanations. Instead, they believed that we are like actors with parts in scripts. These scripts exist for all areas of life, including sexual life. Scripts are involved in learning the meaning of internal states, organizing the sequences of specific acts, decoding novel situations, setting the limits on responses, and linking meanings from other aspects of life to specific experience (Gagnon, 1990, p. 6). A script is a "devise for guiding action and for understanding it" (p. 6). Scripts are plans that people have about what they are doing and what they are going to do. They justify actions that are in agreement with their scripts and challenge those that are not. Scripts are the "blueprints for behavior," that specify the whos, whats, whens, and whys of behavior. ". . . Scripts constitute the available repertoire of socially recognized acts and statuses, and roles and the rules governing them" (Laws & Schwartz, 1977, p. 217).

Scripts operate at social, personal, and intrapsychic levels. They are embedded in social institutions and, as such, are internalized by individuals. The overriding, dominant scripts receive most attention because of their primacy and potency among people's options. It is against the dominant social scripts that people attempt to match or reject their own personal social scripts. But this match is never perfect, and what occurs in actuality is often far from the ideal. These ideal scripts are usually recognizable to us: "the good mother," "the good husband," "the happy marriage." By attempting to make our experiences in accord with our scripts, sometimes we only internalize part of the "ideal" script, or sometimes we reinterpret reality so as to make it "fit" the script better.

In addition, some areas of experience are unscripted. Here there is neither widespread comprehension nor common gauges to facilitate comprehension. Examples are when we are in between scripts, such as the identity transition that occurs during divorce, or in some of the family situations that are presented in this book, such as in backwards scripts, when a child dies before the parents. It is these situations where individuals tend to feel at a loss or report they feel out of control. Scripts also prepare us for events of the future. Rehearsal precedes performance, and while others may coach us or guide us in our parts, it is the social scripts that give us preparation for situations we are about to encounter. Through socialization, we learn the dominant scripts and the expectations that our lives will follow certain scripts. In Figure 1.2 is presented a model of the social constructionist worldview.

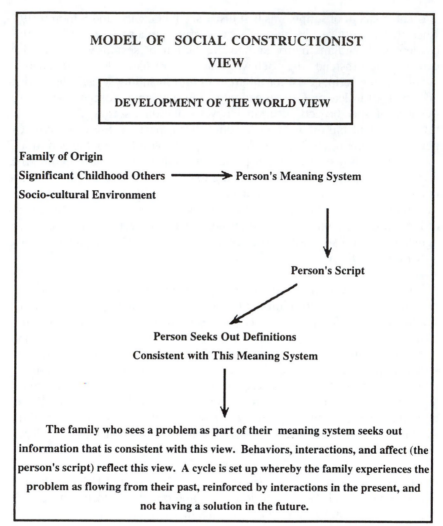

**Figure 1.2.**    Development of a worldview.

**Nondominant Scripts.**    The dialectical relationship between personal realities and social constructions is a recurring focus in this book. While the pluralistic nature of the contemporary American climate is emphasized, it is important to note that not every individual is equally aware of the existence of a variety of life scripts. An individual chooses a particular dominant script generally because of his or her location in the social structure. While some may know that certain other dominant scripts exist, others may not. By the nature of the social construction of reality, the received reality is the only reality; hence, what is different is not merely lacking in validity, but is either hard to imagine, unthinkable, or unacceptable.

So that while the sequences of life stages are scripted and the transitions tend not to be scripted within the dominant scripts, it is not apparent to most individuals that there could be other scripts at each stage. Our socialization makes areas outside the chosen dominant script appear vague—not relevant or appropriate choices. This though is an area that holds promise for the therapeutic setting for it is here where possibilities for new ways lie—in the other, opaque dominant scripts just beyond our view.

**Alternative Scripts.**    Although some persons follow the dominant scripts, this is not an automatic process, like growing taller. It is not a maturational process; it is a social one. Even the majority, for whom inner reality and social reality are in agreement, sooner or later encounter claims for the invalidity of dominant scripts. Any challenge to the accepted social constructions of reality presents a problem for individuals, but unless these alternative scripts have personal relevance for them, they will not be adopted. Even when the individual conforms to the dominant script, awareness of the other scripts has therapeutic relevance because awareness brings awareness of choice. And whenever choice is present, the automatic unquestioned acceptance of social constructions is disrupted. In most cases, the subjective reality of the dominant scripts remains unshaken with the force of primary socialization behind it.

While many individuals find the accepted scripts adequate guidelines for making sense of their own experience and thus form coherent identities basically in line with these scripts, for others, the available scripts do not fit their experience. Sometimes the personal reality becomes a basis for attacking or rejecting the social construction. Sometimes these events are not under our control, i.e., when there is chronic illness in a family member or when a child dies before the parent. It is a fact of the multiply scripted world that many individuals make unscripted transitions in the course of their life histories. And it is even possible to conceptualize a script for being scriptless.

Finding and articulating options outside the dominant script is more risky—both socially and psychologically—than to follow the dominant script. The development of identity for these people is more problematic. They usually suffer from an absence of validation as well as invalidation, or negative sanctions, imposed by those who assume roles in the dominant scripts. There is no standard language to describe or express experiences and identities that are not socially recognized. Consequently, it is difficult for individuals to communicate about such phenomenon. But as Berger and Luckmann (1966, p. 141) pointed out, without such communication, the validation of these experiences by others is practically impossible, and their reality, for lack of verbal recognition, becomes shaky.

Because of the social nature of constructed realities, it is difficult for individuals to achieve and maintain their identities in social isolation. In this case, such persons will generally submit or create alternative lifestyles. Communities where alternative lifestyles are sustained are often sought out or created by such individuals. These communities facilitate resocialization, which can be as intense a process as primary socialization and include mechanisms for displacing or discrediting the reality of the dominant script. This is evident in the lives of many homosexuals. Accounts of publicly "coming out" indicate the powerful process of personal change and the social influence when individuals assume a gay identity and join a gay community.

## Shadow Scripts

As stated earlier, the strength of some social scripts often disallows other scripts to be perceived. Persons use "selective noticing" of experiences, scanning the environment and taking in only those aspects that are in agreement with their socially constructed realities. But in the background, always present, primed to move forward if triggered, are shadow scripts, the scripts just beyond our view, those scripts within which the seeds of change lie. Shadow scripts follow Derrida's (1976) notion of "differance." *Differance* is the tension between what is said and what is not said. Shadow scripts are connected to individuals' dominant scripts because they are composed of the opposite, the trace, of what individuals present to others as their dominant script. They are composed of what is not said, behaviors that are not acted out, gestures that are not made. Therapy in this model then becomes the act of deconstruction, exploring the trace of the script, the part that exists because of the mere mention of the aspects of the person's dominant script. Shadow scripts contain fragments from the past, present, and future, and all exist just outside our awareness at the same time.

Similar to "subjugated knowledges" by White and Epston (1990) or "exceptions" by deShazer (1991), shadow scripts are the opaque elements or fragments that are just beyond our awareness. Shadow scripts are socially constructed and, as such, operate at all levels: the social, the meaning system, the behavioral, and the emotional. Shadow scripts are not similar in meaning to the unconscious because it is not that the individual is unaware of the shadow script; but rather, that the shadow scripts are just outside of, peripheral to, the person's awareness and, if triggered, are accessible. In Figure 1.3 is presented a comparison view of exceptions and shadow scripts.

**Past Shadow Scripts.**     Scripts of the past contain the fragments of our childhoods—those memories we hold that define for us our view of how we were reared, whether we had a happy or sad childhood, and whether we did well in school or not. These scripts are the explicit scripts of our childhood—those that are central to our perception, containing relatively clear definitions of what our experience of our childhood was like. Past shadow scripts are the implicit scripts of the past that are peripheral to our percep-

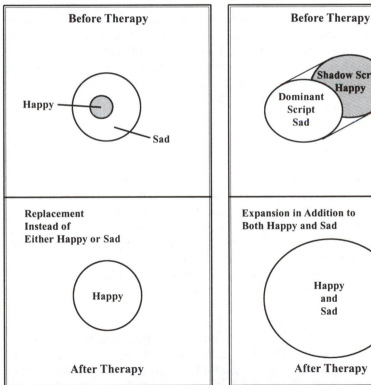

**Figure 1.3.**   Comparison view of exceptions and shadow scripts.

tion but that also affect our current meaning system or behaviors. An example would be implicit, nonverbal negative definitions of sexual expression modeled to us by our parents that affect our sexual expression as adults. While dominant scripts tend to be explicit and direct, shadow scripts tend to be implicit and covert. Shadow scripts represent what information was left out.

**Current Shadow Scripts.** Current scripts give us information about how to behave, what meanings events have for us, whom to date, etc. These are the dominant explicit scripts of society, transmitted to us by our families—the scripts that teach us appropriate meanings and behaviors. Current shadow scripts contain the traces of these scripts. If, for example, we have a current family script that the men in the family are strong, then each family member who has internalized this definition has also internalized the shadow script that contains a model for weak men, along with all the meanings that entails.

**Future Shadow Scripts.** Future scripts hold our vision of how things will be for us in the future. These are fragments of possibility, yet to be developed. Future shadow scripts are the traces of the opposite view. For example, a person could have a future script where he or she sees himself or herself as depressed and alone. This person's view of his or her future then also contains by definition the shadow script where he or she is happy and interacting with friends or family.

**Irrelevant Scripts.** Irrelevant scripts contain fragments of discarded scripts that are no longer relevant. For example, they simply may be age inappropriate, i.e., an adult jumping up and down on the bed. Or they could be role inappropriate—discarded pieces of a couple's premarital scripts, those behaviors, attitudes, or meanings that do not fit well with their newly developed couple script, i.e., going out with the boys on Friday nights. Not as frequent but still possible, irrelevant scripts might be socially inappropriate or unavailable, for example, the person who aspires to be a cowboy or a person who wishes to be a hippie in the '90s. These are the scripts that individuals are aware of, may have experienced, and have discarded because they are unavailable or no longer relevant. In times of stress, these scripts may become relevant again as the person struggles to solve problems. For example, a newly divorced person may revert to adolescent like behavior. In Figure 1.4 are summarized the different types of scripts available to individuals, and in Figure 1.5 is depicted how individuals are only aware of their dominant scripts. Other scripts available to them are either invisible, defined as irrelevant, or seen as inappropriate.

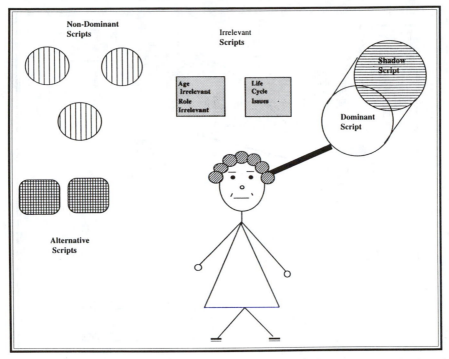

**Figure 1.4.** Many types of scripts exist. They are in constant flux and impact each other and individuals. However, people only "see" scripts that confirm their chosen social script. Shadow scripts contain the opposite, what is not in the dominant script.

## Shadow Scripts Applied to Couples

During dating and marriage, two separate individuals with two separate meaning systems and two separate sets of scripts develop, recognize, and negotiate a coupled or shared meaning system and script. This coupled meaning system now includes not only both of their individual scripts but also contains, like overlapping Venn diagrams (see Figure 1.6), their social scripts that define for them what it means to be a couple. Their view of what it means to become a couple may arise from a similarity in social background characteristics, but as Berger and Luckmann (1966) pointed out, it is more likely that it involves a negotiation of a shared process. Within the newly formed marital relationship, the languaging of the couple leads to new definitions of self, other, relatives, etc. Thus, the two individuals bring two separate scripts into their relationship, then negotiate a newly

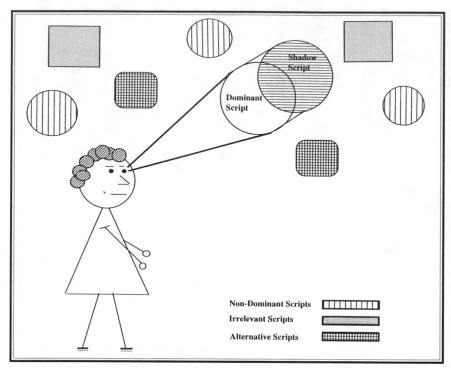

**Figure 1.5.** Depiction of how individuals are only aware of their dominant scripts. Other scripts available to them are invisible, defined as irrelevant, or seen as appropriate.

formed script as a couple. It is this "team" script that they now present to the social world, including their parents, in-laws, bosses, religious figures, etc. As the Venn diagram indicates, however, there still are parts of the diagram where there is no overlap—parts of the individual scripts. These are the remaining individual scripts, those parts that are reserved for when the individuals within the couple pursue their own interests or develop their own individual opinions about topics.

**Couple's Shadow Script.** Shadow scripts have enormous implications for therapy for they indicate from the beginning where the possibilities for change are. Shadow scripts are relevant for couple counseling. For example, a particular couple may have negotiated a couple script that contains what a good marriage entails. For them a good marriage might mean that each person is open to new ideas presented by the other. However, for the couple to have ideas about a good marriage, they also must have ideas about a bad

**Figure 1.6.** Depiction of how two individuals' scripts merge to form a third script, the couple script, when individuals marry.

marriage. That definition might include one or the other being opinionated. These definitions, the definitions that are the opposite of what the couple presents, are part of the couple's shadow script, existing peripherally just below their awareness.

Shadow scripts are also relevant for premarital counseling. Because of the high divorce rate in U.S. society, more and more couples seek premarital counseling. When the therapist asks each partner what he or she likes best about the other, therein lie the seeds of the shadow script—the potential trouble spots of the marriage. A partner who describes the other as having a quiet strength signals that there are traces of "not quiet" and "not strong." A partner who defines her fiancée as protective also announces to the therapist that there might be a time when she defines him nonprotective. The meaning system associated with this also has a shadow script. For example, if she feels safe and cared for when she defines him as protective in premarital counseling, she may later feel unsafe and unloved when she sees him as not protective of her.

Shadow scripts are also those pieces of information that simply do not fit with the individual's definition of the situation. They contain times when one partner felt the argument was unresolved; when the nonjudgmental husband expressed a critical statement; when the passionate, loving wife did not want to have sex; when the laid back wife had a temper tantrum, when one criticized the other in front of friends—all the times when the behavior was discrepant from the ongoing definition of a "good marriage." A couple in therapy because of a boring marriage indicates immediately to the therapist that they have notions of what an exciting marriage is. A couple who reports that there is no passion in their lovemaking verifies to the therapist that they have ideas about passion. These shadow scripts may contain intense emotional material and, similar to White's notions of restraints, require energy to keep them below the surface. Take, for example, the wife who defines her marriage as good and who finds some evidence that her husband is having an affair. When he tells her he is going on a business trip, it might take energy for her to retain her definition of her marriage as good. The more evidence she accumulates, the more difficult it becomes. Eventually the shadow script may become foreground in the relationship. In so doing, the meaning system has been altered as the definition of the "good marriage" changes. This process also works in reverse.

## SOCIAL CONSTRUCTION THERAPY

A model of social construction therapy will be presented based on the above theoretical formulations. Prior to this is a description of the basic premises of a social construction approach: "It is clear that the scripts that individuals bring to treatment exist at the intrapsychic and the interpersonal levels, and most, though not all, interventions involve changes."

### Basic Premises of a Social Constructionist Approach

- There are no absolute truths and there are no absolute realities.
- We co-construct reality through language with another in a continual interaction with the sociocultural environment. Thus, what is "real" is that which is co-constructed through language and interaction with

others in continual interplay with the surrounding sociocultural environment.

- In the social cultural environment are socially created scripts for behavior—those blueprints or plans of action that tell us about behaviors that are appropriate or inappropriate to the given culture.
- Through the process of socialization, which occurs through family interaction, children learn the dominant scripts in society.
- People do not incorporate these scripts in the same way. They tend to select out the information that corresponds to their individual, couple, or family scripts by noticing behavior in others that confirms their self-definitions and definitions of situations and by selectively ignoring disconfirmatory behavior.
- Always present in persons' backgrounds are shadow scripts, scripts that are just beyond their awareness. Shadow scripts contain traces, fragments, of what is not included in persons' awareness. They also could contain repetitive knowledge of behavior that is discrepant or contradictory with the individual's chosen dominant script.
- Shadow scripts hold possibilities for therapeutic change, for their exploration is likely to uncover new knowledges or "unique outcomes." Other possibilities for change are the irrelevant scripts—those that contain the fragments of early, no longer useful scripts; the nondominant scripts—the opaque, tenuous other dominant scripts present in the culture yet outside the person's dominant script; and the alternative scripts—those scripts in society that are not deemed appropriate or normative.
- Individuals, couples, or families who come for therapy are experiencing problems. They have tried many solutions—most of which have been unsuccessful. The problems they report are not seen as being functional in maintaining the system or as a manifestation of underlying pathology. They are seen as problems—problems that have negative effects. The way that individuals, couples, or families language about problems is the way they can use language to co-construct new possibilities.
- Social constructionist therapy focuses on exploring the family's view of the family to bring their shadow scripts to the foreground so that possibilities for new ways to view the family might emerge.

In Figure 1.7 is presented a summary of the therapy flowing from this view.

The view in this book is that of the social construction of scripts. It is assumed that a developmental aspect is dynamic rather than static. It is

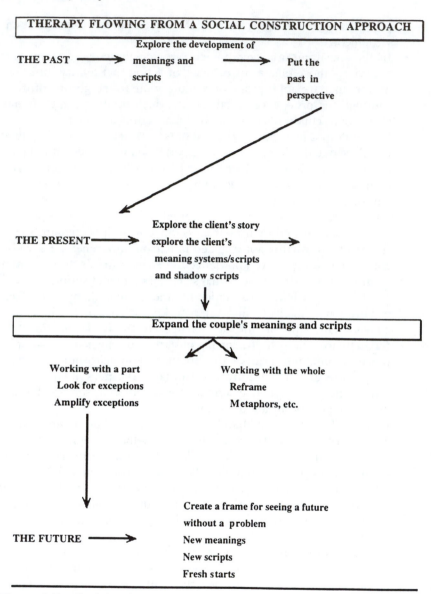

**THERAPY FLOWING FROM A SOCIAL CONSTRUCTION APPROACH**

Explore the development of

THE PAST ⟶ meanings and ⟶ Put the
scripts                                    past in
                                           perspective

Explore the client's story

THE PRESENT ⟶ explore the client's ⟶
meaning systems/scripts
and shadow scripts

Expand the couple's meanings and scripts

Working with a part                Working with the whole
Look for exceptions                       Reframe
Amplify exceptions                        Metaphors, etc.

Create a frame for seeing a future
without a problem
THE FUTURE ⟶ New meanings
New scripts
Fresh starts

**Figure 1.7.**   Social construction therapy.

assumed that change is normal and that choice has a part in change. Our knowledge about how to behave is patterned by family scripts that are in turn embedded in the larger sociocultural environment. It is assumed that multiple family scripts exist in society. However, while a number of family scripts are available to us, some of us are only exposed to some of the family scripts, and only some are acceptable to us. Here is where such factors as socioeconomic status, levels of education, multicultural factors, gender, and unique individual choice come into play. In this book, the editor's aim is to examine the prevailing constructions of some scripts that families bring to the therapeutic situation.

The focus of intervention is on meaning systems and scripts. It is most similar to Epston and White's (1990) recent work whereby the therapist initially assists the person in learning processes that help him or her to amplify (be aware of) process; provides techniques that the person can use to generate new possibilities; and creates a "safe environment" for the person to explore his or her process, generate new possibilities, consider the implications of these possibilities, and negotiate a frame around the chosen change. See also O'Hanlon and Weiner-Davis' notions of possibility therapy, which appears to represent ". . . a balance between acknowledgment of existing realities and the creation of new possibilities" (p. 7). These ways of learning then can be used by the person outside therapy. Over time, as the person learns to rely on his or her own self-healing processes, he or she becomes more confident in the processes and in his or her own abilities to generate growth and change. In this case, the result is new structures that are of a higher order—structures that are more connected and integrated than the prior ones. They are more complex, more flexible, and more susceptible to further change and development.

Stated throughout, the approach to family therapy presented in this book is based on the belief that we create our own reality. Individuals make sense of their ongoing experience, and it is this process of making sense that is the object of this therapy. Social construction therapy takes as its focus the client's meaning system, viewed from the past, present, and future, both negative and positive. The initial focus of the past is affective—understanding how the person's meanings developed and how the person believes these meanings affected him or her in the past. Once the past is put in perspective, the second focus of the approach is cognitive—on his or her scripts for behavior in the present, as well as on the shadow script and on the maintenance of the meaning system—helping the person, couple, or family to be aware of their processes and facilitating learning about and amplifying exceptions to the process in order to provide possibilities for new solutions. Future focus enables clients to image how different meanings and the resultant scripts could affect their lives. Re-visioning their lives, or their relationship, or their family is the last stage of this therapy and emphasizes future visions of life.

Chapter 2 continues to explore some of the theoretical concepts raised in Chapter 1 and provides the reader with an interesting view of "The Script as Life-form." The chapter later explores how some biological ideas have relevance for the field of psychotherapy. Chapter 2 concludes with a metaphor: script as externalized problem. The clinical implications are then discussed.

Chapter 3, Backwards Scripts, explores the times in life when the expected life script does not occur, such as when a child dies before a parent, becoming a parent before marriage, and widowerhood. Social construction therapy with backwards scripts is then presented, along with case material.

Chapter 4, I Demand a Rewrite, explores times when a child does not fit the parent's script, as occurs when a child is born with disabilities. The chapter is explored in terms of the effects of the diagnosis on the marital couple and the siblings. Parenting strategies are presented, along with clinical implications.

Chapter 5, A Multiscript Approach to Adolescence, discusses how the stage of adolescence developed historically and discusses the family life cycle implications. The authors then present three typical adolescent scripts and a model for therapy.

Chapter 6, Exploring Shadow Scripts in Couple Therapy, takes over where Chapter 1 left off in that it applies the notion of shadow scripts to couples. There is first a presentation of the assumptions of this appraoch followed by a description of therapy using shadow scripts. The chapter ends with an application of the theory to case material.

Chapter 7 discusses chemical dependency from a sociocultural context. Chemical dependency is explored in the early adolescent, later adolescent, and adult age ranges. In all cases, the interpersonal scripts are explored and therapeutic implications presented.

Chapter 8 discusses how the AIDS diagnosis in a family member impacts the family. The author suggests that the diagnosis of an HIV positive family member necessitates the devising and revising of life scripts. She explores the family's reactions to the diagnosis and describes the counseling process.

Chapter 9, Scripts for Family Violence, explores the social conditions necessary for family violence to increase. The authors present different types of family violence and provide the therapeutic implications for each.

Chapter 10 explores how mid-life occurances affect family relations.

Chapter 11 considers death as a developmental crisis requiring changes in person's scripts. The author presents this from first a traditional framework and then from a family scripts point of view. Clinical implications are considered throughout.

## A NOTE ON RESEARCH

In general, although family therapy has espoused the process of rigorous scientific research, this has occurred more in theory than in actuality and there is a need for models in family therapy to be empirically tested and examined. In addition, there is also a tendency by family therapy theorists (along with other mental health professionals who see themselves as the "soft sciences") to attribute more authenticity to biologically based events and more artificiality to psychologically or socially based events. For example, many have pointed out that if we compare the study of the family with the study of the aquifer, in examining the family, social forces certainly seem to be more apparent than they are in the explanation of the aquifer. However, if at some point we were to investigate and discover that the aquifer is not the inexhaustible natural resource we once thought it was, but in fact was in danger of extinction, we would have to develop new interpretations and explanations of it and develop new attitudes toward it. In addition, our "knowledge" of the aquifer in the next generation would also have to differ. It is a false dichotomy to regard the social as artificial and the physical as more natural, more real or true.

This false dichotomy in thinking can be particularly misleading in the analysis of the family. Even if we examine what we define as biological "facts," we learn that they do not have a direct effect on experience in humans. With infra human species, researchers have been able to demonstrate rather direct connections between hormones and behavior, but for humans, behavior is mediated by meaning systems. The decision to have a child for women in general is a direct function of the state of the relationship between the woman and her partner. Even the effect of childbirth, a seemingly nonsocial event, depends on social meanings that are attached to it. And we know from Durkheim (1951) that even suicide, a very individual act, is influenced by macrosociological factors. Looking to the "hard sciences" for "social realities" has led family therapists to neglect the study of the meaning systems of the persons. So that while we have accumulated data about who does what, with whom, and where, we still know very little about the ways people learn to consider themselves part of a family, a society, or even married or a parent.

To the extent that we relate to social or physical events in terms of meanings for us, we are acting on the basis of social constructions, that is, knowledge received through socialization.

The exploration of persons' social constructions—definitions of reality under which individuals operate—is one purpose of this analysis. A second purpose is to analyze various current constructions of family scripts and relate them to the social worlds in which they are anchored. A third purpose is to examine family scripts under deconstruction.

## BIBLIOGRAPHY

Andersen, T. (1987). The Reflecting Team: Dialogue and Meta-dialogue in Clinical Work. *Family Process, 26*(4), 415–428.

Atwood, J. (1991). Killing two slumpos with one stone. *Family Therapy Case Studies, 5*(2), 43–50.

Haley, J. (1976). *Problem-solving therapy.* San Francisco: Jossey Bass.

Madanes, C. (1981). *Strategic family therapy.* San Francisco: Jossey Bass.

Minuchin, S. (1974). *Families and family therapy.* Cambridge, MA: Harvard University Press.

Penn, P. (1985). Feed forward: Future questions, future maps. *Family Process, 24*, 299–311.

Watzlawick, P., Weakland, J., & Fisch, R. (1974). *Change: Principles of problem formation and problem resolution.* New York: Norton.

# REFERENCES

Anderson, H., & Goolishian, H. (1988). Human systems as linguistic systems: Preliminary and evolving ideas about the implication for clinical theory. *Family Process, 27,* 371–373.

Atwood, J. (1992). *Family therapy: A systemic behavioral approach.* Chicago: Nelson Hall.

Bateson, G. (1972). *Steps to an ecology of mind.* New York: Ballantine Books.

Bateson, G. (1978). The birth of a matrix or double-bind epistemology. In M. Berger (Ed.), *Beyond the double bind* (p. 97). New York: Brunner-Mazel.

Bateson, G. (1980). *Mind and nature: A necessary unity.* New York: Bantam Books.

Bateson, G. (1991). *A sacred unity.* New York: HarperCollins.

Berger, P., & Luckmann, T. (1966). *The social construction of reality.* New York: Irvington.

Capra, F. (1983). *The tao of physics.* New York: Bantam.

Cooley, C. (1902). *Human nature and the social order.* New York: Free Press.

Dell, P.F. (1982). Beyond homeostasis: Toward a concept of coherence. *Family Process, 21,* 21–24.

Derrida, J. (1976). *Of grammatology.* Baltimore: The Johns Hopkins University Press.

deShazer, S. (1985). *Keys to solutions in brief therapy.* New York: Guilford.

deShazer, S. (1991). *Putting difference to work.* New York: Norton.

Dolan, Y. (1991). *Resolving sexual abuse: Solution focused therapy and Ericksonian hypnosis for adult survivors.* New York: Norton.

Durkheim, E. (1951). *Suicide.* New York: The Free Press.

Epston, D. (1989). *Collected papers.* Adelaide, South Australia: Dulwich Centre Publications.

Epston, D., & White, M. (1990). Consulting your consultants: The documentation of alternative knowledges. *Dulwich Centre Newsletter,* 4.

Foucault, M. (1980). *Power/knowledge: Selected interviews and other writings, 1972–1977* (C.D. Gordon, Ed.). New York: Panthon.

Gagnon, J.H. (1990). Scripting in sex research. *Annual Review of Sex Research, 1,* 1–39.

Gagnon, J.H., & Simon, W. (1973). *Sexual conduct.* Chicago: Aldine.

Gergen, K. (1985). The social constructionist movement in modern psychology. *American Psychologist, 40,* 266–275.

Gergen, K. (1988). Knowledge and social process. In D. Bar-Tal & A.W. Kruglanski (Eds.), *The social psychology of knowledge* (pp. 30–47). Cambridge, England: Cambridge University Press.

Gergen, K. (1992). Toward a postmodern psychology. In S. Kvale (Ed.), *Psychology and postmodernism: Inquiries in social construction* (pp. 17–30). London: Sage Publications.

Gergen, K.J., & Gergen, M.M. (1983). The social construction of narrative accounts. In K.J. Gergen & M.M. Gergen (Eds.), *Historical Social Psychology* (pp. 203–233). Hillsdale, NJ: Erlbaum Associates.

Gergen, K.J., & Gergen, M.M. (1988). Narrative and self as relationship. In L. Berkowitz (Ed.), *Social psychological studies of self: Perspectives and programs* (pp. 17–56). San Diego, CA: Academic Press.

Heisenberg, W. (1958). *Physics and philosophy.* New York: Harper Torchbooks.

Hoffman, L. (1987). Toward a second order family systems therapy. *Family Systems Medicine, 3*(4), 381–386.

Hoffman, L. (1990). Constructing realities: An art of lenses. *Family Process, 29*(1), 1–12.

Hume, R.E. (1934). *The thirteen principal upanishas*. New York: Oxford University Press.

Jones, E., & Gerard, F. (1967). Families in developed countries: Determinants and policy implication. *Family Planning Perspectives, 17*, 53–63.

Keeney, B. (1983). *Aesthetics of change*. New York: Guilford Press.

Keeney, B., & Ross, J. (1985). *Mind in therapy: Constructing systemic family therapies*. New York: Basic Books.

Kelly, G. (1969). Man's construction of his alternatives. In R. Maher (Ed.), *Clinical psychology and personality: The second papers of George Kelly* (pp. 55–70). New York: Wiley.

Kuhn, T. (1970). *The structure of scientific revolutions* (2nd ed.). Chicago: Chicago University Press.

Laws, J., & Schwartz, P. (1977). *Sexual scripts*. Hinsdale, IL: Dryden.

Lipchik, E., & deShazer, S. (1986). The purposeful interview. *Journal of Strategic and Systemic Therapies, 5*(1), 27–41.

Masterson, J. (1976). *Borderline narcissistic personality: An integrated and developmental approach*. New York: Brunner/Mazel.

Maturana, H. (1980). Biology of cognition. In H.R. Maturana & F. Varela (Eds.), *Autopoesis and cognition* (pp. 60–83). Boston: Reidel.

Maturana, H. (1987). The biological foundation of self-consciousness and the physical domain of existence. In E. Caianiello (Ed.), *Physics of cognitive processes*. Singapore, Hong Kong: World Scientific.

Maturana, H. (1988). Reality: The search for objectivity or the quest for a compelling argument. In V. Kenny (Ed.), *Irish Journal of Psychology, Spe-*

*cial Issue on 'Radical Constructivism,' Autopoesis and Psychotherapy, 9*(1), 25–55.

Mead, G.H. (1934). *Mind, self, and society.* Chicago: University of Chicago Press.

Molnar, G., & deShazer, S. (1987). Solution focused therapy: Toward the identification of therapeutic tasks. *Journal of Marital & Family Therapy, 13*(4), 349–358.

Nathanson, M. (1963). *The philosophy of the social sciences.* New York: Random House.

O'Hanlon, W.H., & Weiner-Davis, M. (1989). *In search of solutions: A new direction in psychotherapy.* New York: Norton.

Piaget, J. (1951). *Play, dreams and imagination in childhood.* London: Routledge and Kegan, Paul.

Prigogine, I., & Stengers, I. (1984). *Order out of chaos: Man's new dialogue with nature.* New York: Bantam.

Reiss, D. (1981). *The family's construction of reality.* Cambridge, MA: Harvard University Press.

Reiss, D. (1989). *The social construction of the family.* New Brunswick, NJ: Rutgers University Press.

Tomm, K. (1987). Interventive interviewing: Part I. Strategizing as a fourth guideline for the therapist. *Family Process, 26,* 3–13.

Varela, F. (1979). *Principles of biological autonomy.* New York: Elsevier.

Varela, F. (1981). Describing the logic of the living. In M. Zeleny (Ed.), *Autopoesis: A theory of living organization* (pp. 45–70). New York: Elsevier.

von Foerster, H. (1981a). *Observing systems.* Seaside, CA: Intersystems Publications.

von Foerster, H. (1981b). On cybernetics of cybernetics and social theory. In G. Roth & H. Schwegler (Eds.), *Self organizing systems: An interdisciplinary approach* (pp. 55–67). New York: Campus.

von Foerster, H. (1984a). On constructing a reality. In P. Watzlawick (Ed.), *The invented reality* (pp. 40–71). New York: Norton.

von Foerster, H. (1984b). Apropos epistemologies. *Family Process, 24*(4), 517–521.

von Glaserfeld, E. (1984). An introduction to radical constructivism. In P. Watzlawick (Ed.), *The invented reality.* New York: Norton.

Walter, J., & Peller, J. (1992). *Becoming solution-focused in brief therapy.* New York: Brunner-Mazel.

White, M. (1986). Negative explanation, restraint and double description: A template for family therapy. *Family Process, 25*(2), 169–184.

White, M. (1989, Summer). The externalizing of the problem. *Dulwich Centre Newsletter.*

White, M., & Epston, D. (1990). Consulting your consultants: The documentation of alternative knowledges. *Dulwich Centre Newsletter*, 4.

Zukav, G. (1989). *The dancing wuli masters: An overview of the new physics.* New York: William Morrow.

# Chapter 2

# THE SCRIPT AS LIFE-FORM: PARASITES OF MEANING

*John Mince*

This chapter looks at the process of human scripts from a social constructionist point of view, specifically focusing on the coherence and change of scripts over time. In order to use the script metaphor in a specific manner, the author launches an attack on the dichotomy that has been constructed around modernism/postmodernism, discerning it to be a false dichotomy. A different stance is proposed, one that encourages tacking back and forth between modernist and postmodernist positions, using elements of both domains to create novel metaphors. The remainder of the chapter explores one such metaphor from the field of evolutionary biology. The concept of parasitism as an evolutionary aid is developed, and clinical implications for this extended metaphor are offered as potentially useful in therapy. While not a clinically oriented piece, this chapter offers clinicians another way to think about therapy, and the impact of scripted meanings on clients.

## BACKGROUND

In *As You Like It*, Act II, Scene 7, Shakespeare wrote the following:

> All the world's a stage
> And all the men and women merely players;
> They have their exits and their entrances;

And one man in his time plays many parts,
His acts being seven ages. (Hatcher, 1970)

This famous quotation suggests that for centuries humans have been aware of the power of the script as an organizing element within their lives. The idea that we live our lives partly based upon a number of scripts that have been written for us, or that we have cowritten, is not a new one.

Currently, the field of family therapy is entertaining this entire notion of both story and script through a proliferation of writings on social constructionism (Gergen & Davis, 1985), biological constructivism (von Foerster, 1993; von Glaserfeld, 1987; Efran, Lukens, & Lukens, 1990), and the place of narrative in the act of therapy itself (White & Epston, 1990).

This move from the cybernetic or systemic model toward the narrative or textual model indicates a much larger trend in family therapy. It demonstrates an engagement with a postmodern sentiment and renounces ideologies based upon either scientific or social hierarchies. It is a posture that looks askance at any discussion of structure or scientific findings in human affairs.

## MODERNISM VERSUS POSTMODERNISM

The concept of postmodernism does not imply simply an historical shift. The "post" of the term postmodern implies a far richer and more substantial shift in our thinking. We move away from the taxonomically structured and self-assured knowledge of modernist science, filled with hierarchical correctness and specified moral order, to a more open and randomly organized postmodern posture. The postmodern stance discerns that modernist scientific achievements have failed to produce the world they had promised. There is an increasingly wide recognition now that we humans are a part of every problem in the world and that we actually maintain these problems even while making efforts to solve them. Simple, clear answers based upon technological prowess are no longer considered possible.

Postmodernism often is seen as a viewpoint that allows for and encourages chaos, chance, confusion, multiplicity, and diversity. It searches for many answers instead of one. Rather than attempt to reduce the universe, it expands it in all directions at once. This can be experienced as a very hopeful, or very hopeless, stance depending upon to whom one speaks and which observational point of view one takes.

Distinctions between modernist and postmodern philosophy undergird the current movement in therapy toward narratives and meaning in family life as the most important elements, and downplay notions of family structure, balance, triangulation, and boundaries as purely structuralist conventions.

This chapter looks at the concept of script from this postmodern perspective, while at the same time borrowing a metaphor from biological sciences. We aim to dissuade any "purist" notions of postmodernism by allowing for wide-ranging metaphors and analogies, even if these come from the very sciences that postmodernism has eschewed. Thus our stance in this chapter is to write from the two postures at once, playfully.

Clearly, the distinction between modernism and postmodernism has been constructed in the literature as a dichotomy. But as a dichotomy it may be considered a false one. Consider for example the notion that modernism celebrates structure and that postmodernism celebrates breaking structure. Yet in the field of literature, Conte (1991) has demonstrated compellingly that postmodern poets have defined two new distinct structural forms for their postmodern poetry: the serial and procedural forms. Thus a new formalism arises out of the ashes of the defunct forms.

Watson (1993) has done the same for this modernist/postmodernist dichotomy in philosophy by demonstrating an historical overview of western philosophical thinking that indicates a cyclic occurrence in our thinking that has reiterated itself five times over the last 2,500 years. Watson found that philosophy has moved from questions of being (ontic), to questions of knowing (epistemic), to questions of meaning (semantic), and then back to questions of being again:

ontic > epistemic > semantic > ontic > epistemic > semantic

These kinds of analyses help us see that our current love affair with postmodernism in the writings of family therapists/theorists may be indicating our return to questions of meaning as the most important concern. Yet this focus on "meaning" may once again return to questions of "being" at some point in the future. Watson's work orients us toward a flowing, ongoing trichotomy rather than a static, reflexing dichotomy. Watson's ideas are reminiscent of Hegel's (Edwards, 1967) dialectic, which espouses another ongoing triplicate series:

thesis > antithesis > synthesis > thesis > antithesis > synthesis

Dichotomous notions such as "modern versus postmodern" are always somewhat suspect. They are quite transparent, from this author's point of view, as a set of overly convenient revolutions/revelations about the new, "correct" view replacing the old, "incorrect" view. Dichotomies reek of an oversimplification, one which arrives at distinction through opposition. Such bifurcated ideological revolutions are fundamentally flawed in their vision and sweep.

These revolutions engender the very elements against which the revolutionaries initially fought. Thus does the current modern-to-postmodern revolution fight itself. Literary postmodernist thinking now claims some sort of moral victory over modernist thinking even as it ironically indicates that it has no place for morality or ethics within its purview (Derrida, 1976).

Postmodernism may best be seen as a sentiment *against*, rather than as a verifiable set of new ideas for, the improvement of a culture. Modernism versus postmodernism is fundamentally a polemical device that should be reserved as appropriate to the domains of critical discourse and not as a definitive shift in worldview (Culler, 1975). A polemic is any interactional structure which engages people in argument and debate as the primary goal.

It is within the context of this ongoing dichotomous argument that the notion of script is placed. But ours will be a synthesis attempt, since we do not hold all science to be faulty nor all structure to be hierarchically evil. Rather, the present chapter hopes to pull disparate elements together from modernist and postmodernist perspectives. Therefore, nothing within the present work should be taken as "explanation" by the author about what "really is," but rather as a series of descriptions using metaphor that might prove useful to families and therapists alike.

## DIFFERENCES BETWEEN SCRIPT AND NARRATIVE

Narrative may be seen as the construction of an ongoing set of events including characters, plot, setting, and moral, all developed in a temporal sequence that leads somewhere semantically. That is, it yields meaning.

With the advent of social constructionism and biological constructivism arising within the sentiments of a postmodern epoch, therapists have become more concerned about utilizing the innate narrative productions of individuals, couples, and families as the primary foci for the therapy experience. Since social constructionism emphasizes the interactional aspects of narrative production, it is the client-plus-therapist that become the coauthors of new narratives that now solve or open up possibilities for solutions to the socially problematized narratives brought in to therapy initially.

The concept of script is somewhat different. The script implies an already written set of story lines. A script has a number of actors, places, situations, contexts, etc. that are utilized by an author to bring about drama and entertainment for an audience. The word script implies an actual handwritten document by an author and thus underscores the originality of the writing. The definition of script from Webster (Guralnick, 1980) is as follows:

> 1. handwriting; 2. a written document; original manuscript; 3.
> the manuscript, or a copy of the text, of a stage, film, radio,
> or television show.

Definition 3, script as copy of the text of a show, will be the one used primarily throughout this chapter. The question of audience is more obvious with regard to the term script. A script is for a show, and a show is for an audience. Carse (1986) wrote elegantly of the showy nature of human life in his Finite and Infinite Games. He conjectured openly about the nature of the show and how important the show is for people. The notion of script fits his ideas well. It emphasizes the showy or demonstrative side of people's dwelling in language. People not only dwell in language, but they dwell in a language that must have an audience. From this it follows naturally that one way to insure this is for the human being to follow scripts designed for different audiences.

These ideas cannot help but call the question regarding authorship of the scripts. Who is it that writes these scripts, for whom do they write them, for what audience, and to what purpose?

It would be easiest to posit that we each write our own life scripts individually. But this implies that we each must reinvent ourselves upon being born, that we are cut off from all former writers and former scripts, that we are utterly unaware of the scripts that we have been born into, and that we do not take any advantage of all the script collaborators with whom we live, love, work, and play.

Focusing only on the coherence from generation to generation, it is obvious within this scriptural logic that we may have come into being as just one aspect of our parents fulfilling one or more of their own scripts. Indeed, our parents can then be seen as aspects of their parents' scripts, and our grandparents' births as aspects of our great grandparents' scripts. This image evokes a grand concatenation of scripts, each attached to each other in an organic, unfolding manner throughout time. The sum of such a literary string is nothing less than history itself.

Seen in this way, we are struck with the question, "Where do scripts exist?" Do they exist as remnants within the memories of each generation about the last generation? Do they exist as the product of a set of interactions through which the script then arises anew each generation? We seem to have come to a point where a weaving of the biological and the semantic may be necessary.

## GRAMMAR AND SYNTAX OF THE GENE

The concept of script can and should be opened up to larger forms of coherent messages that are maintained across generations. Biologists have begun to explore the inner molecular workings of the human gene. In so doing they have begun to write of the genome, the specific addresses that the genes take along the chromosome. These addresses and the configurations of addresses of genes are responsible for determining the unfolding of the entire organism over time. Biologists now see the gene not as a simple chemical determinant, but rather as a set of complex and intricate messengers that give information to each other and to the organism regarding its growth and maintenance. By extending their definition and conception of genes in this manner, scientists have begun to speak of genes as having "grammars" and "syntax."

This is quite a leap. It is the leap from determinism to languaging, but at the most fundamental levels of molecular and genetic biology. If we begin to see the intricate and complex informational capacities of genes through the concepts of grammars and syntax, we see them as possessing features of languaging characteristics. If the molecules, bases, and peptides of human genes can be seen as facets of a chemical, informational, languaging system, then the primary metaphor of this chapter is not as strange as it seems upon initial encounter—*The metaphor: script as life-form.*

## NEW CONCEPTIONS ABOUT LIFE-FORMS: MEMES AND ARTIFICIAL LIFE

The notion that ideas may evolve similarly to organic life-forms was posited by an elegant evolutionist, Richard Dawkins. In *The Selfish Gene* (1989) Dawkins coined the term "meme." Paralleling the concept of the gene, the meme was Dawkins' creation emphasizing that at some point in our evolution, human beings no longer needed to find ways to adapt physically. They had invented housing, specialized clothing, food stores, automobiles, central heating, hospitals, and many entertainments. The need for further physical adaptation to an earthly environment became almost nil. However, during this same period in which physical adaptation became less necessary, the evolution of *ideas* became central. Dawkins recognized that evolution did indeed continue for human beings, but now was carried out primarily in the domain of ideas. Most importantly, he noted that ideas are replicators similar to genes. They tend to make copies of themselves as they move through their medium, and their medium is the culture itself. Dawkins (1989) stated

> Examples of memes are tunes, ideas, catch phrases, clothes fashions, ways of making pots or of building arches. Just as genes propagate themselves in the gene pool by leaping from body to body via sperms or eggs, so memes propagate themselves in the meme pool by leaping from brain to brain via a process which, in the broad sense, can be called imitation. (p. 192)

Evolutionary questions could still be asked: Which ideas would be most proadaptive? Which ideas would last as others died out and became extinct? Which ideas would become utilized by the greatest number of people and therefore ensure their continuance in the social fabric? Which ideas would evolve over time to full-fledged ideologies under which vast numbers of people would dwell?

Thus the concept of an ever evolving set of memes was initiated. One could imagine the entire set of ideas existent within a culture being called the "memone," just as the entire set of genes in a human being is called the "genome." This evolutionary framework merges two previously distinct domains of inquiry: (1) organic, biological systems with (2) semantic, meaning systems.

Following Dawkins' lead and to some extent concurrent with it, several unusual groups of researchers had begun discovering events and interactions on their computers that both perplexed and amazed them. These groups, which slowly coalesced over time under various leaderships, came to be known as the discoverers and researchers of *Artificial Life* (Levy, 1992). Note, this is not artificial intelligence. Artificial Life is a far more fundamental research into the formal logic and rules of life.

Artificial Life is a term that implies a life-form that is neither aqueous nor organic. That is, these are life-forms based upon neither water nor organic chemistry, but which exist instead solely on computer screens and within the memory cores of computers. Levy (1992) has written a clear account of the history of this research movement, one of the most unique and promising in decades.

Artificial Life researchers have produced computer programs that emulate evolution (Kelly, 1992). That is, they posit a set of hardware and software environments; they then create a set of digital "organisms" to place in those environment, all via computer programming. Then they switch on their computer and observe what happens to these organisms within a given "run." Amazingly, the "organisms" so created actually carry out the functions and activities associated with evolution, including completely novel and unexpected changes in form and function, adaptation, extinction, and all sorts of population dynamics. Yet none of those processes were programmed in. They emerged naturally as aspects of the infighting of the digital organisms within the computer memory core. Thus self-organization, emergence, novelty, and evolution itself became manifest upon the computer screen.

Artificial Life accounts of digital creature evolution has accorded nicely with the evolutionary theories of Harvard's Stephen Jay Gould (1985), one of the key proponents of punctuated equilibria theory.

There are those within the Artificial Life field who see their research as strictly simulations of "real" life. There are others who are more radical in their approach. They see the self-organizing, rule-governed behavior on their screens as paralleling organic life so accurately that they believe their computer creations *are* in fact another life-form. The digital life-form happens not to be based on water and organic molecules, but on silicon. Yet, the logic and actions by which digital life replicates and improves itself over time is clearly evolutionary in its randomness, unpredictability, self-organization, and adaptive optimization. Artificial Life clearly demonstrates a state or condition on the computer that can only be called perpetual novelty.

The present author has a number of Artificial Life programs on his computer and, having observed them run for many hours, agrees with the radical definition of life maintained by many A-Life researchers:

> Life is best defined as a series of relational rules and interactions capable of producing nondeterministic, self-improving novelty. It does not matter what the material of those interactions is made of. It is the relational, combinatorial, interactional, and perpetually novel qualities of a system that determine whether it is alive.

Using this radical definition, we enter into the script metaphor.

## SCRIPT AS LIFE-FORM

From the above definition of life, and adhering to Dawkins' concept of memes, it follows that scripts can be conceived as life-forms within the semantic environment of human languaging.

Lest any readers revolt at this thought, comforting themselves with the idea that "real" life forms are always autonomous creatures, capable of movement, growth, and action, please consider just how "imprisoned" humans as organic life forms actually are. Humans are anything but free and autonomous. We are constrained to breathing air moment to moment. No air for 10 minutes and we die. No water for 5 days or so, we die. No social interaction for a number of days, we begin to suffer psychologically. No ongoing relationships, we become depressed and perhaps clinically so. Our entire physical makeup consists of the molecules of organic chemistry that must synthesize other molecules and compounds from the surrounding environment. There is nothing genuinely unique about us with regard to chemicals. Even our specific human genes are 95% identical to those of chimpanzees.

Clearly, we are not autonomous beings. We are coupled structurally to a long list of environmental supports, the lack of which would shift who and what we are decisively and profoundly. Paramount among those environmental supports are those of social engagement and interaction. These are based upon and recreate the various scripts within which we dwell throughout our lives.

Maturana and Varela (1980) enabled us to describe life from another perspective, the perspective of its internal logic. Their terms, ***autopoiesis*** and ***structural coupling***, are testament to the rigorous manner in which they defined the processes necessary to ensure living. Autopoiesis implies the self-organizing capacity of life, while structural coupling points to the necessity of all living forms to interact in fundamentally formal ways with their environment.

For the present chapter, it is structural coupling that is of most interest. For it is within this concept that we can see how organic life may parallel nonorganic life forms. It is patently clear that organic life must remain coupled to its environment as well as to other organic life forms for its very survival. Any living organism is seen as a "plastic" entity. By plasticity, Maturana and Varela emphasized the necessity of organic life forms to be changeable, variable. They characterized the environment as having to be "plastic" also. It must be an environment in which change and variation are normal.

Thus, for life to be present, a plastic organism must structurally couple with elements of a plastic environment. While this sounds strange, it is just another way of emphasizing the variability of both, organism and environment. If they were not perpetually variable, there could be no life. It is the plasticity and the coupling that allow life to arise from the complexity and novelty of the ensuing interactions over time. It is plasticity that allows changes, and thus allows improvements. These same requirements of plasticity are necessary for scripts to evolve as living forms.

Scripts are entities that arise only within the domain of languaging and meaning systems. Yet, they are "plastic" in that they are perpetually variable. Scripts can change their leading characters, story lines, endings. They exist over time and demonstrate evolutionary dynamics throughout generations. Scripts move from person to person over time, perpetually shifting and changing as need be to benefit the prime "characters" who carry out the scripts or entire families who dwell around the presentation of scripts. Thus scripts replicate over time, they may improve, they may adapt to changing environments, they may even take on new forms, as they couple themselves to different facets of an ever changing semantic environment, i.e., an environment that supports meaning.

Consider, for example, the script changes necessary during war, during the Holocaust, during slavery by an imperialist regime, during a sibling's death, etc. The scripts' changes, variations, reversals, inversions, and other transformations are especially valuable throughout times of great human exigencies. Such adaptive transformations will tend to ensure that the most robust scripts or ideas for scripts will remain alive and available to a family undergoing great stress. But there may well be produced extremely pernicious scripts during these same stressful times.

When one considers the degree to which scripts can be rearranged, shifted, changed, and made new in order for them and their human hosts to survive, it becomes clear that the script-as-a-life-form metaphor fits almost too well for comfort. Using this metaphor, we can conceive of nearly all scripts as evolving life-forms that now have become coupled structurally to their host human beings, couples, and families. Yet, since humans can only be called humans because they dwell in language, we can punctuate the obverse: humans beings are evolving life-forms that now are coupled structurally to their scripts. It is this reflexive dynamic of human-as-life-form, structurally coupled to script-as-life-form, that is underscored here.

Now that we have pushed the script-as-life-form metaphor to its logical conclusion, demonstrating that it has characteristics of evolution involving perpetual novelty, we can beg the question, "What kind of life-form is the script?"

## PARASITES AS AN EVOLUTIONARY ADVANTAGE

Even the neophyte student of Darwinian evolution theory knows that several possibilities must exist for any creature to evolve. There must be the possibility of selection, which implies that the environment will tend to select out those creatures that are particularly suited to it. Those creatures who had made changes over time that did not help them adapt to the present environment eventually would lose ground and would be dominated by the creatures that had a more fortuitous advantage by virtue of the direction of their adaptations.

Evolutionary theorists have posited two primary means of promoting changes in life-forms over time. One is random change brought about by gene mutation. This can happen through faulty replication processes at the DNA level, or through disintegration of certain genetic material via radiation or other environmental factors. These dynamics guarantee a percentage of change over time. However, a second feature of many living forms that we currently take for granted has been cited as extremely important in the production of more adaptive creatures: sex. The sexual pairing of two creatures in order to produce the next generation may be seen as one of the greatest leaps in evolution. It ensured that the complete set of both sets of chromosomes would have to match up in a combinatoric manner. This combinatorial mixing of the gene materials enabled the evolution of offspring to reach optimal adaptive states within any given environment far faster than might have occurred through mutation or chance gene disintegration alone.

Regarding our script-as-life-form metaphor, it is obvious that over time individuals, couples, families, and other larger systems of people might well have found advantages in the combining of scripts. The combinatorial aspect of enriching scripts, or finding ways to increase adaptational strategies through combining scripts in new and unpredictable ways, may well be seen as parallel to the purely biological evolutionary processes.

More recently, a third, and very interesting possibility has arisen with regard to life-forms reaching optimal adaptive states within a given evolutionary environment. This third feature has been demonstrated very effectively by ecologist turned Artificial Life researcher, Thomas Ray (Levy, 1992).

Ray developed a computer program in the 1980s that demonstrated different properties of evolution by having "digital creatures" compete for space and computational time within the core of a computer. At the rate of many millions of instructions per second, Ray's program, *Tierra*, can show how different adaptations either work to enhance adaptation or can allow a fall to extinction for the creatures on the screen. Because the program can run thousands of generations within as little as 10 minutes, it offers a glimpse into the epochal time of biological evolution in the comfort of a laboratory.

As Ray observed the first set of runs on his now famous program, he was astounded to find that what offered certain creatures a tremendous advantage over the other creatures was the emergence of *parasites*. At first blush, it is difficult to imagine how parasites could possibly help drive evolutionary adaptation, or enable one set of organisms to become rapidly dominant within a given environment. But after many experiments involving the addition or removal of parasites from the evolutionary environment within the computer, this clearly was the case.

Ray concluded that parasites ranked at least as important as sex in terms of driving forward certain creatures to optimal states of adaptation. The creatures who had to not only fight off other creatures, but also fight off the creatures that fed upon them, evolved to become the most robust of the entire group. These alone eventually came to dominate the screen. Indeed, these creatures even came to learn how to utilize their parasites to their advantage.

This insight may be applied to far more obvious and normal biological observations. For instance, we tend to look upon a stand of oak trees as simply that: oak trees. What we fail to take into account because we simplify our observations into unified entities, is that an oak tree is not a stable entity. What we see as an oak tree is a set of relations that are on the way to becoming something else all the time. An oak tree may be portrayed more accurately as a set of interactions between the primary structure of a tree and the sum of all its parasites at any given point of observation.

We tend to toss out time in our observation because of the small temporal scale of a human life. Since we only live about 80 years ourselves, we find it difficult to sense the ongoing changes that are taking place within any evolutionary unit such as the tree-plus-parasites. Clearly no set of oaks on earth will look exactly as they do now in a thousand years, since they are actually a set of relations that are perpetually undergoing change. Thus, the oak specifies its parasites as the parasites specify their oak in an ongoing dance of complication.

An oak forest, from this point of view, may be seen as an emergent feature of all interactions between tree and parasites. An oak forest is thus only a transitory feature that arises out of the mutually specifying interactions of oak trees and parasites. For an elegant description of this enactive point of view, see Varela, Thompson, and Rosch (1993).

Consider the implications if we allow ourselves the luxury of a direct parallel between oak forest and family. The family thus becomes an emergent feature of all interactions between a related group of people and their internalized/externalized scripts—humans specifying scripts and scripts specifying humans in an ongoing evolutionary process of perpetual novelty.

## SCRIPT AS PARASITE

Incorporating Dawkins' notions of memes with Ray's notions of parasites as aids to evolution and optimal adaptation, we postulate that certain classes of memes became structurally coupled to the human being throughout evolution. These memes were the result of ideas that had evolved over time into the form of scripts that were to be played out before an audience of observers. These observers could be the individuals themselves or their friends, partners, family, community, etc. The audience was, in effect, society itself.

This human coupling with scripts may be seen as parallel to parasitic coupling in biological evolution. The script needed the human hosts to continue to survive; the human hosts came to need the scripts to survive.

This stance offers us a view of evolution that emphasizes elements of coevolution. That is, it affirms the idea that no organism evolves by itself within a given environment. Rather, every organism is coevolving along with all the other organisms that share an environment. These coevolving organisms reach a point at which their own adaptational needs become intricately entwined with another organism's adaptational needs in such a manner that the two become structurally coupled to each other.

This process of coevolving parasitism seems compellingly close to the process by which humans began to dwell in scripts and scripts began to dwell in humans. Both are necessary for each other's continuance. Different scripts must have offered certain humans great adaptive advantages over other humans as well as great advantages to some families over other families. One of the great difficulties for anyone attempting to predict an evolutionary advantage from a specific script is the degree to which randomness is necessary for selective processes to take place within evolution.

# BALANCING BIOLOGY AND THERAPY

In this last section we will present biological ideas of parasitism followed by possible clinical considerations that might flow from a parasitic logic regarding problem scripts.

## Biological

Recall that a parasite tends to feed off its host. Scripts that encourage daring deeds or dangerous efforts may be considered to feed off their hosts. Yet, both biological and scriptural parasites may enable the human host to find ever higher adaptive states. There is no way of knowing this in advance, since all of evolution is suffused with random dynamics. So too is the production of scripts. We can never know in advance what script will be most proadaptive for an individual or a family. Only when time moves forward and yields our future world will we learn whether any specific set of scripts have proven helpful or harmful to the persons who live them.

## Clinical

Note the obvious clinical implications. Since randomness is necessary for adaptation, we cannot know precisely what will be best for our clients and families in any future moment. We must not make the error of ever attempting to "infuse" them with our favorite "therapy script." We must allow for multiplicity, diversity, and the random. The impossibility of teleology in biology makes this necessary. That is, none of us can tell the future, not for ourselves, nor for our clients. The way we can increase the likelihood of enhanced choices for them is by admitting this inability and "playing" with ideas, concepts, new scripts, and new possibilities, while never insisting on "correct" ones.

## Biological

Throughout the evolution of earth's current life-forms, many of the viruses and pathogens that invaded and destroyed host organisms through infecting them or parasitizing them became converted into benevolent forms. This certainly is the case with much of the human immune system.

The immune system can be seen as an entire array of different organisms that originally may have been problems for the human body, but that over time became incorporated into the human biological systems as agents of protection. The T-cells and macrophages that race to engulf any foreign invaders are our daily protectors. We scarcely can imagine surviving without them. Yet, at distant past epochs in our evolution, these same cells and "organisms" were themselves a problem to the organism. In the case of specific life-threatening viruses, the evolving human found a way to incorporate and utilize these cells for mutual advantage by incorporating the virus directly into the human genome. This is quite a feat. The virus somehow became a part of the genome itself; thus any organism demonstrating that particular string of genetic proteins became immune from that same viral string of proteins as invaders.

This notion of incorporation as solution is key to understanding the proposition of this chapter. It underscores the notion that any agent that initially seemed pathogenic or dangerous, even linguistic scripts, can be converted and incorporated for our defense and eventual success.

## Clinical

We emphasize this pernicious-to-protective transformation to demonstrate that a similar transformation may occur over time with embedded human scripts. That is, a script may be seen as pernicious or benevolent largely depending on its use by the human host who carries and expresses it. The setting of the script, the audience, and the entire context within which it is expressed, all will have determining features with regard to its benevolence or malevolence for the individual or family who carries the script and plays it out.

There will be times when a parasitic script may prove too much for the human host. Consider all of the clinical cases in which we see a person moving in a clearly self-destructive manner. We are amazed when these persons seem bright, have certain strengths, and even state that they wish to become healthy, happy, and successful. Yet we watch them carry out a set of redundant actions over time that indicate that they are listening internally and at very deep levels to an entirely different script. It is almost as if they must, perforce, follow a script that is directly counter to the one they bring into therapy. Sadly, this pernicious script may be one of self-destruction at a youthful age. It is a script that prescribes that a series of dramatic, even explosive, scenes be played out in full before the family, friends, and professionals who now make up the primary audience.

## SCRIPT AS EXTERNALIZED PROBLEM

Using the script-as-parasite concept, we could conjecture about the virulence of this parasitic script. How did it get so strong? How does it manage to survive our semantic, coauthoring attempts as clinicians? Are there other linguistic/semantic agents that keep it alive? Do other scripts interact with this script in a way that enhances its powers? How can we help rearrange the thinking, the story line, the drama, with our client so that the embedded parasitic script loses its toxicity, its morbidity?

Perhaps this particular script has fooled us using the same technique as the spirochete of malaria. Perhaps the script retreats into an area where we cannot destroy it, as the malarian spirochetes retreat into the deep tissues of the kidneys where medication is useless against them. Since the parasitic script cannot hide in a specified place in the human body, perhaps it embeds itself inside another script that appears more benevolent. Once safely nested within the benevolent script, we can no longer see or experience the virulent script and may even come to feel secure that we have vanquished it. Then, at some later time, when the human hosts and family are unaware, the original script returns with a renewed ferocity. This entire analogy introduces the idea of the script as stealthy, unknown, and possibly pernicious.

There is a dramatic element to this pernicious script concept, an element that is hideous and frightening. We recoil from the concept of a script as stealthy, as concealed, as secret from its host human. There is something very discomforting about this notion, even as metaphor. Yet, there may be utility in it also.

## CLINICAL IMPLICATIONS

Clinical use of this metaphor hinges upon two specific thrusts: (1) Changing our thinking and (2) changing our action.

## Changing Our Thinking about Scripts

- Scripts reside within clients, yet have not been caused or promoted by the clients, their parents, or their children.
- Scripts that reside in the client are likely to be more ancient than we can analyze. So all causal assignments are a waste of time and a mistaken epistemology.
- Problem scripts might be conceived as vestigial organs like the appendix. They no longer are functional, but remain nonetheless. They may remain undiscovered or may erupt into problems, but in no case do we cause them.
- Problem scripts have ways of hiding or being stealthy that is not caused by the client but may be seen as part of their evolutionary ability to cohere over time.
- Problem scripts may have taken up residence in the client's ancestors in the distant past and may have been useful or even enabled them to survive through a dangerous or difficult period.
- No matter how benevolent the scripts may have been in the past, the present clients find them to be pernicious and dangerous to their health or happiness.
- Clients may have found ways already to disempower or tame some of these old scripts. We need to enhance and encourage what they already know how to do.


## Changing Our Therapy with Scripting

- Discover with clients and other collaborators all the ways specific problematic scripts manifest themselves currently.
- Discover strategies the client currently uses to defeat or disable parasitic scripts from achieving toxic potency.
- Discover ways to increase the client's own novel scripts as ways to defend against the older, toxic scripts.
- Observe how parasitic scripts respond to the increased and strengthened dosages of counter-scripts, including the strengthening of scripts that disempower the parasitic script.
- Terminate therapy when the client's confidence in his or her own ability to manage as well as play with these old scripts has arrived at a level satisfactory to client, family, and therapist.
- Ensure creativity by "playing" with the writing of multiple possible scripts for the future, reinforcing the idea of many good answers, never one right answer.

- Consider using a type of homoepathy with the client. In homoeo-pathic medicine, the physician cures like with like. Thus, a dangerous parasitic script might respond best to a similarly constructed new script.

## SUMMARY

Beginning with an attack on the false dichotomy of modernism-post-modernism, the author writes from a postmodernist perspective while si-multaneously using scientific ideas from a modernist stance. The metaphor of the script-as-life-form is proposed. This idea is placed into an evolutionary framework through a review of the research on Artificial Life, particularly the concepts of perpetual novelty and parasitism.

The notion that scripts reside in humans as humans reside in scripts, and that each of these co-specifies the other through interactional and com-binatorial processes, is the fundamental offering of this chapter.

Clinical implications are discussed, the chief of which emphasizing that clinicians and their clients might do well to coauthor multiple scripts that honor randomness, diversity, play, and the impossibility of projecting "cor-rect" solutions into an unknown future.

## BIBLIOGRAPHY

Anderson, H., & Goolishian, H.A. (1988). Human systems as linguistic systems: Preliminary and evolving ideas about the implications for clinical theory. *Family Process, 27*(4), 371–393.

Atwood, J.D., & Ruiz, J. (1993). Social constructionist therapy with the elderly. *Journal of Family Psychotherapy, 4*(1), 1–32.

Atwood, J.D., & Dobkin, S. (1992, October). Storm clouds are coming: Ways to help couples reconstruct the crisis of infertility. *Contemporary Family Therapy, 14*(5), 385–403.

Atwood, J.D., & Dershowitz, S. (1992, Fall). Constructing a sex and marital therapy frame: Ways to help couples deconstruct sexual problems. *Journal of Sex & Marital Therapy, 18*(3), 196–218.

Dawkins, R. (1987). *The blind watchmaker*. New York: W.W. Norton & Company.

Gergen, K.J. (1991). *The saturated self*. New York: Basic Books.

Griffin, R.G., Cobb, J.B., Ford, M.P., Gunter, P.A.Y., & Ochs, P. (Eds.). (1993). *Founders of constructive postmodern philosophy*. Albany: State University of New York Press.

Gould, S.J. (1989). *Wonderful life*. New York: W.W.Norton.

Kelly, K. (1990). Perpetual novelty: Selected notes from the Second Artificial Life Conference. *Whole Earth Review*, (67), 20–29.

Lutz, C.A., & Abu-Lughod, L. (Eds.). (1990). *Language and the politics of emotion*. New York: Cambridge University Press.

Mince, J. (1992). Discovering meaning with families. In J. Atwood (Ed.), *Family therapy: A systemic-behavioral approach* (pp. 321–343). Chicago: Nelson-Hall Publishers.

Mince, J., & Marr, C. (1993). *The fractal narrative process: An endless search for meaning*. Unpublished manuscript. Hempstead, New York: Hofstra University.

Sim, S. (1992). *Beyond aesthetics: Confrontations with poststructuralism and postmodernism*. Buffalo: University of Toronto Press.

Sluzki, C. (1992). Transformations: A blueprint for narrative changes in therapy. *Family Process, 31*(3), 217–230.

Varela, F.J. (1979). *Principles of biological autonomy*. New York: North Holland.

Varela, F., & von Foerster, H. (1993, October). Respective lectures on transitory emergence and non-trivial machines at a conference entitled *Reflecting Observations*, presented by the Forum for Psychotherapy Cybernetics of New York.

von Glaserfeld, E. (1984). An introduction to radical constructivism. In P. Watzlawick (Ed.), *The invented reality* (pp. 17–40). New York: Norton.

White, M. (1989). *Selected papers.* Adelaide, Australia: Dulwich Centre Publications.

Wittgenstein, L. (1953). *Philosophical investigations.* New York: Anscombe and Rhees.

# REFERENCES

Carse, J. (1986). *Finite and infinite games.* New York: Ballantine Books.

Conte, J.M. (1991). *Unending design: The forms of postmodern poetry.* Ithaca, NY: Cornell University Press.

Culler, J. (1975). *Structuralist poetics: Structuralism, linguistics and study of literature.* Ithaca, NY: Cornell University Press.

Dawkins, R. (1989). *The selfish gene.* New York: Oxford University Press.

Derrida, J. (1976). *Of grammatology.* Baltimore: The Johns Hopkins University Press.

Efran, J.S., Lukens, M.D., & Lukens, R.J. (1990). *Language, structure, and change.* New York: W.W.Norton & Company.

Edwards, P. (Ed.). (1967). Hegel, Georg Wihelm Friedrich. In *The encyclopedia of philosophy, vol. 3* (pp. 435–450). New York: MacMillan.

Gergen, K.J., & Davis, K.E. (1985). *The social construction of the person.* New York: Springer-Verlag.

Gould, S.J. (1985). *The flamingo's smile.* New York: W.W. Norton.

Guralnick, D.B. (Ed.). (1980). *Webster's new world dictionary.* New York: Simon & Schuster.

Hatcher, O.L. (1970). *A book of Shakespeare plays and pageants*. Freeport, NY: Books for Libraries Press.

Kelly, K. (1992, Fall). Desktop a-life. *Whole Earth, 76*, 21.

Levy, S. (1992). *Artificial life: The quest for a new creation*. New York: Pantheon Books.

Maturana, U., & Varela, F. (1980). *Autopoiesis and cognition: The realization of the living*. Boston: D. Reidel.

Varela, F.J., Thompson, E., & Rosch, E. (1993). *The embodied mind: Cognitive science and human experience*. Cambridge, MA: The MIT Press.

von Foerster, H. (1993, October). *Reflecting observations*. Lecture at Forum for Psychotherapy Cybernetics of New York conference, New York.

von Glaserfeld, E. (1987). *The construction of knowledge: Contributions to conceptual semantics*. Seaside, CA: Intersystems Publications.

Watson, W. (1993). *The architectonics of meaning: Foundations of the new pluralism*. Chicago: The University of Chicago Press.

White, M., & Epston, D. (1990). *Narrative means to therapeutic ends*. New York: W.W. Norton.

# Chapter 3

# BACKWARDS SCRIPTS

*Joan Ruiz*
*and*
*Joan D. Atwood*

Individuals' meaning systems originally are created by their families of origin and maintained through interactions with significant others and the sociocultural environment. This process begins at birth and continues throughout a person's lifetime. Out of one's meaning system comes the development of his or her life plan or life script (Gagnon & Simon, 1973; Gagnon, 1990). Individuals' scripts are their plans about what they are presently doing and what they plan to do in the future (Atwood & Dershowitz, 1992). Persons will seek out events and other persons that are consistent with their own meaning systems and selectively ignore others who do not fit. By selecting events and persons that "fit," individuals test, challenge, and reaffirm their meaning systems, consequentially internalizing their reality or worldview (Berger & Luckmann, 1966).

It is through this worldview that one develops his or her life script. Scripts guide behaviors and expectations and help persons make sense out of and understand their actions. Life scripts operate at a social, personal, and intrapsychic level (Gergen & Gergen, 1983, 1988). Scripts exist in many areas of individuals' lives. The concept of a life script is analogous to the idea of a blueprint. Persons' scripts prescribe their patterns of interaction in particular contexts. These scripts or "blueprints" for behavior specify who will be part of their lives, what behaviors these persons will engage in, when certain life cycle events will happen or are expected to happen in their lives, and what meaning they will give to the behaviors and events in their lives (Byng-Hall, 1988).

The notion of **backwards scripts** refers to patterns of interaction of life cycle events that do not follow the socially predictable pattern of events. The present chapter explores backwards scripts when individuals', couples' and families' scripts are pulled out from under them. In these instances, the ongoing and present scripts have "flipped," leaving the individual, couple, or family temporarily "scriptless." When a "backwards script" occurs, persons' life scripts become "out of order," "reversed," or "out of sequence." Three examples of life events happening in this order are: (1) when a child dies before the parent, (2) when a child is born before marriage or out of wedlock, and (3) when a wife dies before her husband. This chapter presents information on each one of these situations, giving the reader a "feel" for the intensification of emotionality involved in a backwards script. Therapeutic considerations are explored in each section. The chapter ends with a discussion of social construction therapy with backwards scripts.

Before attempting to understand how adult individuals cope with backwards scripts, an important step is to explore how individuals' concepts of death and their resultant scripts for death develop in childhood and how this influences their reactions to loss and grief throughout the life span (Johnson, 1987). When evaluating individuals' beliefs about death and bereavement scripts, one needs to take into account the effects of culture, media, socioeconomic groups, and religious background, and environmental issues such as parental comfort, schooling, and interaction with friends (Johnson, 1987). Persons' families of origin and cultural influences affect the development of individuals' concepts of death. In addition, McIntire, Angle, and Struempler (1972) found socioeconomic status to be an influencing factor in an individual's development of a concept of death. For example, individuals from urban, low socioeconomic groups are more likely to cite violence as the general and specific cause of death, while middle-class and older children are more likely to cite disease and old age as general causes of death. Religious influences also impact on individuals' development of concepts of death and bereavement scripts. When a child is confronted with death or the concept of death, religious rites, practices, and beliefs typically are taught by the parents. Whatever the religious framework, it becomes a means whereby feelings and reactions become acceptable and expressible. The following section discusses how persons' scripts for death develop. The following sections are relevant when considering the latter sections of this chapter such as when a child dies before the parents or when a wife dies before her husband.

## DEVELOPMENT OF A SCRIPT FOR DEATH

Using a Piagetian framework, Johnson (1987) separated the development of individuals' death beliefs and bereavement scripts into five stages. During the first stage, infancy to two years, the child experiments with concepts of presence and absence. At this age, the idea that people exist even though the infant cannot see them is difficult to master. Until approximately six months of age, the child's belief system is governed by, "Out of sight—Out of mind." Around seven to ten months, separation anxiety peaks in the infant. At this age, the child becomes anxious when an object is removed from his or her view. Once the child "understands" object permanence (that a thing continues to exist even if it is out of view) and experiences separation anxiety, he or she has mastered the notion of presence and absence. A child who is three years old or younger, however, does not comprehend the difference between absence and death, although separation anxiety and object and person permanence are probably the rudimentary beginnings of the concept of death and fear of death. In his study of separation anxiety in young children, Bowlby (1960) described three responses to separation: protest, despair, and detachment. Bowlby's work is important because it indicates that young children respond to loss with feelings of protest, despair, and detachment much earlier than they understand the concept of death.

Johnson's (1987) second stage describes children between the ages of two and seven. This stage is highlighted by the child's tendency to mix magic and reality when thinking about the causes of death. This "magical thinking" about death is exemplified in the idea that death is reversible. Unfortunately this idea often is supported in cartoons and other media. A child sees a character explode or killed in one scene only to see it reappear in another seconds later, leaving the child to conclude that people die but they will return later. Unfortunately, this concept is also present in many adolescents who take their own lives. Magical thinking at this age may influence the child's inability to understand the difference between reality and fantasy, possibly lending the child to believe that he or she had the ability to cause the death of a loved one. In this case, the resulting guilt and pain may be acted out in other areas of the child's life and may have a negative influence on the child's psychological development.

In the third stage, children become aware that death is permanent, irreversible, and universal. Here, because of cognitive and emotional growth, they are better able to develop a concept of the permanence of death. A child in this stage is able to utilize logic and reason as he or she processes information. At this age, when someone in a child's life dies, he or she will give a "logical" concrete answer or reason for the death. For example, "He was a mean, uncaring person and that is why he died." The problems in this stage arise when a person dies who does not fit into the child's logic or meaning system around death. Here, the child may say, "I do not understand why Mary died. She was a really nice person." Adults will give similar reasons, indicating that chronological age is not necessarily indicative of cognitive or psychological age. Adults also may exhibit child-like questions about death when there is no answer or reason for the loss. Sadly, oftentimes the answer for people at this stage is to shoulder the blame themselves. Kushner's (1981) book described helpful coping skills for persons who feel that there are no answers to death.

Johnson's (1987) fourth stage involves adolescents and their concepts and meanings surrounding death. During adolescence, individuals continually are searching for self and developing emotional and intellectual tools. At this age, persons may vacillate; while they are strongly influenced by cultural mores, at times they also will exhibit thinking indicating their belief in immortality. In other words, during this stage, even though adolescent's fantasize about death, they also believe they cannot be touched by it. If faced with death, they may tend to believe that they will be rescued at the last minute. This often is given as a factor in the shockingly high adolescent suicide rate in this country (Jersild, 1978). The final stage, adulthood, brings with it an internalized comprehension that death is universal, irreversible, permanent, and a certainty to all. These beliefs, while often accompanied by deep feelings of grief, also are manifested by death-denying behaviors. Here, the concept of death is intellectually understood, but the emotional process—the feelings and reactions—is denied.

The development of a person's concepts of death and bereavement scripts is continually changing throughout the life cycle as the individual physically, emotionally, and mentally matures. Throughout development, a person's present meaning systems about death are examined, questioned, and challenged. Novel thoughts and ideas that do not coincide with present incoming beliefs are sometimes added, forcing individuals to modify their old beliefs and scripts into new ones that can incorporate and accommodate the newly acquired "knowledge," rendering the old beliefs obsolete. von Glaserfeld (1984) redefined "knowledge" as pertaining to invariances in the living organism's experience rather than to entities, structures, and events in an independently existing world. Correspondingly, we redefine "perception." It is not the reception or duplication of information that is coming in from outside, but rather the construction of invariances by means of which the organism can assimilate and organize its experience. When individuals develop their beliefs about death, they are not looking for truth but merely for a "fit" in their attempts to understand the world (Hoffman, 1986, 1988). When a piece is found that does not fit the overall puzzle, either the person will discard the piece rendering it as unimportant (if they noticed it in the first place) or the possibility for growth emerges (Atwood & Dershowitz, 1992).

# FIVE GRIEF SCRIPTS

Five scripts frequently utilized by families dealing with death are (1) the *scapegoating script*, (2) the *conspiracy of silence script*, (3) the *detachment script*, (4) the *guilt script*, and (5) the *masochism script*. These scripts are seen in families where death occurred after a long illness or where death was sudden. Maintaining these scripts over a long period of time can be detrimental to healthy bereavement.

## Scapegoating Script

The scapegoating script refers to a process of singling out one or more persons to bear the brunt of the family's dissatisfaction. In this type of situation, further exploration of the family of origin typically will reveal that the family has used scapegoats in the past as a means of coping with difficult situations. The scapegoating script utilizes two primary defense mechanisms: projection and displacement. *Projection* occurs when a feeling or attitude is emotionally unacceptable in oneself, is unconsciously rejected, and then is attributed to another. *Displacement* permits emotions or reactions to be transferred from the original object to a more acceptable substitute. Scapegoating has the potential to be destructive to individuals and families. If the family has adopted a scapegoating script, they should be encouraged to and given permission by the therapist to express their anger appropriately so that this script is not perpetuated (Johnson, 1987).

## Conspiracy of Silence Script

Generally speaking, persons who have suffered death of a loved one eventually develop a primary and fundamental need to talk about their experience. They develop an intense desire or need to reveal their sadness, to release their anger, to allay their guilt, and to have others understand their reactions. In some cases, though, persons feel unable to discuss their losses and feelings at a time when such a discussion would be most appreciated and needed, such as at the time of death. This inability generally stems from either the persons' reluctance to upset others or from the refusal of other significant people to enter into a meaningful and helpful discussion of the event. This inability or refusal to communicate often amplifies the emotional feelings, causing them to extend over a much longer period of time. The longer the silence continues, the more difficult it is to deal with. Persons in this situation often report feeling alone, isolated, and guilty. This "conspiracy of silence script" may lead to the terrible fears so often verbalized by bereaved persons that everyone is forgetting about the dead person, that people's memories are fading. It may produce a burning desire to keep the memories alive by vowing never to forget (Knapp, 1986, 1987).

## Detachment Script

The detachment script refers to the process whereby people "pull away" from each other because of their own bereavement pain. This script usually happens with people who have had a close bonding prior to the death of the family member. The primary reason given for the incorporation of this script is that people are in such pain that they are incapable of administering support to others. Additional reasons for the adoption of this script are (1) protection of self or others, (2) testing behaviors, (3) shock, (4) people grieve in different ways at different times, and (5) the marriage or relationship may have been unstable or detached before the death. The detachment script can assist persons through the bereavement process if it is not lengthy. Once persons feel healthier and stronger, they should be encouraged to reattach. At this time, they also appear to be more willing and able to provide support to others (Johnson, 1987).

## Guilt Script

The guilt script is one most commonly associated with the grieving process. This script is often a difficult one to deal with in that it must be contended with on a continual basis. When a child dies, he or she does not die from old age or from a "natural death." Parents *know* that their child died from some "cause," and this often leads to overwhelming inescapable feelings of guilt that they have failed to eliminate or recognize that cause beforehand. They believe that if they had recognized early symptoms or signs, if they had been more perceptive in regard to some of the dangers all children face while growing up, or if they had made one decision rather than another, their child might still be alive. Here it would be helpful to encourage parents to deal openly with their guilt. If buried, it can greatly complicate a healthy grieving process (Knapp, 1986).

## Masochism Script

The final script, the masochism script, refers to the process whereby an individual learns and is reinforced through various external stimuli that suffering, submission, and self-punishment are ways to respond to, internalize, act, and interact with others. Persons adopt this script because their meaning systems and the resultant scripts dictate that a way of coping with crisis is to suffer (Johnson, 1987). Other behavioral characteristics often manifested in individuals following a masochism script are (1) a desire for approval; (2) fears of offending others, fears of authority, and fears of abandonment; (3) self-doubt; (4) self-punishment; (5) nightmares of helplessness and flight; and (6) a sense of being the center of critical attention. This script, although sometimes adopted by men, is adopted most often by women (Shainess, 1984).

In the case of a death of a loved one, the love object is gone and the family member often feels helpless, defenseless, powerless, and physically and emotionally ill. In some cases, there is a refusal to go on with life or to give up his or her grieving. For this person, the grief will be as potent today as it was 10 years ago. Long-standing masochistic scripts can lead to health- and life-threatening situations. For example, unresolved grief and continued mourning has been linked to ulcers, colitis, and arthritis as well as to noticeable physical, emotional, and relationship deterioration (Johnson, 1987).

# WHEN A CHILD DIES BEFORE THE PARENTS

Nothing is as inappropriate, unnatural, and unacceptable to a mother and a father as the death of their child. Youthful deaths in our society, particularly of infants and young children, are regarded as ultimate tragedies (Knapp, 1986). The death of a child is said to be the most devastating death; it is the one we least expect, the one we deny and fear the most (Bordow, 1982). Our life scripts dictate that children are to outlive their parents. The idea of children dying before their parents is philosophically unintelligible and incomprehensible. It defies the natural order of things. When a child dies, the dominant beliefs and scripts are uprooted, leaving the family in a state of disequilibrium. The parents' thoughts, judgments, considerations, and beliefs are swirling; the order of life events, reversed. Because a child dying before his or her parents is not the typical or dominant script, many significant adjustment problems are present. The death of a child thrusts those who are left into a reevaluation of everything in their lives—its meaning, its purpose. The events, ideas, thoughts, expectations, hopes, and dreams that once fit into their script no longer do. The parents and family members now must create new individual and family scripts from the ruins of their old scripts. They often are struck now by the flimsiness of their assumptions, their expectations, and their reality and are more able to notice the integrity and love often left unobserved in life's fast pace (Bordow, 1982).

Immediately after a child's death, the parents and family are at a loss as to what to do next. The family is usually in shock even if they were aware of the impending death (Johnson, 1987). Their individual and family's script has been pulled out from under them; they are left, for the time, "scriptless," in a state of anomie or disorganization. This is not the way it was supposed to be. How each person copes at this time depends on the individual's unique coping skills. How each family copes at this time depends on the particular family's coping skills. There is no one way to grieve and no one grief script. Families and individuals are social systems with their own internal structure of positions, norms, roles, values, and beliefs. They also have their own set of defensive techniques for coping with problems that they encounter (Knapp, 1986).

## The Script Immediately after the Death

Although no single script or single way to grieve exists, a "pre-scripted script" for behaviors immediately after a death does. The first scripted behavior is to inform family and friends of the death. Johnson (1987) believed an important procedure is to encourage families and individuals to find a helpful person who can assist with arrangements and provide comfort. It is important, however, that this person does not become "too helpful." The helper should not feel the need to rescue or overprotect family members. If the immediate family wants to inform other family and friends about the death, they should do so. This can be very helpful because it is a chance to tell and retell the story. The more often the story is told, the more "comfortable" the family members then become with it. It also can assist in promoting the reality of the loss. The family also should be encouraged to participate in the making of funeral arrangements (Johnson, 1987). Encouragement can help; pushing does not.

The funeral is a tragic time for parents, and the entire family should be involved. Parents and siblings eventually must come to deal with the reality of the death. By enabling family members freedom of choice with regard to funeral arrangements, and by being open and truthful with them at all times, therapists can assist families in decreasing some of the stresses that are usually present at this time (Knapp, 1986). The family can be encouraged to discuss memories, both good and bad; to think of special music or verses for the service; and to assist in any of the tasks to make the funeral as meaningful as possible. Important components of the behavioral script following a death are the rituals. The writing of the obituary, the ordering of the flowers, the planning of a memorial, and the visitation of the grave are all important scripted ritual behaviors that occur in the event of a death. These scripted ritual behaviors assist the family through healthy bereavement (Johnson, 1987).

### Scripted Feelings Following a Child's Death

No matter what script an individual or a family adopts, there are feelings existent in those scripts that are similar. People generally experience a number of feelings when coping with the death of a loved one. But when a child dies, these feelings are intensified. The initial feeling is often numbness, characterized by a sense of shock and unreality. Shock is a universal feeling that is found to exist in all individuals who have lost someone close to them. Here, the bereaved person suffers emotional confusion and tenseness (Alexy, 1982). Initially, these feelings of numbness or shock protect the person so that he or she may slowly process the reality that the child has died (Johnson, 1987).

While some persons experience numbness and shock, others experience anger. Individuals may manifest anger in different ways. Anger may be directed outward toward others or inward toward oneself. Anger is a normal and healthy emotion if expressed appropriately (Johnson, 1987). Anger outbursts are aroused by frustrations resulting from futile yearnings and searchings for the lost person (Alexy, 1982). As stated earlier, guilt is another feeling experienced by grieving individuals. Guilt is a complicated feeling in that it is learned through socialization. Therapists can assist persons in expressing their guilt feelings so that they eventually can move toward responses that will help them undo their guilt (Johnson, 1987).

Feelings of disorganization, sadness, and despair usually result from the bereaved person's realization that attempts to recover the lost child are hopeless. At this time, there is a painful lack of capacity to initiate and maintain organized patterns of behavior (Alexy, 1982). Persons often express that they feel as though there is no hope left in life, that there is nothing left. Persons also may experience helplessness and terror, overwhelming rage, guilt, and an intense yearning for the child who is dead. As the bereavement process continues, hope begins to grow slowly, and the person gets closer to the time when he or she starts to think and talk about his or her life continuing (Johnson, 1987). Individuals and families who have had to cope with a child who had a long terminal illness often experience anticipatory loss and may feel relief at the time of death. This relief often is followed by feelings of guilt as they wonder how they can feel relief over death (Rolland, 1990).

Anxiety is a universal feeling that often is felt by individuals who have experienced a death of a loved one. Here, individuals experience symptoms such as restlessness, difficulty concentrating, difficulty sleeping, diarrhea, vomiting, sudden increased heart rate, dizziness, frequent urination, and sweaty palms and feet. Anxiety is a normal feeling in any bereavement script. At this time, the therapist can assist the person with the anxiety so it will not become debilitating. If individuals are helped to verbalize, resolve, and make sense of their feelings, they will be able to move toward reorganization. Then the bereaved individuals can first begin to accept their loss as permanent (Alexy, 1982). These symptoms, while general and applicable to all grieving situations, are intensified tremendously when the death involves a child.

## Society's Unspoken Script

Culture and society have a silent but very powerful script that affects and greatly influences the behaviors, thoughts, and feelings of those individuals and families who are trying to cope and work through the grieving process. One socially scripted messages is that grief should not last "too long." This script leaves those who are grieving with the belief that there must be something wrong with them if they are unable to pick up the pieces of their lives and move on shortly after the death. Another socially scripted behavior is that family and friends will take care of the bereaved family for a short time after the death. These behaviors are considered acceptable if they continue for about two weeks after the death. The myth is that after two weeks the bereaved are supposed to be "over the worst" and "should be getting on with their lives." Unfortunately, at this time, not only are persons not through with the grieving process, all too often they have just begun. If the death was sudden, persons often continue in a state of acute grief for well over a year. Frequently, friends and relatives of the family may become uncomfortable and exasperated by this intense mourning. As the months go by, they may begin to admonish the family members to get on with their lives. When the admonishments prove fruitless, friends and relatives often begin to withdraw, compounding the isolation and loneliness of the family. Responding to these socially created ideas about bereavement, many grieving people cut off their pain. This can be very detrimental to individuals. They need to feel their pain. When distracted or dissuaded from their grief by well-wishers, persons' recovery most definitely will be hampered (Johnson, 1987).

An individual's or a family's bereavement script also depends on the occurrence of the death: Was the death sudden or expected? Most research suggests that sudden loss is initially more difficult to cope with and is more likely to lead to long-term problems than a death that is anticipated (Lehman, Lang, Wortman, & Sorenson, 1989; Knapp, 1986; Parkes & Weiss, 1983; Bordow, 1982).

## Anticipatory Death Script

When the family or individual is anticipating the death of a child, their lives are lived in the present; all future plans are canceled. Their relationships and all interactions become laden with overtones of feelings, both positive and negative (Knapp, 1986). The bereavement process begins as soon as the individual or family learns the child is going to die. They begin to mourn the loss of their child and along with it the death of their dreams for a future with their child (Soricelli & Utech, 1985). Understanding and support is crucial at this time for it helps to maintain open lines of communication for the parents, the ill child, and the siblings. Often, the child who is dying knows that he or she is dying. This creates a unique problem in that the child must deal with his or her own feelings as well as the family's feelings. In the anticipatory bereavement script, there is the opportunity to openly discuss, share, and deal with the child's feelings. The ideal psychological situation is that the child and the family work toward the final stage of acceptance of death together and before it occurs. Problems can occur when communication is blocked and the parents and child are not moving through the stages of death together (Knapp, 1986). For example, a child may have reached the acceptance stage of his or her own death while the parents are still in denial. In general, the stages are denial, anger, bargaining, depression, and acceptance (Kubler-Ross, 1969). However, not everyone goes through these stages, nor do they necessarily go through them in order. These stages are part of the socially defined bereavement script and, as such, are useful as guidelines in the bereavement process.

Another valuable element of the anticipatory bereavement script is the parents ability to involve themselves in a support group that can afford them the opportunity to express and work through their feelings with other parents who are in a similar situation (Soricelli & Utech, 1985). The more the parents can work through their own emotions, the better able they are to assist their child.

Dealing with a terminally ill child is without a doubt one of the hardest ordeals any family will experience. Even so, there are some benefits to this experience that parents who are faced with a sudden and unexpected loss do not have. Parents involved in an anticipatory death script have the opportunity to adjust to the impending death of their child. These families have less difficulty accepting the loss when it occurs; they tend to show little evidence of guilt or self-blame, little extreme emotional or stressful reaction at the time of death, less anger, far fewer depressive symptoms, a greater tendency to formulate some way of handling the event that makes it more real, less likelihood of reacting with disbelief and shock, greater tendency to involve themselves in after-death ceremonies such as grave visits, fewer problems with role functioning, and less likelihood of developing a fixation to the past (Knapp, 1986).

## Sudden Death Script

Unlike the anticipatory death script, the sudden death script leaves no time for preparation. There is no warning, no plan, and no known words, feelings, or behaviors (Miles & Perry, 1985). One day the family's script is intact, and the next day it has crumbled. The sudden death script is a surprise attack on everyone's psyche, a frontal assault on everyone's ego (Knapp, 1986). Imagine an actor being handed a script while at the same time being told, "You go on stage in two seconds." There are no words to describe the next moment. The person is left standing with few or no options for success. No plan of action. He or she feels trapped—he or she is script-less. Similarly, a person faced with the sudden death of a child experiences many different feelings and behaviors than those in the anticipatory death script. They were unable to say good-bye to their child, so there might be more unfinished business than where families had preparation time. They have difficulty accepting the loss, there is a lot of self-blame and guilt, they experience intense physical and emotional pain, and they are in shock. The sudden death is so unbelievable, so utterly shocking, so devastating, and so traumatic that denial becomes the dominant reaction. Behavior in this script is disorganized and confused and, unlike those in the anticipatory script, there was no opportunity to say good-bye, no sharing of feelings, no time to adjust. Feelings of anguish, despair, shock, anger, guilt, sadness, and immense pain have not been worked through previously. They are just beginning. A problem unique to the sudden death script is the question of "Why?" Every parent asks, "Why did this happen to my child?", "Could I have prevented it?", "Why am I being punished this way?" These questions are basically unanswerable and impinge on the thought patterns of many parents for weeks, months, and all too often, years. They riddle the mind and complicate the grieving process (Knapp, 1986). It is not incorrect to say that the sudden death of a child creates chaos, mass confusion, and many indescribable behaviors and emotions.

Most often when a child dies, it is because of a terminal illness. As stated earlier, this situation at least allows for the child and the family to grieve together, to say good-bye together. If a child dies from an accident (i.e., hit by a car), the family is not afforded this luxury, and the shock is sudden, devastating, and overwhelming. If a child is murdered, additional internal feelings are experienced. During the initial stages, families react similarly to other grieving families. However, the unexpected nature of the homicide increases the family's shock and denial. Here also, they did not have a chance to say good-bye. These families tend to be more disorganized and disoriented because they also must deal with an unfamiliar system, the criminal justice system. It is here that they often will focus their anger. They may become impatient with the pace of the system to process the assailant, if found. The mere presence of an assailant may prevent the family from accepting the finality of the death. They may tend to focus on the last moments of the possible pain, anxiety, or fear of the victim. This may increase their own anxiety. They also may feel more vulnerable and feel that other family members are at risk. During the last stages of the criminal justice process, they may be forced to relive the experience of the death.

## The Marital Relationship

The couple who once laughed together, vacationed together, and parented together realize suddenly when their child dies that they are two separate individuals who must mourn individually and alone. They may expect to lean on each other in this time of crisis, but quickly learn that their mate is equally devastated and absorbed in his or her own pain. Seventy percent of marriages end when there is a death of child (Schiff, 1977). Schiff (1977) estimated that 90% of couples experience serious marital difficulty when their child dies. These couples have shared tragedy, disaster, and grief, but these emotions do not necessarily create a bonding. In some cases, the bond becomes so taut that it snaps. Individuals grieve differently, and couples may have different ways of grieving, making it more difficult for the couple to support each other. One parent may feel better one day and feel resentful that the other is "down in the dumps." One parent may want to discuss the dead child; the other may not. One may want to socialize; the other may refuse. One may become very protective; the other may be resentful and feel smothered. One may refuse to participate in sex. One may turn to religion for comfort; the other may begin drinking. One may become depressed; the other may become obsessed. It is important for the therapist to be aware of the many issues that the couple experiences. They are extremely vulnerable and frightened. If the couple can recommit to their marriage, they will be better able to grieve together.

## Rebuilding the Family and Individual Scripts

After the individual or family works through the immediate grieving process, the family's new script that develops is never the same as the script the family had before the death. Although most bereaved parents claim that the intensity of their grieving lessens over time, the impact of their loss is such that many parents resign themselves to never being the same again. Often, changes in fundamental life values and philosophical beliefs are reported as a consequence of experiencing the death of a child (Alexy, 1982).

During this time when the family is rebuilding their script, they generally will search for some cause or rational reason for the loss. They have a need to make the loss intelligible. They search for assurances that the loss was not in vain. This frantic search influences the creating of the new family script. Many families turn to their religious faiths for answers and comfort. This may occur even in those who had not placed much credence in religion in their old family script. In some cases, religious revitalization may be incorporated into the new developing script; in others, it may take the form of a belief in some sort of reunification with the child after the parent's own death or in an afterlife of sorts. Another change in the family's new script may be in their values. New commitments and more intangible values may be brought into the new script. Many families may no longer have the need to strive in the way they did in the past. Family goals as opposed to individual ones may become primary. Parents may tend to become more concerned with cultivating and strengthening family relationships, and remaining family members gradually may be viewed in a different light, with new emphasis on their importance as people. Doing things with the family rather than for the family and taking a genuine interest in each other may become the new values incorporated into the family's new script. Many parents become less concerned with appearances and with materialistic things. Family concerns in the new script may move toward caring about the family's health and happiness. Not only may the family's internal script change, but the script that they use to interact with society also may be affected. Loss of a child may tend to make parents more tolerant of other people outside of the immediate family. Here, they may be more willing to listen to others express their problems and more willing to develop a sense of understanding (Knapp, 1986, 1987).

## BECOMING A PARENT BEFORE MARRIAGE— PREMARITAL BIRTH SCRIPT

A person's backwards scripts can occur at many different points and for many different reasons during a person's life cycle. One such instance is when a person has a child before marriage, "out of wedlock." In this case, the socially approved script—getting married and *then* having a child—no longer applies, and the person must incorporate new ways of behaving into his or her life. In the United States, the typical social script for young adults involves completing their education, beginning a first full-time job, courtship, marriage, the birth of a first child, etc. These events, either singly or in combination, mark transitions between important roles in American society (Teachman & Polonko, 1984). Over the last two decades, however, the United States has witnessed a striking increase in the proportion of young women who deviate from the normative timing and sequencing of roles pertaining to family formation and become pregnant and give birth prior to marriage (Yamaguchi & Kandel, 1987). The problem is one of adolescent pregnancy, which has reached epidemic proportions in our society. Approximately one million pregnancies are expected among 15- to 19-year-olds each year, resulting in the United States having the highest teenage pregnancy rate in the developed world (Jones, 1985), reporting 96 pregnancies per 1,000 (or 1 in 10) in young women between the ages of 15 and 19, with the highest rates among low-income black adolescents (Franklin, 1987), resulting in the premarital birth script being greatly overrepresented among blacks. The birth rate for black adolescent women in 1984 was twice as high as the rate for whites. Black adolescents were far more likely than whites to have nonmarital births—89% of births to black adolescents compared to 45% of births to Hispanic teenage women and 34% to non-Hispanic whites in 1984. This differential among black women has been attributed to the greater acceptability of childbirth (either legitimate or illegitimate) as a means of establishing adulthood (Teachman & Polonko, 1984 ). For some black women, a premarital birth script may be a natural life transition script signifying maturity.

Perhaps one of the reasons so many young women are choosing the premarital birth script is because of changes in the social definitions in premarital sexual scripts. Generally speaking, males always have had a script for premarital coitus, usually called the casual-sex script. This social script assigns to men the role of initiating and pursuing sexual activity until stopped by their partners. Women, on the other hand, at least "nice" women, until the 60s, did not have a prescribed script for premarital coitus. The script for women was, "Nice girls don't" (Reed & Weinberg, 1984). With the sexual revolution of the 60s, mainly a revolution in the sexual behavior of women, female incidences of premarital intercourse approached that of men. At this time also, technology ushered in "the pill," and women's contraceptive needs were potentially met. However, adolescents use contraceptives sporadically at best, and the situation was ripe for an increase in adolescent pregnancy rates. This in fact is what did occur. Research evidence shows that most births to teenagers are unplanned (80%) and tend to result from unprotected sexual intercourse (fewer than 25% of sexual encounters among adolescents are reported as planned). Two thirds of teenagers who have had intercourse either never use contraception or use it poorly (Zelnick & Kantner, 1980). Many of these young women were not using the most effective methods: 36% used withdrawal and 5% used the rhythm method (Zelnick & Kantner, 1980). About 50% of premarital teenage pregnancies in the United States occur during the first six months of sexual activity and 20% occur during the first month (Zabin et al., 1986). For those young women with premarital sexual experience, about 60% are not protected against pregnancy the first time they have intercourse. (See Gold & Berger, 1983, for a review of single males' contraceptive behavior.)

Unlike the "backwards death script," the "backwards premarital birth script" has factors that contribute and influence the formation of this backward life transition script. For example, more choice is afforded to those in the "backwards premarital birth script." When the pregnancy is realized, options are available, i.e., adoption or abortion. There are no options when a child dies. There are variables that influence individuals' adopting a script whereby they have a child before marriage. These variables allow for some element of predictability. There are no predictable factors available for the death of a child. The multiple predictors of having a child before marriage range from behavioral characteristics to social and family background variables. Since individuals learn their scripts from their family of origin, significant childhood others, and the sociocultural environment, it seems only natural to predict that those who have a lower commitment and attachment to conventional values and institutions (such as family, school, and religion) and lower psychological well-being will be the ones who will opt for a premarital birth script (Yamaguchi & Kandel, 1987). Biological variables of race and age, and the sociological variables of low parental education and low educational aspirations and performance, are also among the identified risk factors (Teachman & Polonko, 1984). From a review of studies, Chilman (1979) suggested that the family characteristics associated with adolescent pregnancy are alcoholism on the part of one or both parents, family violence, incest, severe conflict in parental marriage, chronic physical or mental illness on the part of a parent or sibling, authoritarian and punitive parent(s), low family communication, conflict-ridden and/or rigid family systems, families with ambiguous boundaries, and neglecting or rejecting parents. According to the perspective of problem behavior theory, those individuals who take part in deviant behaviors hold attitudes and values that are nonconforming to the values of society (Yamaguchi & Kandel, 1987). By adopting this backwards script, these individuals are rebelling against the socially defined appropriate script.

### Consequences of Adolescent Pregnancy

Deviations from social timetables and normative sequences of role participation generally have negative definitions and consequences for individuals. For the majority of those who adopt this backwards script, there is a drastic shift in their life script. Education may have to be postponed or forgotten; the American dream of a big wedding is shattered. After the child is born, the mother's wishes, aspirations, needs, and wants become secondary to the child's. For most, the single-parent script must be learned and implemented. The consequences of teenage pregnancy are often disastrous. It increases the health risks to both mother and child. Several studies (Gunter & LaBarba, 1980; Hamburg, 1989; Hayes, 1987) have shown that adolescent prenatal care is inadequate in most cases. Adolescent mothers have a death rate 60% higher than the rate among older women (Thorburg, 1985). They also are liable to have numerous health problems and are at high risk for abuse and neglect of their children (Alan Guttmacher Institute, 1976). Single adolescent mothers have less of a chance than their peers of getting married and a much greater chance of divorce if they do. Among girls who keep their babies (90%), only two out of ten marry the father (Furstenberg, Brooks-Gunn, & Morgan, 1987a, 1987b; Norton & Glick, 1986; Hayes, 1987).

The young woman who chooses a premarital birth script generally has a social life that is altered drastically, most likely for the worst. Dependable peer relationships are critical for proper psychological development of the adolescent. However, the script that the teenage mother assumes changes her position in the social group in a variety of ways. First, it is unlikely that she will be able to engage in the amount of interaction as she did previously. Secondly, her peers may become intimidated by her and her situation and, as a result, avoid contact. This can be emotionally painful to her, because the support of peers in a time of crisis can be helpful for the maintenance of her emotional well-being. Thirdly, peers may change their feelings about her, denigrating her character as possibly immoral, irresponsible, or promiscuous, adding to her emotional isolation. Finally, opposite sex relationships may cease to exist for the teenage mother, as adolescent males make similar assumptions. And, if the teenage father is not supportive, the adolescent mother may be bereft of any social support whatsoever.

Adolescent fathers face similar problems. Along with experiencing similar peer attitudes as the teenage mother, the teenage father also may be estranged from the family of the girl, even if he desires to be supportive

(Cervera, 1991). The father may want to participate in the caretaking of the child but may be prevented from doing so as much as he would like. He also may have the financial burdens of raising a family at a very young age when he is emotionally, physically, and/or financially unable to do so.

The baby also faces increased risks. Babies born to adolescent mothers are more likely than babies born to older mothers to have low birth weights, neurological defects, and childhood illnesses, all of which are major causes of infant mortality (Bolton, 1980). The social and economic consequences can be enormous. Adolescent mothers are twice as likely to drop out of school, less likely to be employed, and more likely to be dependent on welfare. Fully half of all payments made under the Aid to Families with Dependent Children (AFDC) go to women who bore children during their adolescent years (Gilchrist & Schinke, 1983).

Furstenberg et al. (1987a, 1987b) reported on their 17-year followup study of women who had been teenage mothers. The authors emphasized the tremendous variability of the group and warned against stereotyping the so-called consequences of adolescent parenthood. Although the literature and some mental health professionals emphasize the highly adverse effects of teenage parents on their youngsters, much of the research evidence has failed to support this generalization as it applies to young children. However, by the time these children reached adolescence, they were more likely to have academic and behavioral problems at school when they were compared to children whose mothers were older when they gave birth.

Many factors exist that influence and contribute to the creation of a new life script due to a premarital birth. Some important influences are the assistance and support the mother has from her family of origin—both financially and emotionally. Young single mothers who remain home and have the support of their families are more likely to return to school and graduate. In these cases, more of these mothers become employable and fewer receive welfare. These mothers exhibit better parenting skills, have help with child-rearing, and are less socially isolated from their peers than those who receive no familial support (Jemail & Nathanson, 1987). Here, mothers are able to salvage some of the socially approved dominant script by finishing school and establishing themselves in a job or career. However, the birth of the child to an unmarried young woman also could create a prolonged dependency on the parents and possibly can function to maintain the possible preexisting dysfunctional organizational and communication patterns in the original family.

Family therapy researchers have identified variables strongly associated with a premarital pregnancy script. They include growing up in a single parent household and coming from homes and family systems marked by a high degree of family disruption (Zongker, 1980). Family environment factors are related to the decisions made by pregnant adolescents. Held (1981) found that pregnant adolescents viewed their mothers as important (often more important than themselves) and disapproving. Coblener (1981) also found problematic relationships with mother to be prominent and described three profiles of these relationships: the retaining or binding mother, the controlling mother, and the abandoning mother. Other studies have shown no differences in family environment between groups of pregnant and nonpregnant adolescents (Honeyman, 1981). Hatcher (1973) linked the motivation of adolescents for becoming pregnant with the desire to break away from the mother (early adolescents) and the desire to compete with her (middle adolescents). Fox and Inazu (1980) found that an association existed between more responsible patterns of daughters' sexual behavior and frequency of parental communication. Olson and Worobey (1984) found that pregnant adolescents perceived less love, attention, and interdependence in their relationships with their mothers than did their nonpregnant peers. Thus, the quality and degree of parent-daughter interaction (Rawlins, 1984) and the presence of both parents in the home (Gispert, Brinich, Wheeler, & Krieger, 1984) are important variables associated with regular use of contraception among adolescents.

Once again, though, we need to be careful about generalizing these studies on premarital pregnancy scripts to mean that faulty relationships with the adolescent's mother creates the script conducive for the daughter to become pregnant. There are very few studies that examined the relation between the adolescent's father and the likelihood of her becoming pregnant. And it is only recently that feminist family therapists have pointed out the sexist assumptions in family therapy theory and practice (Goldner, 1985). One study by Zongker (1980) pointed to the impact of the father's absence on the teenage daughter. This author asserted that the deprivation of a male parental relationship with the daughter during these formative years impels her to seek compensatory masculine attention through precocious sexual relations. In addition, to date, no one has examined the relation between the adolescent boy's family characteristics and his likelihood of impregnating an adolescent girl.

Regardless of whether or not the single mother has the support of her family, there are many changes that must occur: she no longer only has her individual script; she has a single-parent family script as well. Her world becomes "we" instead of "I." Brown (1989) believed that many single mothers experience a number of problems in establishing themselves as a viable unit. Three new problems must be incorporated into their new life script: money, parenting, and social relationships. Generally speaking, creating a new script was not expected nor planned for. Financially, even if the young mother obtains a job, it still will be difficult for her to "make ends meet" without additional public assistance. It is probably true that she will be unable to maintain her prior standard of living. She must now consider child-care costs; free time is almost an impossibility. Time for relaxation, socializing, hobbies, and other interests, which may have been in abundance in the old life script, is rarely found in the new script. Instead the new script generally involves task overload. In addition, she may experience new feelings such as guilt, fatigue, shame, anger, resentment, and anxiety. Learning the role of a parent—caretaking, loving, disciplining, and nurturing—must be accomplished. The young woman generally makes many sacrifices where she perhaps never did before. In addition, she may feel socially isolated. For someone who possibly had many friends, peer relationships, and social activities as part of her life script prior to the pregnancy, feelings of social isolation, loneliness, depression, and fear now may be experienced (Brown, 1989; Young & Ruth, 1983).

When a young woman has a child before marriage, many life scripts are affected. For example, not only is the woman's individual script affected, the family of origin script may be affected as well. If her family is providing support, they also must deal with their own role changes and their own script modifications. Parents who were looking forward to their children growing up may have major role adjustments when the new infant is introduced into the immediate family.

## WIDOWERHOOD—A BACKWARDS SCRIPT?

Most marriages end with a partner's death. Although a spouse can die during early or middle adult years, widowhood usually occurs later in life. In most cases, it is the man who dies first, a tendency that has become more pronounced in this century. The ratio of widows to widowers has increased from less than two-to-one in the early 1900s to five-to-one in the 1970s (Hoult & Smith, 1978). Of the more than 22 million people in the United States who are 65 years old and older, almost one-half of the women and one-fifth of the men have lost their marital partners (Leslie & Leslie, 1977), resulting in over 11.5 million widows and widowers in the United States. This represents approximately 13% of all women over the age of 18. Growth in the number and proportion of women who are widows is likely to continue for the rest of this century, since census projections indicate an increase of 43% in the size of the total population over 65 by the year 2000.

Most preindustrial societies have very clear scripts for widows. This is not the case in industrialized societies. In fact, to a large degree, widowhood can be defined more by the collapse of old scripts, roles, and structural supports than by norms and institutions that specify or provide new scripts, role relationships, and behavior patterns. Lopata (1975) concluded from her data that American society has been phasing out the traditional status role of "widow" as an all-pervasive lifelong identity: "Usually, widowhood is a temporary stage of identity reconstruction, and this is a major problem. The direction of movement out of it is not clearly defined" (p. 47). It is even less clearly defined when the person left behind is a man.

The death of a spouse is one of the most serious life script crises a person may face. The immediate emotional crisis of bereavement, if not fully worked through, may result in psychological symptoms. As stated in earlier sections of this chapter, during the first few days of bereavement, sacred and secular guidelines define the proper mourning script. However, over the longer term, there is generally a need for the restructuring of the person's life script as persons often find themselves much poorer if they are female, socially isolated, and left without a meaningful lifestyle. Whether the survivor is a man or a woman, the death of a loved one deprives the survivor of various kinds of satisfaction. Generally speaking, the deceased served as a satisfier of the physical needs of the bereaved as well as a source of emotional gratification. As a consequence, over the years, the bereaved's sense of identity and the meaning of his or her life may have become intertwined with the personality of the deceased. Somehow the individual must now learn to cope with the loss and the resulting stress.

The period of greatest stress for the bereaved is usually immediately after the death of the deceased. This is the time when the reactions of the bereaved are most intense. Among the behavioral reactions observed during the first month of mourning are periodic crying, difficulty sleeping, loss of appetite, and problems in concentrating or remembering. A study of 109 widowed persons found that the emotional disturbances and insomnia associated with bereavement also can lead to dependence on tranquilizers, sleeping pills, and/or alcohol. The emotional reactions of a surviving spouse, who in 75% of the cases is the wife, may be so intense that severe physical illness, a serious accident, or even death—occasionally from suicide—occurs. It was found in a study of 4,500 British widowers aged 55 and over, for example, that 213 died during the first six months of their bereavement (Parkes, Benjamin, & Fitzgerald, 1969). The rate of death, most instances of which apparently resulted from heart problems, was 40% higher than expected in this age group. Concluding from a series of related investigations that grief and consequent feelings of helplessness make people more vulnerable to pathogens, Seligman (1975) suggested that individuals who recently have lost a spouse would do well to be very careful about their health. He recommended monthly medical checkups during the first year after the loss.

Although anxiety and depression are the most common reactions to bereavement, anger, guilt, and even psychotic symptoms have been observed. Depression is a normal response to any severe loss, but it is augmented by feelings of guilt in cases where interpersonal hostilities and conflicts with the deceased have not been resolved. Anger may be expressed—toward nurses, physicians, friends, and family members whom the bereavement believes to have been negligent in their treatment of the deceased. For various reasons, survivors also may experience anger toward the deceased or relief at his or her death—both of which can lead to feelings of guilt. The emotional and psychological traumas of grief and mourning involve "letting go" of the emotional ties and roles—the script—centered on the loved one. If this working through of grief is accomplished successfully, the widow(er) can face a second set of problems having to do with building a new life—a new script—including a new set of role relationships and a new identity.

Theorists have discussed stages in the grief process. For example, Bowlby (1960) found evidence for five stages in mourning: (1) concentration on the deceased, (2) anger toward the deceased or others, (3) appeals to others for help, (4) despair, withdrawal, and disorganization, and (5) reorganization and direction of love toward a new object. Relatively little research has been done on Bowlby's stages, but it is recognized that not all mourners go through them in the order listed. Kavanaugh (1974) also described stages in the process of grieving or mourning for a loved one: shock, disorganization, volatile emotions, guilt, loss and loneliness, relief, and reestablishment. Kavanaugh (1974) also recognized that a particular mourner may not go through all these stages and not necessarily in the order listed. Gorer (1979) also presented a three-stage conception of mourning: (1) Initial shock is the first stage, which lasts only a few days and is characterized by loss of self-control, reduced energy, and lack of motivation. The mourner is bewildered, disoriented, and looses perspective. The person cannot accept the fact that "he/she is really dead, gone forever." This numbness often extends for several weeks beyond the funeral. (2) Stage 1 is followed by intense grief, the second stage. This stage is characterized by emotional reactions such as crying, a confused inability to comprehend what has actually happened, often accompanied by such psychosomatic symptoms as headache and insomnia; feelings of guilt ("If I had done so and so, maybe he wouldn't have died."); expressions of anger ("Why me! It is so unfair!"); hostility or blame ("The doctors killed her."); and often preoccupation with memories of the deceased and an idealization of him or her. The second stage can last for several months, but it gradually gives way for the third stage. (3) During the third stage, feelings of sadness and loneliness, which are often incapacitating, surface, along with feelings of extreme depression and loss of customary patterns of behavior and of motivation to try to go in living. This is followed by a recovery phase. Here there is a general recovery of interest. During this final phase, the mourner accepts the reality of the loved one's death and all that it means. As Glick, Jerussi, Waters, and Green (1974) have concluded from their extensive studies on bereavement, "the death of a spouse typically gives rise to a reaction whose duration must be measured in years rather than in weeks" (p. 10).

A variety of grief reactions may occur when the mourner does not express emotions or refuses to deal with the loss. These include delay of the grief reactions for months or even years, overactivity without a sense of loss, indefinite irritability and hostility toward others, a sense of the presence of the deceased, acquisition of the physical symptoms of the deceased's last illness, insomnia, apathy, psychosomatically based illnesses such as ulcerative colitis, and such intense depression and feelings of worthlessness that suicide is attempted (Parkes, 1972, p. 211). One tendency is to reconstruct an idealized script of one's deceased spouse and of the role relationship with him or her before the death. Referring to this as "spouse sanctification," Lopata (1975) reported that three quarters of the Chicago area current and former beneficiaries of Social Security define their late spouses as having been extremely good, honest, kind, friendly, and warm. Sanctification is especially likely among women. It is an attempt to continue defining oneself primarily in terms of the now-ended marital script, and Lopata (1975) viewed this as an effort to "remove the late spouse into an other worldly position as an understanding but purified and distant observer" (p. 30) so that the widow(er) is able to go about reconstructing old role relationships and forming new ones.

## Prolonged Grief

Several factors are related to severe or prolonged grief. Sixty-eight widows and widowers under the age of 45 were interviewed shortly after the spouse died and again a year later. Three classes of strongly correlated variables predicted continued severe bereavement reactions 13 months after the death (Parkes, 1975, pp. 308-309): (1) Low socioeconomic status, i.e., low weekly income of the husband; (2) lack of preparation for the loss due to noncancer deaths, short terminal illness, accident, or heart attack, or failure to talk to the spouse about the coming death; and (3) other life crises preceding spouse's death, such as infidelity and job loss. Another problem is the amount of unfinished business (Blauner, 1966) left by the removal of the husband through death. Parkes (1975) concluded that for his young respondents, including widowers as well as widows, "When advance warning was short and death was sudden, it seemed to have a much greater impact and lead to greater and more lasting disorganization" (Parkes, 1975, p. 313).

## Gender Differences

The specific impact of widowerhood on men has received little systematic attention, and the role of widower is probably even vaguer than that of the widow. Because widowers who have not remarried are not very common in the community until after about age 75, they are not as likely to join each other in groups. Like widows, their script dictates that they are expected to preserve the memories of their wives and are expected not to show interest in other women. Indications are that many widowers adhere to the former but ignore the latter, as can be inferred from the remarriage rates cited earlier.

It appears that women who are widowed do not experience that life event in the same way that men do. For example, in a study of 403 community residents aged 62 and over, six major areas of life functioning were assessed: psychosocial needs, household roles, nutrition, health care, transportation, and education (Barrett, 1978). Widowers were found to experience lower morale, to feel lonelier and more dissatisfied with life, to consider community services more inadequate, to need more help with household chores, to have greater difficulty getting medical appointments, to eat more poorly, and to possess stronger negative attitudes about continued learning than widows. Moreover, widowers were more reluctant to talk about widowerhood or death than widows were and stated that they did not want a confidante.

Based on available research, widows seem to fare better than widowers after the death of a loved one. Clearly something other than simple numbers is operating with respect to sex differences in coping with widow(er)hood. It is the contention of the present authors that persons experiencing backwards scripts tend to experience intensification of the emotions typically encountered in bereavement situations. In addition, men who have led their entire lives playing instrumental, at the expense of expressive, marital roles, have poorly prepared scripts for widowerhood. On one level, these men probably have been dependent upon their wives for the performance of the most basic maintenance tasks, such as preparing a meal or running a washing machine; they may feel helpless in tending to daily necessities. Then, too, a general unwillingness exists among some of these men to perform "women's work" if there is any way they can avoid it. They may have difficulty breaking lifelong scripts toward sex role behaviors.

Also, those men who have taken most seriously the traditional cultural script of emotion or sensitivity among males may not have developed genuinely close friendships. One might argue that they have been preoccupied with their script of what it means to be a man at the expense of true same-sex intimacy. Another reason might be that their script does not include feeling comfortable risking their feelings or expressing fears and concerns to peers, whereas within a traditional/subordinate type marriage, a wife can be used as confidante without the husband fearing a loss of face (Balsweick & Peek, 1971). For whatever reasons, studies indicate that among middle and lower socioeconomic groups, male friendships resemble play or meet work oriented goals rather than genuine interpersonal needs. There is evidence that men, especially in late middle age, experience awareness of the superficiality of their friendships and express regret (Lowenthal & Weiss, 1976).

Perhaps because women have been permitted, indeed have been culturally coerced, to play expressive roles within families and have been socialized to display such attributes as emotionality and sensitivity to others, they show more flexibility in the object of their close relationships. Women often have intimate same-sex friendships at various life stages. Thus, the prevalence of friendships among older widows not only reflects the dearth of available widowers at that age but also their prior experiences and comfortability within such relationships. Both in terms of same-sex friendships and in ability to run a household on a day-to-day level, widowed women tend to be better prepared for living alone than their male counterparts. This is one reason why the great majority of widowers remarry within a year or so after their wife's death.

Glick et al. (1974) reported that widowers have more difficulty on jobs than do widows during the mourning period. Because jobs are primary in men's lives, widowers may be more sensitive to job disruption than are widows. Widowers do not differ from widows in feeling isolated from kin or friends. Nor are widowed men and women, on the whole, more isolated than are their married peers. In fact, after being widowed, those who have friends tend to see them more often (Petrowsky, 1976). When Atchley (1975) controlled for social class, he found that widowhood tends to increase contacts with friends among middle-class widowers and to decrease contacts among lower-class widowers. It could be that the large surplus of women in senior centers and similar social groups for older people—generally used more by working-class people than by middle-class people—may inhibit working-class widowers from developing new kinds of community activities. Widowers tend to be embarrassed and even to feel harassed by the competition among widows for their attentions. Moreover, they are unaccustomed to participating in such preponderantly female gatherings, where women dominate discussions and other activities. Petrowsky (1976) found that widowers were less involved in religious activities than were widows, an effect that probably is due to a continuation of religious participation sex differences established earlier in life.

As stated earlier, the male's life expectancy is shorter than the female's, and generally speaking wives expect to outlive their husbands. When the reverse is the case, the situation may be considered a backwards script. For many men, the expectation that they will die before their wife is part of their life script. Often they prepare for this by making all sorts of financial arrangements in order to ensure that their wives will be taken care of after they are gone. Few men consider or plan for the time when they may be left alone without their spouse, and few give thought to the possibility of their wives dying first. Bowling (1988–89) believed that widowhood has a more deleterious effect on men than on women. He believed that the loss of a spouse in old age is harder for men to cope with than women. This makes sense considering that most men have not planned for this event to take place in their life script. For many men, it is planned and expected that they will retire and die before their wives. This is the "typical" script reinforced by the statistics for life expectancy. Not often do elderly women worry about whether or not they have big enough pensions or enough savings to support their husbands after their own deaths; yet men often voice these concerns.

Many of their behaviors in life reflect their concerns about ensuring that the loved ones they leave behind are provided for. When an elderly man's wife dies before him, he is left scriptless.

Death of a marital partner is less unexpected and untimely than the death of a child; however, this anticipatory preparation does not necessarily protect persons from equally intense separation anxiety, sadness, loneliness, and despair when the loss finally does occur. Sociologists Jacobs, Kasl, Ostfeld, Berkman, and Charpentier (1986) have observed that sex-determined role expectations for men emphasize the importance of appearing competent, independent, under control, and unemotional. Given these social expectations, it is reasonable to speculate that the expression of grief may be suppressed in men when they experience the death of their wives.

Evidence suggests that the mortality risk is greater for men up to the first six months of widowerhood. This risk might be increased due to the stress of bereavement, lack of adequate social support, and/or the stresses of role changes (Bowling, 1988–89). It also can be affected by the loss of care that was given by the deceased wife or the poor baseline health status for men in general (Jacobs et al., 1986 ). Role theory argues that the death of a spouse not only removes the protective buffer of a partner, but also leaves the widowed in a worse position than the never married. The widowed may find themselves suddenly not only lonely and deprived of their major source of support, but also confronted with the loss of material and task supports. This is especially true for men who, in many cases, must not only take over the share of the household tasks that had been performed previously by the spouse, but must learn them as well. For a widower this can mean the homemaking and housekeeping. Older men are probably the least prepared for coping alone in terms of cooking for themselves and performing household chores. In such circumstances, it is possible that feelings of inability to cope, self-neglect, and malnourishment may occur (Bowling, 1988–89).

**Redefining the Script**

Before widowers can begin to redefine their relationships with family and friends, or begin to form new adult relationships, they first must come to terms with the loss of the previous spouse. With the death of a spouse, the external reality of the widower is permanently altered: a partner is absent, economic status generally changes, there are fewer people available to complete requisite tasks, etc. Relationships with in-laws, with one's own family, and with coupled and single friends may change to the degree that they had previously been predicated upon the presence of the now absent partner. The successful redefinition of these relationships is of central importance to the well-being of the person.

The memory of what used to be can create an alternative, subjectively held reality for some widowers. For these persons the maintenance of a relationship with the "ghost" of the absent partner can become a central therapy issue; living with ghosts while ignoring the living does not represent an adequate adjustment to an altered lifestyle. Redefining relationships with family and friends in the present becomes impossible for those who refuse to acknowledge the differences between then and now. The clinical picture is different for those persons who, at the level of the unconscious, refuse to give up the ghost of the past. For these persons, the ghost becomes a demon who makes impossible an adequate adjustment to life's reality demands.

The present authors do not agree with the position taken by many theorists (e.g., Pollock, 1975) that one of the reasons for studying loss reactions following death is that such study will inform the understanding of reactions to all forms of loss. Franz (1984) wrote, "Coping and grieving are things we learn, we are taught, and we develop from the time we are infants. By the time we are adults we've all had a lot of experiences with loss starting with the rattle in our own crib, up on through our baseball gloves, dolls, teddy bears, high school boyfriend or girlfriend, graduation from high school or college, moving away from friends, and grandparents dying" (p. 21). The implication seems to be that a loss is a loss is a loss, regardless of whom or what was lost. We believe this to be true in only the most general way: all losses involve the breaking of an attachment bond (Bowlby, 1969). Not all bonds are equally strong; neither are all equally desirable. It seems reasonable, therefore, that loss reactions are moderated by these variables.

**Creating a New Script**

In order for a widower to continue living without his spouse, he will have to incorporate a new life script. Since grief and depression resulting from bereavement can be assumed to provide stress, stress theory would have no problem accounting for the increase in mental and physical disorders and even mortality in grieving men (Bowling, 1988–89). In order to create a new life script successfully, a widower must conquer a series of complex tasks. In order to begin the construction of the new script, the widower should reconstitute a coherent and consistent self-concept, including addressing feelings of grief and mourning and reintegrating these feelings into an ongoing psychological portrait of himself. He should examine the meaning and importance of the lost relationship as well as the new importance he has found in his life to continue living. He must negotiate a new "single" role that is not based on being a couple. He should explore any feelings of stigmatization associated with being widowed in our culture as well as, for many, the loosening of old ties with friends and family. If these tasks can be accomplished, the widower can then renegotiate old relationships and develop new social linkages (Lieberman, 1989).

Mourning is the process through which the subjectively held internal reality of the widower becomes aligned with external reality. The burden of change is upon the mourner. Parkes and Weiss (1983) wrote, "Those who recover from bereavement do not return to being the same people they had been before their marriages or before their spouses' deaths. Nor do they forget the past and start a new life. Rather, they recognize that change has taken place, accept it, examine how their basic assumptions about themselves and their world must be changed and go on from there" (p. 81). Most people do not give up the ghost as easily as may be implied from this citation.

Walsh (1991) posited that three primary tasks must be accomplished. They are the reorganization of the roles of the remaining members of the family in order to accomplish necessary tasks, the shared acknowledgment of the loss, and the reinvestment of energy into new relationships and activities. The therapist must help the client focus on the necessary family structural changes and create an atmosphere where the widower is free to openly express any and all feelings of loss and is open to the possibility of new satisfactions. The therapist must be aware that many of the most powerful behavior-directing relationship rules are covert and below the level of the client's consciousness. Here it is helpful for the therapist to help the client make the covert overt.

The therapist serves an educational function when he or she is able to take what is known from theory (Bowlby, 1969; Parkes & Weiss, 1983) and apply it to the client's experience. In so doing, the therapist not only normalizes the widower's experience, but also provides a unifying theme for the many disparate and distressing manifestations of loss. In adopting a developmental stance with regard to widowhood, the therapist assists the client in becoming aware of the possibility of new and satisfying relationships in the present and in the future. In helping the client renegotiate old relationships and establish new ones, the therapist is aware of the dyadic nature of relationships. In taking this position, the therapist helps the client explore the renegotiation from a systemic as well as from an individual perspective. The therapist thus remains open to the possibility and desirability of conjoint sessions with the widower or extended family members and friends.

The therapist should be aware that the impact of the dissolution of the marital bond in the present may be exacerbated by whatever family of origin legacies the person brings to his or her own situation. Does the death of a spouse rekindle previous unresolved loss? The therapist helps the client understand these historical issues not only through insight oriented counseling, but also through the use of sessions with the client's family of origin if they are available, or with the client's own family. For those persons who need help in dealing with the ghosts of past relationships, McGoldrick (1987) placed great emphasis on the open flow of information among family members. In the relationship review technique, the individual or family member tells the story of his or her own relationship with the former spouse. The review begins with each individual's first memory of the relationship. Ghost-related issues are often highlighted by an unrealistic view of the person; the former spouse often is seen either as an angel or as a demon. The open expression of these misrepresentations allows other family members to serve as reality checks for one another and to dispute irrational beliefs. The authors also suggest that asking the family very specific questions concerning the details surrounding the loss also serves to open up the system. Visits to the cemetery, writing letters to the deceased, making picture albums, and keeping a journal of memories and feelings are also suggested.

Parkes and Weiss (1983) separated the process of recovery from loss into three phases. The goal of the first is intellectual recognition. During this phase, the therapist helps the person formulate a story that settles the question of "why" the loss occurred. Without such an account, the ability to reinvest in new relationships is diminished. If people do not know why they have suffered a painful loss, they will be loathe to form new attachment bonds that may again, for no reason, be taken from them. The goal of the second phase is emotional acceptance. Operationally, emotional acceptance implies a diminished fear of being overwhelmed by grief, pain, or remorse. Part of the recovery process involves the working through of what Parkes and Weiss (1983) referred to as the obsessive review—the painful and time consuming task of dealing with each and every memory trace of the former relationship, grieving over it, and ultimately neutralizing it. No change in the content of the review is contraindicative of growth. In the third phase, identity transformation, the person creates new self-definitions that are not predicated on the previous relationship. When a widower reports, "I want to find another wife," the therapist sees the meaning behind the words: The ghost has been exorcised.

# SOCIAL CONSTRUCTIONIST THERAPY WITH BACKWARDS SCRIPTS

Social constructionist therapy explores the individual's or family's meanings and beliefs that are present in person's backwards scripts as well as how these meanings "fit" into and influence persons' behavior. The dialectical relationship between individual realities and the socially constructed meanings around the "backwards script" is the focus of this form of therapy.

In order for a therapist to be most effective, he or she should begin therapy by joining with the individual's or family's meaning system, or constructing a workable reality. It is important to join with each member of the family, to be an active listener, and to be nonjudgmental. The therapist must work at not imposing his or her own reality, values, beliefs, and meaning system on the family. Instead, he or she should listen to the family's language, learn it, and use it in order to create a comfortable and safe environment that will foster change and growth. The individual or the family will feel comfortable if they feel that the therapist is empathic and if they feel that they are being heard, validated, and respected.

Sally is a 20-year-old college student. She lives with her widowed father and her 18-year-old brother. Ed is Sally's boyfriend. They broke up last month when Sally informed Ed that she was pregnant and was keeping the baby. Sally stated that although this baby will "throw off her life and plans completely," she would not and could not consider an abortion. "It would be like killing a member of my own family." The belief and value that a child needs and deserves its mother is very deep and emotional for Sally. She believes that her mother's death, when Sally was only four, contributes to this outlook on life. Sally also strongly believes that with enough support, love, and determination, a single parent can "successfully" raise a child. "Just look at my father; he raised two children on his own."

It is important in this first stage of therapy that the therapist listen to and hear the client's beliefs and language about the problem. The therapist needs to join with Sally and her family and respect and support the decision to "add another member to the family." Joining is the process by which empathic rapport is developed through socialization with the clients. The therapist's reflections serve to create an environment conducive to change. The basic assumption is that the client is expert in knowing what is best for him or her. If the therapist doubts the client's competency or challenges the client's views, beliefs, and values, this will make for an uncomfortable environment and will not foster change and growth. In these cases, it is most likely that the therapist will lose the client.

In the next phase of therapy, the therapist allows those individuals in the family to each tell their "story." It is the stories that people have about their lives that determines the meaning that they ascribe to their experiences (White, 1989). The plotting of experiences or events into stories or "self-narratives" is necessary in order for people to make sense of their lives, provides them with a sense of coherence and continuity, and is relied upon for the achievement of a sense of purpose (Gergen & Gergen, 1988). During the family's storying, the therapist takes the role of a curious observer, one who listens to the family's story about their experiences with their families of origin, their present relationship, and their views about the future. "Problems are stories people have agreed to tell themselves" (Hoffman, 1990, p. 3), and by hearing these stories, the therapist can gain a clearer understanding of the family's frame of the problem. An example of a therapist understanding a client's belief or story is exemplified by a session that involved an elderly widower. When listening to the client's story about his family of origin, the therapist learned that his client's mother was a widow at age 53. The client stated that his mother's life was full of grief and despair, "she was just going through the motions of existing day by day," until she herself died 2 years later. This elderly widowers belief was that "life ended" with the death of one's spouse. He also believed that "life could never again be fun" without his wife (Florsheim & Gallagher-Thompson, 1990). Being aware of this belief, the therapist now can challenge the client's thinking and views and provide opportunities for alternative beliefs containing hope and possibility.

Once everyone's past stories are told, it is important to concentrate on the family's present meaning system. If a family is rooted and stuck in the past, it is beneficial to spend a session or two exploring these past meaning systems. If the family is forced to move on before they are ready, therapy can be hindered due to unresolved issues resurfacing and halting the process. This is very important to remember when working with the backwards script of losing a child. Society and possibly the therapist himself or herself may feel and deem that the family is ready to move on. The therapist must respect each client's grieving process and time period as to not disrespect or devalue the client's need to hold on to the past a little longer. The child's father may be ready to move on and may want to discuss his relationship with his new wife and how it was changed by the tragedy, while the child's mother cannot yet hear let alone discuss her new marriage when she is still focused on the stories, memories, and lost hopes and dreams she had for her child. It is important that the therapist be aware of the different ways and different rates that the family members grieve so as not to disrespect or ignore anyone's pain and/or reality. Once the past story is explored and put into perspective, the family will feel more comfortable burying it and moving on. A ritual might be appropriate at this time. One family who was dealing with the death of their 12-year-old daughter/sibling together redecorated her bedroom. The bedroom was an important part of the discussion since it had not been touched or rearranged in any way since the child's death. The room was honored as a shrine and was bringing uncomfortable memories and feelings to all who viewed it, including the family. The family moved forward by having a portrait of the lost loved one made and displayed in the "family room"—"She will always be remembered as part of our family."

At this point in therapy, now the present can be concentrated on with less distraction. Here, the constructed family meaning system about the issue is explored and uncovered. At this time, the therapist pays attention to family myths, legends, and metaphors while languaging with the clients about the problem. Some relevant questions are, "How do you view the event that brought you all here? What solutions have you attempted to help the situation? What other options do you feel you can try? What attempts were made that you felt were beneficial?" When families learn about their meaning system and see that they each "view" their problems differently, they gather information about how each of them inadvertently contributed to and perpetuated the existence of the problem.

Once the family accepts that their meaning system about the problem is socially constructed, it becomes possible to deconstruct. Ways of doing this can involve learning about the origins of their meanings around the situation and their attempted solutions to it and exploring the extent of their meanings' validity and usefulness. A family's meaning system can be challenged and/or recombined to create new experiences. The goal is for the therapist to see or view the clients' experience through their eyes and to help them develop alternative perspectives. Some ways of challenging the family's meaning system and amplifying their process are tracking, exaggeration, and circular questioning. Tracking the story about the problem sometimes helps the family to see the redundancy and recursiveness of their actions, beliefs, and language around the problem (Atwood & Dershowitz, 1992). Exaggeration of the family's beliefs and meaning system sometimes can assist the family in realizing the discrepancies and inconsistencies in their story. The widower, in the example cited earlier, repeatedly stated how his life is "no longer fun" and how he is "always depressed." By questioning the client about his weekend, the therapist uncovered that his daughter invited him to his granddaughter's birthday party. It was apparent from the client's body language and lively discussion about the party that this was a happy event for him. The therapist pointed out this discrepancy, "How did you manage to not have fun and be depressed while you were happy and enjoying yourself?" The client realized the inconsistency in what he said and how he felt and behaved over the weekend with his family. A change of perception is now possible for the client since he can no longer say he is *always* depressed and that life is no longer fun. Once the family's story ceases to make sense to them, it becomes impossible for them to continue to tell it the same way. Once the story begins to fall apart and the family holds different views of their problem that also make sense to them, they must work at constructing a new frame for their family system. White (1989) proposed the process of "externalization" to assist people in the reauthoring of their lives. "Externalizing" is an approach that encourages people to objectify and, at times, to personify the problems that they experience as oppressive. In this process the problem becomes a separate entity and thus external to the person who was, or the relationship that was, ascribed the problem. Problems are thus rendered less fixed and less restricting: ". . . this new perspective enabled the development of an alternative story of family life, one that was more attractive to family members" (White, 1989, p. 5).

It is the therapist's choice as to how to intervene in the family's meaning system around the "backwards script." The therapist may choose to amplify exceptions to the presenting problem by working on a part of the family's meaning system around the "backwards script" or a part of the "backwards script" itself. Or, the therapist can work on the family's meaning system as a whole. Both ways eventually will lead to change: ". . . working with a part is like chipping away at a brick wall while working with the whole is like tearing down the wall all at once (Atwood & Dershowitz, 1992). "It is never the size of the step that a person takes that counts, but its direction" (White, 1989). At this point, the role of the therapist is to notice competing constructions or exceptions in the family's meaning system. An example of this is evident with the mother/family whose child died. The mother believes that she no longer feels like being a mother. A piece of her motherhood has been taken from her, and she feels she can no longer function as such.

Through questioning, the therapist learned that the mother defined motherhood as a loving devoted person who is available to her children for love, guidance, support, and advice. The other two children in the family then provided her with examples of her mothering to them in the past week. The children's examples fit perfectly with the mother's definition of motherhood. Her children provided her with the exceptions to how she was viewing herself since her daughter's death.

Change requires a two-sided perspective, and a therapist may seek to construct a relational definition by developing two (or complementary) descriptions of the problem (White, 1986). As the family receives competing constructions about their "backwards script," their frame or "brick wall" begins to crumble and leave spaces for new constructions, new frames, and growth. No family is comfortable with being "scriptless," so when their script no longer fits, they are left with no choice but to construct a new workable reality for their family system that they all can contribute to, make sense of, and accept as their new world view or reality.

The therapist needs to amplify the family's new meaning system so that their new more constructive view seems reachable, realistic, and inevitable. This gives the family hope for their future and control over their lives. If the family has the opportunity to deepen their relationships with each other without the problem, their new reality and view will be much more positive and forthcoming.

Before terminating with clients, it is imperative that their new meaning system be stabilized. In order to accomplish this, the therapist can focus on the future. For example, the therapist can ask questions about how the family sees their future without the problem. By concentrating on the future, the family's hopes for a future without the problem become possible. When faced with questions about the future—even if that future is hypothetical—the system is free to create a new map" (Penn, 1985).

## DISCUSSION

By no means is it being suggested that by simply communicating and creating a new narrative, a family can overcome easily the shock and overwhelmedness of a "backwards script." As discussed earlier, many stages must be completed successfully in order for a family or individual to be able to cope with and make sense out of a life cycle tragedy. A "backwards script" can leave a family or individual with many realistic and tangible problems such as financial and economic difficulties and social constraints. These very real life crises are by no means being minimized.

What is being suggested here is that social constructionist therapy can help clients reconstruct what is important to them in order to provide them with more options for action. Clients are provided with alternative perspectives of their view of their "backwards script" in order to change their behavior if they choose to do so (Viney, Benjamin, & Preston, 1988). The successful functioning of families who experience a "backwards script" requires a flexibility in structure and roles. One will always remember and sometimes even continue to feel the pain caused by a "backwards script." One also has the opportunity to process the pain and emotions it brings forth. What hopefully can follow is a shift in the manner in which the person dealt with the problem or tragedy. Growth seldom comes without pain and conflict, and there is no conflict that cannot lead to gain. We have to increase our recognition of the occurrences of "backwards scripts" and use the unavoidable confusion, conflict, and pain to help us grow as individuals and families (Pincus, 1974).

## REFERENCES

Alan Guttmacher Institute. (1976). *Eleven million teenagers: What can be done about the epidemic of teenage pregnancies in the U.S.?* New York: Alan Guttmacher Institute.

Alexy, W.D. (1982). Dimensions of psychological counseling that facilitate the grieving process of bereaved parents. *Journal of Counseling Psychology, 29*(5), 498–507.

Atchley, R.C. (1975). *Social forces in later life.* Belmont, CA: Wadler.

Atwood, J.D., & Dershowitz, S. (1992, Fall). Constructing a sex and marital therapy frame: Ways to help couples deconstruct sexual problems. *Journal of Sex & Marital Therapy, 18*(3), 196–218.

Balsweick, B., & Peck, G. (1971). The inexpressive male: A tragedy of American society. *The Family Coordinator, 20*, 363–368.

Barrett, J. (1978). *Individual goals and organizational objectives: A study of integration mechanisms*. Ann Arbor, MI: Center for Research on Utilization of Scientific Knowledge, University of Michigan Press.

Berger, P., & Luckmann, T. (1966). *The social construction of reality*. New York: Irvington.

Blauner, R. (1966). Death and social structure. In B.L. Newgartin (Ed.), *Middleage and aging* (pp. 531–540). Chicago: University of Chicago Press.

Bolton, F. (1980). *The pregnant adolescent*. Beverly Hills, CA: Sage.

Bordow, J. (1982). *The ultimate loss: Coping with the death of a child*. New York, Toronto: Beaufort Books.

Bowlby, J. (1960). Grief and mourning in infancy and early childhood. *Psychoanalytic Study of the Child, 15*, 9–52.

Bowlby, J. (1969). *Attachment and loss, volume 3*. New York: Basic books.

Bowling, A. (1988–89). Who dies after widow(er)hood? A discriminant analysis. *Omega, 19*(2), 135–153.

Brown, F.H. (1989). The postdivorce family. In B. Carter & M. McGoldrick (Eds.), *The changing family life cycle* (pp. 92–95). Boston: Allyn and Bacon.

Byng-Hall, J. (1988). Scrips and legends in families and family therapy. *Family Process, 27*, 167–179.

Cervera, N. (1991). Unwed teenage pregnancy: Family relationships with the father of the baby. *Families in Society, 72*(1), 29–37.

Chilman, C.S. (1979). *Adolescent sexuality in changing American society*. Bethesda, MD: USDHEW.

Coblener, G. (1981). Who is the most at risk? *Female Patient, 6*, 63–68.

Florsheim, M.J., & Gallagher-Thompson, D. (1990). Cognitive-behavioral treatment of atypical bereavement: A case study. *Clinical Gerontologist, 10*(2), 73–76.

Fox, G.L., & Inazu, F. (1980). Patterns and outcomes of mother-daughter communication about sexuality. *Journal of Social Issues, 36*, 7–29.

Franklin, D. (1987). Black adolescent pregnancy: A critical review of literature. In S. Battle (Ed.), *The black adolescent parent*. New York: Haworth Press.

Franz, G. (1984). The family's influence on adolescent sexual behaviors. *Children Today, 3*, 21–25.

Furstenberg, F., Brooks-Gunn, J., & Morgan, S.P. (1987a). Adolescent mothers and their children in later life. *Family Planning Perspectives, 19*, 142–151.

Furstenberg, F., Brooks-Gunn, J., & Morgan, S.P. (1987b). *Adolescent mothers in later life*. Cambridge, MA: Cambridge University Press.

Gagnon, J.H. (1990). Scripting in sex research. *Annual Review of Sex Research, 1*, 1–39.

Gagnon, J.H., & Simon, W. (1973). *Sexual conduct: The social sources of human sexuality*. Chicago: Aldine.

Gergen, K.J., & Gergen, M.M. (1983). The social construction of narrative accounts. In K.J. Gergen & M.M. Gergen (Eds.), *Historical social psychology* (pp. 73–79). Hillsdale, NJ: Erlbaum Associates.

Gergen, K. & Gergen, M. (1988). Narrative and the self as relationship. In L. Berkowitz (Ed.), *Social psychological studies of self: Perspectives and programs* (pp. 17–56). San Diego, CA: Academic Press.

Gilchrist, L.D., & Schinke, S.P. (1983, October). Coping with contraception: Cognitive and behavioral methods with adolescents. *Cognitive Therapy and Research, 7*(5), 379–388.

Gispert, M., Brinich, P., Wheeler, K., & Krieger, L. (1984, July). Predictors of repeat pregnancies among low-income adolescents. *Hospital and Community Psychiatry, 35*(7), 719–723.

Glick, S., Jerussi, T., Waters, D., & Green, J. (1974, November). Amphetamine-induced changes in striatal dopamine and acetylcholine levels and relationship to rotation (circling behavior) in rats. *Bio-chemical Pharma-cology, 23*(22), 3223–3225.

Gold, D., & Berger, C. (1983, Summer). The influence of psychological and situational factors on the contraceptive behavior of single men: A review of the literature. *Population and Environment Behavioral and Social Issues, 6*(2), 113–129.

Goldner, V. (1985, March). Feminism and family therapy. *Family Process, 24*(1), 31–47.

Gorer, S. (1979). Marring, divorcing, and living together in the U.S. today. *Population Bulletin, 32*, 1–40.

Gunter, N.C., & LaBarba, R.C. (1980, July). The consequences of adolescent childbearing on postnatal development. *International Journal of Behavioral Development, 3*(2), 191–214.

Hamburg, D. (1989, April). Preparing for life: The critical transition of adolescence. Special issue: Preventive interventions in adolescence. *Crisis, 10*(1), 4–15.

Hatcher, S.L.M. (1973). The adolescent expense of pregnancy and abortion: A developmental analysis. *Journal of Youth and Adolescence, 2*, 53–101.

Hayes, C. (1987). *Risking the future: Adolescent sexuality, pregnancy, and child bearing.* Washington, DC: National Academy Press.

Held, B. (1981, Winter). Self-esteem and social network of the young pregnant teenager. *Adolescence, 16*(64), 905–912.

Hoffman, L. (1986, Winter). Beyond power and control: Towards a "second order" family systems therapy. *Family Systems Medicine, 3*(4), 381–396.

Hoffman, L. (1988). A constructivist position for family therapy. Special issue: Radical constructivism, autopoiesis, and psychotherapy. *The Irish Journal of Psychology, 9*(1), 110–129.

Hoffman, L. (1990). Constructing realities: An art of lenses. *Family Process, 29*(1), 1–12.

Honeyman, B. (1981). A multivariate investigation of the family system in families of unwed pregnant and nonpregnant adolescents. *Dissertation Abstracts International, 43*, 872–875.

Hoult, P., & Smith, M. (1978). Age and sex differences in the number and variety of vocational choices, preferences, and aspirations. *Journal of Occupational Psychology, 51*(2), 119–125.

Jacobs, S., Kasl, S., Ostfeld, A., Berkman, L., & Charpentier, P. (1986, December). The measurement of grief: Age and sex variation. *British Journal of Medical Psychology, 59*(4), 305–310.

Jemail, J.A., & Nathanson, M. (1987). Adolescent single-parent families. In J.C. Hansen & M. Lindblad-Goldberg (Eds.), *Clinical issues in single-parent households* (pp. 50–59). Rockville, MD: Aspen Publishers.

Jersild, A. (1978). *The psychology of adolescence* (3rd ed.). New York: Macmillan.

Johnson, S.E. (1987). *After a child dies: Counseling bereaved families.* New York: Springer Publishing.

Jones, E.F. (1985). Teenage pregnancies in developed countries: Determinants and policy implication. *Family Planning Perspectives, 17*, 53–63.

Kavanaugh, J. (1974, October). Issues and needs in research. *Language, Speech, and Hearing Services in the Schools, 5*(4), 258–262.

Knapp, R.J. (1986). *Beyond endurance: When a child dies.* New York: Schocken Books.

Knapp, R.J. (1987, July). When a child dies. *Psychology Today, 21*(7), 60–63, 66–67.

Kubler-Ross, E. (1969). *On death and dying.* New York: Macmillan.

Kushner, H.S. (1981). *When bad things happen to good people.* New York: Avon Books.

Lehman, D.R., Lang, E.L., Wortman, C.B., & Sorenson, S.B. (1989, March). Long-term effects of sudden bereavement: Marital and parent-child relationships and children's reactions. *Journal of Family Psychology, 2*(3), 344–367.

Leslie, F., & Leslie, F. (1977). *Unplanned parenthood: The social consequences of teenage childbearing.* New York: Free Press.

Lieberman, M.A. (1989, April). Group properties and outcomes: A study of group norms in self-help groups for widows and widowers. *International Journal of Group Psychotherapy, 39*(2), 191–208.

Lopata, H.Z. (1975). On widowhood: Grief work and identity reconstruction. *Journal of Geriatric Psychiatry, 8*(1), 41–55.

Lowenthal, M.F., & Weiss, L. (1976). Intimacy and crisis in adulthood. *Counseling Psychologist, 6*(1), 10–15.

McGoldrick, M. (1987, May–June). On reaching mid-career without a wife. *Family Therapy Networker, 11*(3), 32–35, 38–39.

McIntire, M., Angle, C., & Struempler, L. (1972). The concept of death in Midwestern children and youth. *American Journal of the Diseases of Children, 123,* 527–532.

Miles, M.S., & Perry, K. (1985, June). Parental responses to sudden accidental deal of a child. *Critical Care Quarterly, 8*(1), 73–84.

Norton, A.J., & Glick, P.C. (1986, January). One parent families: A social and economic profile. Special issue: The single parent family. *Family Relations Journal of Applied Family and Child Studies, 35*(1), 9–17.

Olson, C.F., & Worobey, J. (1984, Winter). Perceived mother-daughter relations in a pregnant and non-pregnant sample. *Adolescence, 19*(76), 781–794.

Parkes, K. (1972). Adolescent pregnancy: Implications for prevention strategies in educational settings. *School Psychology Review, 17*(4), 570–580.

Parkes, C.M. (1975). Determinants of outcome following bereavement. *Omega Journal of Death and Dying, 6*(4), 303–323.

Parkes, C.M., & Weiss, R.S. (1983). *Recovery from bereavement.* New York: Basic Books.

Penn, P. (1985, September). Feed forward: Future questions, future maps. *Family Process, 24*(3), 299–310.

Petrowsky, M. (1976, November). Marital status, sex, and the social networks of the elderly. *Journal of Marriage and the Family, 38*(4), 749–756.

Pincus, K. (1974). *Death and the family.* New York: Pantheon Books.

Pollock, G.H. (1975). On mourning, immortality, and utopia. *Journal of the American Psychoanalytic Association, 23*(2), 334–362.

Rawlins, J.M. (1984, Spring). Parent-daughter interaction and teenage pregnancy in Jamaica. *Journal of Comparative Family Studies, 15*(1), 131–138.

Reed, D., & Weinberg, M.S. (1984, June). Premarital coitus: Developing and established sexual scripts. *Social Psychology Quarterly, 47*(2), 129–138.

Rolland, J.S. (1990, September). Anticipatory loss: A family systems developmental framework. *Family Process, 29*(3), 229–244.

Schiff, S. (1977, October). Personality development and symbiosis. *Transactional Analysis Journal, 7*(4), 310–316.

Seligman, L. (1975, November). Skin potential as an indicator of emotion. *Journal of Counseling Psychology, 22*(6), 489–493.

Shainess, N. (1984). *Sweet suffering: Women as victims.* New York: Bobb Merrill Publishers.

Soricelli, B.A., & Utech, C.L. (1985, September–October). Mourning the death of a child: The family and group process. *Social Work, 30*(5), 429–434.

Teachman, J.D., & Polonko, K.A. (1984, September). Out of sequence: The timing of marriage following a premarital birth. *Social Forces, 63*(1), 245–260.

Thorburg, H.D. (1985, Spring-Summer). Sex information as primary prevention. Special issue: Sex education—past, present, and future. *Journal of Sex Education and Therapy, 11*(1), 22–27.

Viney, L., Benjamin, Y.N., & Preston, C. (1988, December). Constructivist family therapy with the elderly. *Journal of Family Psychology, 2*(2), 241–258.

von Glaserfeld, E. (1984). An introduction to radical constructivism. In P. Watzlawick (Ed.), *The invented reality* (pp. 91–104). New York: Norton.

Walsh, A. (1991, October). Self-esteem and sexual behavior: Exploring gender differences. *Sex Roles, 25*(7–8), 441–450.

White, M. (1986, June). Negative explanation, restraint, and double description: A template for family. *Family Process, 25*(2), 169–184.

White, M. (1989). *Selected papers.* Adelaide, Australia: Dulwich Centre Publications.

Yamaguchi, K., & Kandel, D. (1987, May). Drug use and other determinants of premarital pregnancy and its outcome: A dynamic analysis of competing life events. *Journal of Marriage and the Family, 49*(2), 257–270.

Young, H.H., & Ruth, B.M. (1983). Special treatment problems with the one-parent family. In B.B. Wolman & G. Stricker (Eds.), *Handbook of family and marital therapy* (pp. 215–222). New York, London: Plenum Press.

Zabin, L.S. et al. (1986, March). Adolescent pregnancy prevention program: A model for research and evaluation. *Journal of Adolescent Health Care, 7*(2), 77–87.

Zelnick, M., & Kantner, J. (1980). Sexual activity, contraceptive use, and pregnancy among young unwed females in U.S. In *Research Reports, Volume 1, Commission on Population Growth and the American Future.* Washington, DC: U.S. Government Printing Office.

Zongker, C.E. (1980, April). Self-concept differences between single and married school-age mothers. *Journal of Youth and Adolescence, 9*(2), 175–184.

# Chapter 4

# I DEMAND A REWRITE: WHEN YOUR CHILD DOES NOT FIT YOUR SCRIPT

*Ann Marie Sturniolo*

I went to the mall recently. I was looking for pot holders and passed a store called "Kitchen Express"; I decided to take a look inside to see if they had what I wanted. I walked through the door expecting to find gadgets, dishes, pots, and other kitchen paraphernalia. Instead the store was actually a restaurant, decorated in a retro-diner look straight out of the 50s. I immediately turned to leave, feeling disappointed that I wouldn't buy my pot holders here. Then something caught my eye.

Based on a lifetime of experience, I expected that store to sell pot holders. Before I entered that store I became conscious of a meaning system, a construction, a script, for this type of store. This is a common phenomenon that humans experience constantly, without thought. "The terms in which the world is understood are social artifacts, products of historically situated interchanges among people" (Gergen, 1985, p. 5).

I decided to examine what had taken my attention away from pot holders. It was a beautiful display of 50s era kitchen knickknacks. As I admired the display, I started to feel happy that I had stumbled upon this place. I explored for a while, then decided to stay for lunch. What started as a disappointment became a lovely experience.

As we mature, our parents and others who influence us give us messages that become our life scripts (Dusa & Dusa, 1979). We decide as children to plan our lives based on these messages. We concoct our own meaning system for living and thinking (our life script) based on these messages and our own immature constructions. We are rarely conscious of this decision, and usually our lives develop to our satisfaction. An important message that often is incorporated in our life scripts involves the decision to bear children and create a new family. When children are included in our life scripts there are automatic expectations for them.

I am reminded of children playing with dolls. The child decides that the doll will (or will not) get married, what the wedding will be like, and what the dress will look like. Then the child decides that the doll will (or will not) have a child of her own. The child does not need an actual doll to enact this stage because the child already has decided that the baby will be a boy or girl and that the baby will be a carbon copy of either the mommy doll or the daddy doll. Based on his or her own experience of babies, the child decides if the doll's baby will be a "good" baby or a difficult one. Of course the child also decides if the doll will be a "good" parent or not.

As people approach the decision to bear children, few realize that their decision actually was made long ago and filed away in their life script. As the birth of the child becomes imminent the new parents call on their scripts to help them with the responsibilities of their new roles. This is not usually a conscious process, although very often new parents become aware that they somehow are using familiar scripts. With the birth of the infant, new parents sometimes find that their expectations have been fulfilled. More often than not, new parents are disappointed to find that their infant is not at all what they expected. We all have heard anecdotes about new fathers who were certain they would have a son. When their daughters were born instead, there was usually a run to the sporting goods store to return the baseball bat they had bought for early batting practice. I am sure we also have heard stories about new mothers in the throes of postpartum depression who cry when they discover that the daughter they thought they were carrying for nine months turns out to be a son.

As the child becomes older, the opportunities for thwarted expectations become greater. An important part of becoming a nurturing parent is learning how to value the child for himself or herself in spite of what our scripts tell us. Hopefully, our scripts have that assumption built in. The diagnosis of one's child as disabled or handicapped is an event that is challenging to even the most healthy of scripts.

The diagnosis of a child as handicapped or disabled presents most family systems with a milestone for which they have no script. This generates enormous stress within the system as it struggles to adjust to this unexpected event (Cavanagh & Ashman, 1985; Dyson, 1991; Farran, Metzger, & Sparling, 1986; Frey, Greenberg, & Fewell, 1989; Wilton & Renaut, 1986). While there are often discrepancies between the child one's script is ready for and the actual child, the system that is incorporating a disabled member faces an often overwhelming task. Researchers have described this task as grieving for the "perfect child" who was not born (Ellis, 1989; Featherstone, 1980). Additionally, the family is forced to examine consciously their meaning systems for the concept of a handicapping condition.

What attitudes has this family encoded for people who are handicapped? How will this influence their effectiveness with their diagnosed child? This information must be examined for perhaps the first time as the family begins to write a new script for itself. Family scripts for loss also must be examined, as the grieving process proceeds (Byng-Hall, 1991). This reference to birth does not suggest that this stress occurs only at the bearing children stage of the life cycle (Turnbull, Summers, & Brotherson, 1986). Many children in fact are not diagnosed at birth. Children with learning disabilities most often are diagnosed during the elementary school years. Some disabilities are missed at those ages and not diagnosed until much later. This chapter describes the process that family systems encounter when their child is diagnosed at any age, as most systems are not scripted for this occurrence at any stage in the life cycle.

## EFFECTS OF THE DIAGNOSIS

According to the *Concise Encyclopedia of Special Education* (1990, John Wiley and Sons), approximately 10% of the total school-age population now receives special education services in the public schools. In 1989, 4,587,370 students were enrolled in educational services for the handicapped. There were over four million families who had negotiated the diagnostic process. One study (Mahoney, O'Sullivan, & Dennebaum, 1990) estimated that 64% of the service providers surveyed used family-based interventions. Clearly the need exists to service the families of diagnosed children. Kazak (1986) reported a decrease in secondary psychological problems in that segment of this population that received family-based interventions along with school-based ones. The United States government is committed to providing an education to handicapped and disabled children; family services ensure that education will be integrated into a cooperative, effective system, to the maximum benefit of the handicapped child.

In order for parents to become most effective with their diagnosed child, they must write their own script. This script then will provide them with the direction they will need as they encounter each successive life stage (Dusa & Dusa, 1979). In order to develop their script, parents must accept their imperfect child. Psychoanalysis offers a theory base that attempts to explain this process.

The birth of any child initially is seen as an extension of the parent's self (Bloch, 1989). As the child matures, the parent's task becomes one of separating and allowing the child to individuate. When the child is disabled or handicapped, this process is complicated by the parents' tendency to view the child as a representation of that which is most negative in themselves. The child even may be viewed as an assault on the parent's self. A good illustration of this process is the feeling voiced by some parents that "God has punished me, and I deserve it" (Featherstone, 1980; Pueschel, 1986; Stewart, 1986).

The task for these parents becomes one of adapting to their particular situation. In order to adapt, the parents must overcome the identification of their child as their own worthlessness personified. They must grieve for the child who never can be in order to fully accept the child they have. As the parents' self-esteem grows, they will become better able to handle their child's special needs.

The need for professional assistance at this stage in the acceptance process is great (Crutcher, 1991; Seligman, 1985). Research has shown that the successful adaptation of the parents is a key factor in the development of the handicapped or disabled child (Frey et al., 1989). Unfortunately research also has shown that most assistance is focused on the child, particularly on school-based interventions. Seligman (1985) asserted that counselors have shown little concern for the families of handicapped children. He makes the point that school-based counselors have the expertise to help these families and therefore should use their expertise in this way.

Systems theory provides an alternate framework for understanding the process of assimilating a handicapped or disabled child. Systems theory teaches that the addition of any new member requires the system to expand and adapt. The system accomplishes this by redefining each member's role and function (Turnbull et al., 1986). When the new member is diagnosed as handicapped or disabled, additional responsibilities are created for each family member. As the system struggles to adapt, stress is increased throughout the system. Although it is the inherent nature of systems to adapt, this process repeats itself at every developmental stage of the family. McCubbin (1989), in comparing single- and two-parent families with handicapped children, stressed the family's cohesiveness as the key to successful adaptation. Their ability to remain invested in their system as each redefined his or her role and function in response to the stressor of the handicapped child was an important indicator of their effectiveness. Those families who scored high on the adaptability sub-scale were also able to obtain outside (or ecosystemic) support, a crucial factor in the effective management of the special issues encountered by these families.

Most research has focused on the family with a handicapped child on the macrosystemic level (Kazak, 1986). Relevant macrosystem variables include social policies, language and attitudes toward the handicapped, and the legal system. The lack of research combining systems theory and families of handicapped children on the more immediate microsystemic level is noted. Kazak (1986) described several methodological deficiencies regarding this area. The field of family systems primarily lacks a unified research methodology. This has led to much research with no coherent model to relate the diverse findings. Another lack in the research noted by Kazak is the reliance on mother-reported data rather than on direct observation of the system or comparison of mother and father reports. This may tend to skew overall results toward validating the stereotypical mother-child over-involvement.

Systemic researchers are in agreement with psychoanalytic theorists over a significant part of the adaptation and acceptance process; that is, the process of grieving. Pueschel (1986) discussed the impact on the family of living with a handicapped child. He described parental responses to the birth of a handicapped child that are applicable to all ages of diagnosis. Those responses are feelings of inadequacy and shame, depression, rejection of the child, death wishes, anger, retribution, punishment, and self-pity. Pueschel felt that professional assistance and supportive resources as well as the passage of time are all beneficial. Ellis (1989) presented a wholistic model for the grieving process that occurs when a handicapped child is born. His model is wholistic in that it incorporates biological, intellectual, emotional, behavioral, and spiritual aspects. He used case examples to illustrate this model that encompasses six phases: initial awareness, strategies to overcome loss, awareness of loss, completions, resolution and reformulation, and transcending loss. Seligman (1979) listed Kubler-Ross' now well known stages of mourning and adapted them to the families of handicapped or disabled children. Denial occurs immediately upon diagnosis. This may be manifested as parents repeatedly have their child reevaluated, seemingly searching for some positive news or hope that the diagnosis is in error. This stage may last indefinitely; some parents never fully accept the diagnosis of their child and thus never are able to view their child as just another child.

Bargaining may occur next. Seligman noted that this stage is particularly individual. He quoted a study that found that Catholic mothers are more accepting of their handicapped children than non-Catholic mothers. He stated that this is because Catholic mothers report that they are more religious than non-Catholic mothers. Certainly religion is an important part of this stage as it offers its own hopeful script to those who are suddenly without the one on whom they usually rely.

Anger is the next stage. It may take the form of generalized anger with no conscious sense of where to direct the anger. It may be displaced onto the child and take the form of child neglect or abuse (Fine, 1986). Typically the anger is projected on others who are seen as responsible for the child's handicap. Most often the physician is made the scapegoat for this anger (Quiney & Pahl, 1986).

The potential exists for angry feelings to become feelings of guilt and shame. This potential is greatest when the family has little support and learns to keep their feelings to themselves (Cavanagh & Ashman, 1985). Depression may result if the script for guilt, and shame calls for denial of those feelings. As a stage in the grieving process, depression can be an expected reaction that is usually of short duration. Depression that becomes chronic should definitely be treated professionally. Acceptance is the final stage in the mourning process. At this stage, the family has been able to formulate their new script and become effective advocates for their child (Stewart, 1986). Families should be cautioned that this stage is subject to challenges. Symptoms of grief often return unbidden, causing renewed guilt and sadness (Seligman, 1979; Turnbull et al., 1986). The script the family writes as it first experiences the mourning process serves the family well when these same symptoms return.

# THERAPEUTIC IMPLICATIONS

The process these families endure holds many opportunities for therapeutic intervention. As simply a supportive service, family therapy offers many useful interventions for helping the family negotiate their new script (Bailey & Simeonsson, 1988; Boer, 1986; Somers, 1987). Family therapists can help families with handicapped or disabled children identify their unique systemic frailties as well as develop positive functioning patterns.

Gooder (1986) discussed the role of family therapy as one part of a clinical team approach. He included the importance of identifying the family processes that impede the handicapped child's cognitive and social development and asserted that family therapists are usually the most effective professionals at this task. He also stressed the need for viewing the disabled child as a member of a family as well as an individual. Kazak (1986) reported that the chief modalities for working with families with a handicapped or disabled child remain individual work with the child and separate parent counseling and behavior management techniques. She asserted that what often is needed is an ongoing integrated program of treatment that treats the family as the system that it is. This program of treatment would help to forestall the occurrence of secondary psychological problems that often become the primary handicap for these children.

I recently began working with a man who is the personification of Kazak's assertion. This man was diagnosed as handicapped at age 13 due to an accident. From that day forward he has been taught to view himself as handicapped first. His life script was overridden by this handicapped construction. Although he was able to graduate from college, he has never been able to assimilate in the nonhandicapped world. His disabled script was written in a way that would forever set him apart. I only can wonder how different his life might have been had his family been offered support to work through their grief. I suspect that his script today would have allowed him to see himself as a man first.

Supportive services can take many forms. Many researchers have explored ways in which families of handicapped and disabled children receive the support they need (Kirkham, Schilling, Norelius, & Schinke, 1986; Werth & Oseroff, 1987; Winton, 1990; Zeitlin, Williamson, & Rosenblatt, 1987). Informal social support seems to have more benefit than school-based support groups (Frey, Fewell, & Vadasy, 1989; Kazak, 1986, 1987). Families with a broader social network were able to cope with the adjustments associated with the handicapped member better than families with a narrow social base.

Support services focusing on parent counseling were seen as limited in their usefulness (Mueller & Leviton, 1986). This approach often excludes other family members. The handicapped or disabled child usually is treated individually with no provisions made for the input or reactions of the family. The family therapist can serve as a link between school-based interventions and home-based ones (Boer, 1986; Seligman, 1979). Remember, the goal is to assist the family as they write their new script, not to impose a different set of school-generated scripts for handling this life event.

## MARITAL EFFECTS

One area that school-based interventions rarely affect is the marital subsystem. The diagnosis of one's child as handicapped or disabled places enormous strain on the marital subsystem. Featherstone (1980) wrote extensively about this particular strain. She listed four basic ways that the marriage is strained by the diagnosis. The diagnosis awakens powerful emotions in both parents, the child may become the symbol of a shared failure, the organization of the family is altered completely, and the diagnosis creates a multitude of opportunities for conflict.

Script theory tells us that each partner's life script is formed by messages received by the child aspect of the personality. The adult aspect attempts to apply this child-formed script to current, adult situations. When two scripts marry, they must adjust to the wants and needs of not just their adult aspects but also to the insistent wants and needs of two child aspects. The third part of script theory is the parent aspect of the personality. This aspect attempts to continue the messages that formed the script, in spite of what the more rational adult aspect attempts to accomplish. One can see the potential for maladjustments that exists in the average marriage. When the diagnosis of a child as handicapped or disabled occurs, the three personality aspects of each partner are thrown into conflict as they scramble to find a new script. The mourning process is a natural adaptation effort to form a new mutually satisfying script.

A separate but related issue is the increased responsibility a handicapped child bears on the marriage. There are usually medical issues that must be handled; evaluations and other appointments that must be attended to; an increase in financial considerations; and practical considerations, such as a loss of privacy for the couple and lack of time to pursue former pleasures. "If a handicap constricts a couple's life at every point, the marriage becomes a prison" (Featherstone, 1980, p. 91).

The task for the marriage becomes one of balancing the needs of the diagnosed child with the needs of the family and the needs of the couple themselves. Parents must try to remember that they were a couple before the diagnosis and are still a couple. Parents without a diagnosed child often have trouble paying attention to each other, particularly when the events of daily living become temporarily overwhelming. Parents of a diagnosed child who successfully adapt to their situation come to the realization that they have the potential to be their own best support system. They realize that although the handicapped child can bring division to the marriage, they are more effective if they learn to face the challenge together.

Of course not all parents learn to adapt. The rate of divorce of parents of diagnosed children has been estimated at twice the rate in the general population (Kazak, 1986). This may be an indication of the degree of stress this life event places on a marriage. When observing that many children diagnosed with learning disabilities came from single parent homes, Featherstone (1980) was told that the constant conflict over the disabled child was probably the mitigating factor in the high divorce rate of that population. Kazak (1986) also quoted research that found a correlation between the severity of the handicap and the presence of marital discord. This parallels the finding that more severe handicaps are related to greater parental stress (Dyson, 1991). It appears that Featherstone's anecdotal correlation is supported by research.

## SIBLING EFFECTS

Along with research on the effects of the diagnosis on the marital subsystem, several studies have examined the effect of the diagnosis on the siblings of the handicapped child. Featherstone (1980) wrote from her own experience about the reactions of her other child. These reactions range from embarrassment to loving acceptance to rejection of the handicapped sibling. She made the point that the majority of siblings' reactions parallel those of their parents, indicating that as the parents come to accept the diagnosis so will the siblings.

Some of the research does not support this point. Seligman (1979) quoted research that found that although the strongest factor in sibling acceptance was parental acceptance, overall siblings of diagnosed children responded in significantly different ways. Some siblings exhibited bitter resentment of their family's situation along with extreme guilt for having these feelings. Other siblings were comparatively well-adjusted, exhibiting tolerance about prejudice and its consequences. Also, a definite correlation existed between family income and sibling acceptance; higher income families were able to spare the siblings more of the responsibility of the handicapped child than lower income families. Hannah and Midlarsk (1985) supported these findings. They found the same socioeconomic correlation that Seligman reported. Additionally, they reported that older female siblings are more affected than male siblings, as they seem to take on more responsibility for their handicapped or disabled sibling. Hannah and Midlarsk advocated working with siblings as well as parents of diagnosed children as a preventative to psychological problems.

Rodger (1985) discussed the effects of a handicapped child on siblings in terms of arrested life cycle development. According to this model, the handicapped child becomes the youngest child regardless of his or her birth order position. This arrests family development because a dependent child remains a constant in the family. Rodger reported that according to this theory (first expounded by B. Farber in 1959) young siblings must adapt to losing their birth order position, to increased responsibility and decreased parental attention, and to increased parental expectations of academic performance.

Stewart (1986) outlined some guidelines that are useful to remember when dealing with siblings. The first is the feeling among siblings that they might "catch" the disability in some way and the fear that accompanies this feeling. The second is the lack of communication among family members. Stewart reported that in their attempts to protect siblings by withholding information parents actually set up a family dynamic of exclusion to which siblings are sensitive. The third guideline involves the need for siblings to be able to express openly their feelings about their family's situation, regardless of how negative those feelings may be. Stewart concurred that parental attitudes and adjustment are an important indicator of siblings' attitudes.

Lobato (1990) discussed sibling effects extensively. She began by outlining the functions of siblings in the family system. These functions are of developmental importance, such as providing emotional experiences and opportunity for expression, providing social experiences and skills, helping in the formation of personality, and attaining language and other social skills. Siblings are the first peer group to which children belong. As such, Lobato listed the importance this peer group has on influencing relationships with others. Some examples include disseminating information, maintaining secrecy and alliances, and setting expectations for the group as a whole. The diagnosis of a child as handicapped or disabled formerly was thought to adversely affect these processes in nonhandicapped siblings.

Lobato (1990) disputed that dated research. She presented more current research that overall does not support the presumption that siblings of the handicapped are automatically adversely affected. Studies are presented that are broken down by disability or handicap. She reported that although siblings may have special concerns and feelings, this finding does not translate into psychological problems. Lobato supported the conclusion reached by other researchers (discussed previously in this chapter)that parental attitudes seem to be the key to overall adjustment in the family.

Byng-Hall (1988) wrote about the power of family myths and legends and their effect on life scripts. The sibling of a handicapped or disabled person finds himself or herself thrust into the position of living a family legend as it unfolds. To experience the adaptations that the family lives through and create a new myth inevitably alters the siblings' life script and creates new beliefs that are shared among the family. Byng-Hall's perspective is unique in that it looks toward the future rather than remaining in the present.

Featherstone (1980) made one more interesting point that I feel is important to relate. She briefly discussed an issue called stoppage. This is the decision not to bear more children after the diagnosis of one child as handicapped or disabled. I find this an interesting phenomenon related to the family's level of coping and adaptation to the diagnosis. Unfortunately, I have not been able to locate any research that supports or disputes (or mentions) this issue.

This inability to locate further information seems to be characteristic of the general lack of research on families with a handicapped member. In organizing this chapter, my own search for current, valid research uncovered much research that was only partially applicable to families. There is much research that needs to be done that can assist professionals in servicing this population of families that is so often in dire need of such services.

## PARENTING STRATEGIES

This section is about strategies that can be helpful to parents who are negotiating the script generating phase after the diagnosis of the child as handicapped or disabled. Indeed, the one area that seemed to be crowded with research was the effect of stress on the family and its members. Virtually every reference made in this chapter has referred to the stress that the diagnosis places on the family system. Wikler (1986) reviewed family stress theory research as it is applied to families with a handicapped member (specifically, a mentally retarded member) and made several conclusions. A primary conclusion Wikler reached concerns the general state of research in this field. She asserted that little research is available on successful family functioning, making comparisons of different family types difficult. This difficulty is compounded by the lack of research on the family with a handicapped member over time. Current research does not address the accumulated stresses resulting from the chronicity of the diagnosis and the ways in which the family continues to adapt at each life cycle stage. She advocated a much more thorough and detailed approach to research in the field.

Dyson (1991) reported on the association between families with a handicapped child and parental stress and family dysfunction. She compared families with a handicapped child to statistically matched families with nonhandicapped children. She found that although families of handicapped children appeared to have high degrees of stress, this did not correlate well with substantial increases in family dysfunction. Dyson concluded with a plea for increased family intervention to alleviate parental stress. She felt that individualized programs are suited better to this task as they are able to incorporate each family's strengths and other unique attributes.

Carr (1990) reviewed literature on the effect on the family of a person with learning difficulties and behavior disorders. She reported that studies show that behavior problems have a greater effect on families than learning problems. Behavior problems were shown to have a significant effect on family functioning and family stress. Carr reported success with the use of behavioral management techniques by parents of problem children and noted the lack of research on families with handicapped adults. Fish (1990) noted the particular stress that is generated by the individualized education program (I.E.P.) conference between the parents and the schools. Parent-school conflict places stress on the family, which is mediated by the level of family functioning and may be manifested in family interactions and/or work. She noted that this stress affects all family members. Fish stated that the family's ability to generate adaptive responses greatly affects the impact of this type of stress.

McCubbin (1989) used the typology model of adjustment and adaptation that she developed in 1987 to explore differences between single-parent and two-parent families who had a child with cerebral palsy. The groups were matched on the severity of the child's handicap and on the age and gender of the parents. Both groups reported high levels of stress. However, contrary to predictions, there was no significant difference between single- and two-parent families in family strain or other family variables such as degree of cohesion. Although single-parent families were significantly lower on financial well-being and parental coping in relation to maintaining family integration, they were higher on adaptability scales. This finding suggests that under the most extreme stress (i.e., separation and/or divorce and the diagnosis of a handicapped child), families develop the capacity to success-fully adapt.

Foster (1988) asserted that what appears to be pathology or dysfunction in families with retarded children is actually an aspect of adaptive function-ing for these families. She corroborated other evidence (Hampson, Hulgus, Beavers, & Beavers, 1988) that families of retarded children are actually quite proficient at incorporating the stress of the diagnosis. These families are often quite effective and functional.

Zeitlin et al. (1987) described a counseling approach for parents of a handicapped child that is based on coping with stress. They described a four-step process that can be utilized to cope with a stressful event. This process is described as transactional and includes the cognitive appraisal of the event, decision making, acting on the decision, and evaluating the out-come. Zeitlin et al. included a case study that illustrated the approach. Farran et al. (1986) proposed the stress-adaptation model for parents of handicapped children. This is a linear model that offers an outline for a predicted sequence of adaptations that these parents can expect to cycle through in response to many events in their child's life. The model focuses on the event (its occurrence), the changes it produces, the adaptive capacity of the family, and its impact on both the adults and the children in the family. The model points to two specific places for professional intervention:

at the event stage, parents can be helped to alter the demands of the event thereby reducing the number of changes to which the family must adapt; and at the level of individual adaptability, professionals can help by providing individual and family therapy and parent support groups.

An important issue to include in this section is the potential for child abuse that exists in families with a diagnosed child. Fine (1986) reported that abuse of the handicapped child can be viewed as symptomatic of how the family is coping with the stress of the diagnosis. Fine advocated a family focus to intervention and outlines a multilevel model for change. He recognized that an important potential for change exists on the attitude/belief level. This speaks directly to the concept of meaning systems and life scripts. Families of the handicapped need to alter their perceptions of the diagnosis (the meaning system) in order to become or remain effective via the enactment of their rewritten life script.

What does the family that is living with a newly formed script for their handicapped or disabled member look like? How does a professional assess the level of adaptation the family has attained? A family who is negotiating successfully their new scripts has been able to generate new constructions about the handicapping condition. They will be able to convey their views fairly objectively, absent of excess emotion (such as defensiveness). They will respond to routine inquiries about their handicapped child with responses that are appropriate to any child. The handicapping condition will be an additional piece of their child and not allowed to define who their child is or how their family adapts to it. Adult scripts in the family will seem appropriate for the family's situation. If the parents are married, there will be evidence of a healthy marital subsystem (such as opportunities to spend time alone, agreement on major issues in the family's life, etc.). The siblings will evidence age appropriate developmental milestones. Conflict in the family would be manifested generally and not focused solely on the handicapping condition or the member who bears it. Research reports that have been reviewed here all agree on one point that bears emphasis: the process of adaptation undergone by families with a handicapped member is not a finite one. No final adaptation exists, no end to the process. The family must learn to adapt continually to events and situations that simply do not occur in other families. As such, the professional's role must be one that can also adapt to the family's changing needs.

## CASE ILLUSTRATION

A mother was referred to our agency to seek treatment for her 15-year-old son. During her first contact with the agency, she persistently quizzed the program director about the qualifications of the agency's therapists. She was insistent that the therapist assigned to her son be experienced with adolescents and knowledgeable about the effects of substance abuse. Before I contacted her, I was armed with information about her scripts for seeking help and her relationship with her son. That telephone call illuminated the part of her mothering script that called for a "take charge" behavior.

I was prepared when I returned her call and introduced myself as the therapist who would be working with her son. I politely answered her questions about my credentials and experience. I joined her around the difficulty she faces as a parent of an adolescent. She expressed concern that her son would became his father, a man she had divorced when her son was a very small child because of his alcoholism and antisocial behavior. She admitted she felt trapped in a continuing stream of overpowering behaviors and admitted that she felt powerless to pull herself out of this vicious cycle with her son. I recommended family sessions; she was skeptical but agreed to allow me to interview the family. She casually asked if she should bring her husband (her son's stepfather) to the sessions.

This exchange added detail to what I already had surmised about her mothering script. She was living out a script that demanded that the mother handle all matters pertaining to her children. She married her husband when her son was three years old. He had no memory of living with his biological father. Yet the family's system was arranged to present the stepfather as a benevolent visitor to the family. The couple's scripts had merged and supported this notion. I knew that the adolescent's script would include powerful messages about the nature of fathering.

The first therapy session included L (mother) and B (stepfather). L had assumed that because I asked for her husband to be present that precluded her son's attendance. This event reinforced my previous observations of this family's script: son and stepfather could not appear together at our first session. The invitation to treatment had gone through L to the family. I made certain to request specifically the presence of all three members of the family at all future sessions.

The second therapy session included the couple and the adolescent, N. I was surprised to encounter a rather tall young man with a youngish face. When I expressed my surprise to L, she admitted that she tends to paint a picture of a much younger boy. He sat in the session slumped backward in his chair, conveying an openness and weightiness at the same time. At the content level, this session focused on the litany of complaints against the adolescent, including his recent experimentation with alcohol and marijuana and his truancy. At the process level, more evidence emerged to support the analysis of this family's predominant scripts. But why was this child the one that the system focused on? The family reported that there was an older brother living in the home as well as two step-siblings who lived in another town. Life cycle theory suggested that because he is the youngest in the family, this child has the greatest potential for delayed launching. Script theory suggested that something about this particular child offered his mother's script a reason to become dominating.

The third session began with L reporting that N's behavior had begun to escalate. This was expected: from a systemic perspective, escalation occurs when systemic anxiety is increased. This was accomplished for this family simply by attending two sessions. Then L confirmed my overriding hypothesis for this family: she revealed that N was diagnosed as having attention deficit disorder and significant learning disabilities at age six or seven. He had been attending school in a self-contained special education class until the last school year, when he requested a chance to mainstream. His mother not only supported his request, she characteristically forced the school to comply. In his second year of mainstreaming (his first year on the secondary level), his behavior began to worsen.

The therapeutic direction began to shift after these revelations. It was apparent that L's mothering script required that she take over her son's disabilities. It precluded the formation of new script that would allow her to help her son appropriately. Instead she began to do his school work for him and inappropriately allowed him to define his own educational plan. She was inadvertently sending N the message that he would never be able to achieve success; he would eventually become like his biological father.

Once L was able to explore her family scripts and their meanings, she was able to allow her husband to take a more active role in he family. She and B both negotiated a new script for their relationship with N, which allowed him the room to concentrate on overcoming his disabilities. When I last spoke to them, N had resumed playing baseball, which he had a natural talent for and had abandoned previously. While he still manifested severe learning disabilities, his mother ceased doing his school work for him. The family reported there was a much more relaxed atmosphere at home.

## SUMMARY

This chapter has described the process that family systems encounter when their child is diagnosed as handicapped or disabled. This process involves examining the family's meaning systems that have evolved into its life script. This examination facilitates the mourning of the "perfect child" that was not born. Once this stage has been negotiated, the family constructs a new life script incorporating a meaning system that they have developed in response to the diagnosis.

I wish to emphasize that this is a process of adaptation that does not necessarily have a finite beginning, middle, and end. In this chapter has been presented various research that illustrates this point. The script for life with a handicapped or disabled child is generated over a lifetime and is subject to constant revision. Each stage of the life cycle presents a potential meaning system with a life of its own, forcing the family to adapt once more.

Stress is a fact of life for these families. The successful handling of stress seems to have a positive correlation with parenting effectiveness. As such, it seems that services provided to families of the handicapped should incorporate strategies for successful stress management. Families who are not naturally skilled in this area would benefit from formal instruction in stress management, as would all families faced with what all the research agrees is an extremely stressful life event.

I used to read a comic strip that had a character who always was followed by a black cloud. Most of the time the other characters dreaded his appearance as it always was accompanied by rain or thunder or some other dire consequence. I remember once there was a drought in the comic strip. Then this character was greeted as the savior of the land. The child with the handicapping condition reminds me of that character. We cannot avoid noticing the handicapping condition (the cloud). We perceive it differently based on our meaning systems, on how our life scripts are written. In order to be an effective parent, one must reject the socially defined "handicapped" script and construct a new reality that accepts the child in spite of the cloud. A black cloud does not always have to be seen as a negative; very often good things happen as a result of a black cloud.

# BIBLIOGRAPHY

Mahoney, G., & O'Sullivan, P. (1990, June). Early intervention practices with families of children with handicaps. *Mental Retardation, 28*(3), 169–176.

Mahoney, G., & Powell, A. (1988). Modifying parent-child interaction: Enhancing the development of handicapped children. *Journal of Special Education, 22*(1), 82–96.

Quiney, L., & Pahl, J. (1985, October). Examining the causes of stress in families with several mentally handicapped children. *British Journal of Social Work, 15*(5), 501–517.

Rodger, S. (1987, March). A comparison between parenting a normal and a handicapped child throughout a life span. *British Journal of Occupational Therapy, 50*(5), 167–170.

# REFERENCES

Bailey, D.B., & Simeonsson, R.J. (1988). Assessing needs of families with handicapped infants. *Journal of Special Education, 22*(1), 117–127.

Bloch, J. (1989, July). Parents as assessors of children: A collaborative approach to helping. *Social Work in Education, 16*, 229–241.

Boer, P.A. (1986). The role of the family therapist in supportive services to families with handicapped children. *Clinical Social Work Journal, 14*(3), 250–261.

Byng-Hall, J. (1991). Family scripts and loss. In F. Walsh and M. McGoldrick (Eds.), *Living beyond loss* (pp. 130–143). New York: W.W. Norton.

Byng-Hall, J. (1988, June). Scripts and legends in families and family therapy. *Family Process, 27,* 167–179.

Carr, J. (1990). Supporting the families of people with behavioral/psychiatric difficulties. *International Review of Psychiatry, 2*(1), 33–41.

Cavanagh, J., & Ashman, A.F. (1985, September). Stress in families with handicapped children. *Australia and New Zealand Journal of Developmental Disabilities, 11*(3), 151–156.

Crutcher, D.M. (1991, February). Family support in the home: Home visiting and public law 99-457: A parent's perspective. *American Psychologist, 46*(2), 138–140.

Dusa, J., & Dusa, K.M. (1979). Transactional analysis. In R.J. Corsini (Ed.), *Current psychotherapies* (pp. 374–427). Itasca, IL: F.E. Peacock Publishers.

Dyson, L.L. (1991, March). Families of young children with handicaps: Parental stress and family functioning. *American Journal on Mental Retardation, 95*(6), 623–629.

Ellis, J.B. (1989). Grieving for the loss of the perfect child: Parents of children with handicaps. *Child and Adolescent Social Work Journal, 6*(4), 259–270.

Farran, D.C., Metzger, J., & Sparling, J. (1986). Immediate and continuing adaptations in parents of handicapped children. In A.P. Turnbull (Ed.), *Families of handicapped persons* (pp. 142–158). Baltimore, MD: Paul H. Brookes.

Featherstone, H. (1980). *A difference in the family: Life with a disabled child.* New York: Basic Books.

Fine, M.J. (1986, October). Intervening with abusing parents of handicapped children. *Techniques, 2*(4), 353–363.

Fish, M.C. (1990). Family-school conflict: Implications for the family. *Journal of Reading, Writing, and Learning Disabilities International, 6*(1), 71–79.

Foster, M.A. (1988, September). A systems perspective and families of handicapped children. *Journal of Family Psychology, 2*(1), 54–56.

Frey, K.S., Fewell, R.R., & Vadasy, P.F. (1989). Parental adjustment and changes in child outcome among families of young handicapped children. *Topics in Early Childhood Special Education, 8*(4), 38–57.

Frey, K.S., Greenberg, M.T., & Fewell, R.R. (1989, November). Stress and coping among parents of handicapped children: A multidimensional approach. *American Journal on Mental Retardation, 94*(3), 240–249.

Gergen, K.J. (1985). Social constructionist inquiry: Context and implications. In K.J. Gergen & K.E. Davis (Eds.), *The social construction of the person* (pp. 10–24). New York: Springer-Verlag.

Gooder, I.M. (1986, April). Family therapy and the handicapped child. *Developmental Medicine and Child Neurology, 28*(2), 247–250.

Hampson, R.B., Hulgus, O.F., Beavers, W.R., & Beavers, J.S. (1988, September). The assessment of competence in families with a retarded child. *Journal of Family Psychology, 2*(1), 32–53.

Hannah, M.E., & Midlarsk, E. (1985). Siblings of the handicapped: A literature review for school psychologists. *School Psychology Review, 14*(4), 510–520.

Kazak, A.E. (1986, June). Families with physically handicapped children: Social ecology and family systems. *Family Process, 25*(2), 265–281.

Kazak, A.E. (1987, March). Families with disabled children: Stress and social networks in three samples. *Journal of Abnormal Child Psychology, 15*(1), 137–146.

Kirkham, M.A., Schilling, R.F., Norelius, K., & Schinke, S.P. (1986, September/October). Developing coping styles and social support networks: An intervention outcome study with mothers of handicapped children. *Child Care, Health, and Development, 12*(5), 313–323.

Lobato, D.J. (1990). *Brothers, sisters, and special needs*. Baltimore, MD: Paul H. Brookes.

Mahoney, G., O'Sullivan, P., & Dennebaum, J. (1990). A national study of mothers' perceptions of family-focused early intervention. *Journal of Early Intervention, 14*(2), 133–146.

McCubbin, M.A. (1989, April). Family stress and family strengths: A comparison of single- and two-parent families with handicapped children. *Research in Nursing and Health, 12*(2), 101–110.

Mueller, M., & Leviton, A. (1986). In-home versus clinic-based services for the developmentally disabled child: Who is the primary client—parent or child? *Social Work in Health Care, 11*(3), 75–88.

Pueschel, S.M. (1986, November). The impact on the family: Living with the handicapped child. *Issues in Law and Medicine, 2*(3), 171–187.

Quiney, L., & Pahl, J. (1986). First diagnosis of severe mental handicap: Characteristics of unsatisfactory encounters between doctors and parents. *Social Science and Medicine, 22*(1), 53–62.

Rodger, S. (1985, March). Siblings of handicapped children: A population at risk? *Exceptional Child, 32*(1), 47–56.

Seligman, M. (1979). *Strategies for helping parents of exceptional children.* New York: The Free Press.

Seligman, M. (1985, December). Handicapped children and their families. *Journal of Counseling and Development 64*(4), 274–277.

Somers, M.N. (1987, September). Parenting in the 1980s: Programming perspectives and issues. *Volta Review, 89*(5), 68–77.

Stewart, J.C. (1986). *Counseling parents of exceptional children.* Columbus, OH: Charles E. Merrill Publishing.

Turnbull, A.P., Summers, J.A., & Brotherson, M.J. (1986). Family life cycle: Theoretical and empirical implications and future directions for families with mentally retarded members. In A.P. Turnbull (Ed.), *Families of handicapped persons* (pp. 234–269). Baltimore, MD: Paul H. Brookes. US. Bureau of the Census Statistical Abstract of the United States, 1991 (111th ed.), Washington, DC.

Werth, L.H., & Oseroff, A.B. (1987). Continual counseling intervention: Lifetime support for the family with a handicapped member. *American Journal of Family Therapy, 15*(4), 333–342.

Wikler, L.M. (1986). Family stress theory and research on families of children with mental retardation. In A.P. Turnbull (Ed.), *Families of handicapped persons* (pp. 179–192). Baltimore, MD: Paul H. Brookes.

Wilton, K., & Renaut, J. (1986, June). Stress levels in families with intellectually handicapped preschool children and families with non handicapped preschool children. *Journal of Mental Deficiency Research, 30*(2), 163–169.

Winton, P.J. (1990). Promoting a normalizing approach to families: Integrating theory with practice. *Topics in Early Childhood Special Education, 10*(2), 90–103.

Zeitlin, S., Williamson, G.G., & Rosenblatt, W.P. (1987, April). The coping with stress model: A counseling approach for families with a handicapped child. *Journal of Counseling and Development, 65*(8), 443–446.

# Chapter 5

# SCRIPTS, SCRIPTS, AND MORE SCRIPTS: A MULTISCRIPT APPROACH TO ADOLESCENTS

*Joan D. Atwood*
*and*
*Susan Dershowitz*

Throughout history, the period of development between childhood and adulthood has not been given a lot of attention. Individuals seemed to go from childhood to adulthood in a blink of an eye. However, within the past 100 years or so, because of many social and cultural changes that have taken place, such as longer life span and increased need for specialized training in the economic arena, the period of the life cycle between childhood and adulthood has lengthened and has come to be recognized as a separate stage of development called "adolescence." This chapter describes the period of adolescence in the family life cycle as a time of multiple scripting pressures that "invade" the family. Although there are families who adapt easily to the additional stressors of this period, these pressures typically result in a disruption of the current family script, often creating conflict within the family. This chapter first places the stage of adolescence in a socio-historical perspective, exploring how a multitude of scripting forces impacts the family. The roles of sexuality, peers, media pressures, the family's covert and overt scripts, prejudice, career choices, social norms, the self, feelings, perceptions, and gender are considered. Next a therapeutic model is presented taking the aforementioned into account.

## STAGE SETTING

### Scene 1

Imagine a surprise family birthday party. Picture family members scurrying around preparing and eating the food, getting the presents out of the way, trying to hide the birthday cake covered in white frosting and pink roses with the words "Happy Birthday" written in pretty pink lettering. Imagine the decorations—the pink and white balloons, the pink and white streamers, the white paper tablecloths covering the tables surrounded by bridge chairs, and the pink papier-mache ballerina decorations in the center of each table. Hear the buzz of excitement brewing as members catch up on each other's lives and reminisce about the birthdays and the special days of the past. Feel the happiness that the family feels of being able to celebrate a happy occasion together and the excitement of the anticipation of the arrival of the birthday person. As the time approaches, imagine everyone huddling in a corner of the room trying not to be seen. Hear the sounds of shh!!! as the birthday person approaches.

### Scene 2

Now move your attention to a birthday party for a young girl who is just turning 12 years old. As she walks around her home, she comes across relatives stirring, ready to pounce on her with affection and good wishes. Her immediate thought is, "Yuck! Get me out of here!" She tells her mother that she is supposed to meet her friends down at the mall for pizza. She thinks out loud, "If my friends ever found out about this, I would die!" Discontent is written all over her face. She forces a smile. She shies away from the hugs and does not answer many of the questions people ask her about her life. She sneaks away to use the phone or to sit alone in her room with the radio on. Her parents and other relatives cannot understand what has happened to her. She has always loved and looked forward to her family birthday parties, but for some reason today she is acting very aloof. Some family members leave feeling confused, thinking something must be wrong with her. Some question what they might have done to make her feel or act differently at the party. Some brush it off as her just having a bad day. Her younger brother, age seven, cannot understand how she was not upset when everybody left, especially Grandma and Grandpa. Her brother was in tears.

This supposedly happy ritual has turned this family into an adolescent family. What used to be a joyous event for all has somehow changed. Although the above scenario has been fabricated for its point, the content of its message can be painfully true for many families with an adolescent. Adolescence is generally the first time when the family scripts are scrutinized and questioned, signifying to the family that a change is occurring.

## SOCIO-HISTORICAL CONTEXT

The adolescent stage of development has not always existed and for some cultures still is not as disruptive as what typically occurs in Western cultures. For different cultures and even in our recent past history, the transition period between childhood and adulthood was much shorter and smoother. In the early twentieth century, many theorists began to study human development, and some theorists began to speak of a new stage of development termed "adolescence." The length of time between childhood and adulthood was increasing. G. Stanley Hall (1904), one of the first to speak of adolescence as a distinct stage of development, termed his theory "recapitulation theory." He believed that the period of adolescence corresponded to the period in history when the human race was in a turbulent, transitional stage. Hall described adolescence as a period of upheavals, suffering, passion, and rebellion against adult authority and of physical, intellectual, and social change. He was the theorist who popularized the words "storm and stress" in describing this time period (Sisson, Hersen, & Hasselt, 1987).

Once the notion of adolescence as a distinct stage of development was accepted, theorists began to ponder whether the behavioral manifestations of the stage were due to biological or social forces. The cultural studies by Margaret Mead (1950, 1953) in Samoa and New Guinea challenged Hall's ideas about adolescence being a universal stage of storm and stress as she found that young people in primitive societies seemed to make the transition from childhood to adulthood with relative ease. She concluded that stress and alienation were not universal characteristics of adolescence driven by biological forces, but rather that the nature of adolescence was a "cultural invention." She believed that young people experience adolescence differently according to their culture, concluding that there were many determinants to the notion of adolescence.

Hollingshead (1949) and Havighurst, Bowman, Liddle, Matthews, and Pierce (1962) conducted comprehensive investigations specifically designed to determine the effects of social class on adolescent behavior and found that adolescent behavior patterns differed predictably according to social class. Adolescent boys and girls from lower socioeconomic levels were more likely to drop out of school, show aggressive maladjusted tendencies, and engage in delinquent behavior. Hollingshead (1949) and Havighurst et al. (1962) explained their findings by proposing that different social expectations yielded different results.

Bandura (1969, 1973; Bandura, Ross, & Ross, 1963; Bandura & Walters, 1959) extended this research to pinpoint the environmental events that caused certain behaviors said to characterize adolescents. These researchers concluded that factors such as imitation, modeling, and reinforcements were the major contributors to the development of adolescent behaviors. Young persons begin to reenact that which they see. In sum, the data from these and other observations and experiments highlight the importance of recognizing the family and social influences on adolescent behavior (Sisson et al., 1987). This information adds to the idea that adolescence is a culturally defined term. The increases in technology and the resultant needs for increased specialization of training, the need for increasing numbers of people in the work force, the longer life span, and the ever changing roles of the family all have added to the development and lengthening of the adolescent stage of development. Although adolescence is a time of "raging hormones" and unprecedented biological growth and maturity, the behavioral manifestations and, to a large degree, the psychological experiences of adolescence are determined by the sociocultural environment.

## FAMILY LIFE CYCLE

Because the focus of life cycle research is on how generations of families move through time, research on the family life cycle yields understanding of this stage of development. Transition points from one stage to another of the life cycle are called "nodal points," and during these points life cycle researchers hypothesize that symptoms are most likely to appear due to the interruption or dislocation of the unfolding life cycle (Carter & McGoldrick 1989). During these transition points, the developmental task of families is to aim toward flexibility, adjusting to the new roles and rules.

Preto (1989) discussed how adolescence impacts on a family, believing that the origins of this family transformation begin with the adolescent's development of rapid physical growth and sexual maturation during puberty. As a result of physical and sexual maturation, the adolescent moves toward solidifying an identity that includes establishing autonomy from the family.

## SCRIPTING THEORY

Scripting theory assists in our understanding of how families experience disruptive events and helps us see adolescence as a period of exploration and questioning. Throughout the life span, people learn scripts for all types of social interactions by both observing and interacting with others (Abelson, 1976; Simon & Gagnon, 1986). Family life, school, work, experiences with peers, and exposure to the mass media all produce information about how people are supposed to relate to each other (McCormick, 1987). Social scripting theory is a cognitive model used to explain why sequences of social behavior occur. Social scripting theorists view social interactions as everyday dramas that people use to play out their beliefs about the expected sequences of events. This dictates the roles they as actors should assume within well-known situations (Abelson, 1976; Nisbett & Ross, 1980; Schank & Abelson, 1977, McCormick, 1987). Simon and Gagnon (1986) described people's cognitions about their social transactions as being similar to the set of flexible stage directions that actors might follow when doing improvisational theater. According to social scripting theorists, individuals are able to imagine a script or a typical sequence of events which outlines what is happening now, what happened before, and what is likely to happen next (Abelson, 1981). A script guides behavior.

Gergen (1985) and Gergen and Gergen (1983) used the term "self-narratives" to describe the social psychological processes whereby people tell stories about themselves to themselves and others. These belief systems originally are created by and maintained by interactions with significant others. As stated throughout this book, the process begins at birth and continues to death. When someone holds a particular meaning, he or she will seek out events and people that are consistent with that belief system.

The belief system then sets the stage for individuals' emotional reactions, called the "meaning state." Individuals behave in ways that are consistent with their meaning systems (Atwood & Dershowitz, 1992). During the stage of adolescence, external and internal social and behavioral interactions and pressures begin to weigh heavily on the adolescent.

## FAMILY SCRIPTS

Family scripts provide blueprints for actions that are necessary for every family (Ferreira, 1963; Gagnon, 1977). Family scripts usually are learned through repetition over many years. Family scripts "write" the patterns of family interaction for particular events. Each member of the family has mental representations of the family relationships. Each member of the family builds up these mental images and uses them to predict sequences of interaction in particular situations (Byng-Hall, 1988). A cue-reaction cycle emerges and repeats itself. Thus, patterns are formed with each member continually performing his or her part. From a generational viewpoint, each generation can either replicate those earlier scripts or work toward changing parts of scripts where a person may have felt there were mistakes made by his or her parents (Byng-Hall, 1988).

## SCRIPTS AND ADOLESCENTS

Havighurst (1972) identified seven life tasks that adolescents can expect to master during their transition into adulthood. They are

- accepting one's body,
- choosing sex roles,
- establishing peer relationships,
- resolving dependence on family,
- choosing a career,
- planning a family, and
- achieving socially responsive behavior.

These tasks are viewed in terms of the many multiscript pressures that influence adolescents. More generally, the tasks adolescents face are the development of scripts for autonomy, scripts for sexuality, and scripts for the future. As adolescents are impacted by these multiscripts, they begin to select out of the larger sociocultural scripts the script that fits into their individual and familial meaning systems. In addition, they reject or rewrite those scripts that do not fit into their belief systems. As adolescents are trying on these multiscripts, the family reacts and adjusts. This then leads to multi-feedback for adolescents. For example, one possibility is that there pressure may exist for adolescents to continue to follow their original scripts, i.e., remain as children. Or, there may be reinforcement of the adult aspects of adolescents' scripts. This could lead to continued growth on the part of the adolescents or, if reinforced to the exclusion of the still remaining child-like aspects, may propel the adolescents forward, in some cases creating a situation of "too much too soon." These reactions to pressures appear both overtly and covertly.

## ADOLESCENT SCRIPT #1: AUTONOMY

The push toward autonomy is one of the most critical psychosocial developments of adolescence (Pardeck & Pardeck, 1990), but it also can be one of the most painful experiences for the whole family, as was so elo-quently expressed by this poem. Adolescence is a period in which the child perceives that he or she has control over his or her own behavior. This belief is relayed to the family in various ways. Related factors are

- the family myths regarding separation,
- the current socially agreed upon norms of the adolescent peer group,
- the current media hype, and
- the social consensus of the socially accepted behaviors and deviant behaviors.

Add to these the idea that social norms change—what was acceptable or deviant during one person's adolescence can be drastically different in his or her child's generation—and the pressures increase. Take for instance the wearing of all black. Not too long ago wearing all black symbolized rebellious or nonconformist attitudes. Recently, however, dressing in all black was a fashion statement of style of all adolescent groups, not just those of rebellious groups.

## "Exploratory interaction is not scripted" (Byng-Hall, 1988)

There are many influences on the development of autonomy, and one such element is the exploration of the family's scripts. During adolescence, a person begins to explore actively the social environment and the self in order to formulate his or her own identity. This generally leads to an evaluation of family scripts. Adolescents are aware of the roles, rules, meaning systems, and behaviors of the family. They begin to explore whether or not they feel comfortable with the present family scripts or if there are areas that they feel need improvement or rewriting. It is here that adolescents may begin to think about intimate relationships and begin to examine and evaluate the quality of their parents' relationship. Also at this time, the family may feel themselves—their attitudes, their values, and behaviors—under close scrutiny by their 14-year-old! Sometimes, this may lead to a defensive reaction on the family's part, causing a further entrenchment into the original family script. This can involve increased pressures on the adolescent to conform, which in turn can lead to a more rebellious stance on the part of the adolescent. In order to accomplish the healthy adolescent developmental task of autonomy, he or she must be an "individual" who is "different/separate" from the family of origin. In some extreme cases, the family stance may become more and more rigid and static (frozen in time so to speak), where no independent behaviors on the part of the adolescent are acceptable. In some extreme cases, the psychological suffocation becomes so severe in the adolescent's mind, there are only drastic ways out— suicide or self-starvation.

The exploratory phase may entice the adolescent to experiment with ideas and behaviors that are either acceptable and fitting to the family scripts or those that are questionable or taboo. For example, the family scripts may include a rule that dictates, "we stay with our own kind," meaning that relationships, platonic or romantic, are with individuals of the same ethnicity or race. At school, work, socializing, etc., the adolescent comes into contact with people of other ethnicities and colors. Whether the adolescent is cognizant of the thought processes involved or not, a decision is made whether or not he or she will become involved with the person(s). At some junction, a decision to adhere to the approved family scripts or not is made. Generally, the decision to interact with the "other" types of people is made. Making a decision to alter or even question the family scripts is a push toward autonomy that generally results in an editing process to the childhood scripts. The individual's and the family's reaction to the editing process is more apt to be received positively if there is flexibility in the family definitions and flexibility in the family roles and beliefs.

External pressures, such as verbalizations, reinforcements, and punishers also may impact the adolescent, causing him or her to be loyal to the family scripts. The family may exert pressure in covert ways such as withdrawal, nonverbal gestures, or secretive activities. At other times, both overt and covert messages may be given to the adolescent, for example, a father who verbally and nonverbally discourages socialization with other races while a mother verbally encourages the same. This family may then consider themselves in a crisis situation because their son is dating a girl of a different race.

According to Becker, (1964), Kelly and Goodwin (1983), Fleming and Anderson (1986), and Allen, Aber, and Leadbeater (1990), parenting styles and the adolescent's perceptions of his or her respective parents' parenting styles, play a significant role in the achievement of the autonomy scripts from the family of origin. Part of developing scripts for autonomy is developing a sense of autonomy. This involves developing individuality that does not threaten the relationship with parents or violate any major social norm (Allen et al., 1990).

Many articles and ideas about differentiation from the family of origin have been written and expressed in family therapy literature, and words such as "fusion" (Guerin & Guerin, 1976; Karpel, 1976), "triangulation" (Bray, Williamson, & Malone, 1984), and "scapegoating" (Anderson & Bagarozzi, 1983; Bowen, 1978) have been used to describe some of the processes that occur in families that "debilitate" the individuation/differentiation process. It has been hypothesized that children who perceive themselves as more triangulated or fused with their family members are more likely to experience difficulty in solving some of the developmental tasks such as college adjustment, development of high self-esteem, and feelings of mastering their environment. In addition, they report a greater number of health problems (Fleming & Anderson, 1986). What the struggle *really* is for adolescents is how to balance a sense of closeness with their family of origin while still remaining autonomous—how to develop a sense of an autonomous self so that they are free to feel and act independently, yet stay connected enough to feel a part of the family. The adolescent and his or her family of origin's task is to renegotiate and edit the original family scripts so that the scripts can incorporate an adolescent member.

## ADOLESCENT SCRIPT #2: SEXUALITY

As was stated earlier, individuals learn their sexual scripts by interacting with their social environment. The major pressures involved in adolescents developing their own sexual scripts are family scripts, peer pressure, social norms, the exploration of self, and gender. Concerning sexuality, adolescents have multiple sexual scripts from which to choose, spanning a spectrum from advocating celibacy to total permissiveness. Parents themselves may be inconsistent in the messages they send to their children (i.e., wanting their children to be popular, accepted, and liked by their peer group but being hesitant and fearful of that position) (Weinstein & Rosen, 1991). As persons' sexual belief systems are developing, they select people and exhibit behaviors that fit with their developing meaning systems.

Although sexual scripts are not as rigidly defined as we once thought, they do dictate within a range the appropriate people, acceptable kinds of sexual activity, appropriate times and places of sexual activity, and the meanings the activity has (Gagnon, 1977). Specifics may include items such as sexual activity is acceptable with someone of the opposite gender, of the same race and culture, close in age and attractiveness, and in a monogamous relationship. Although scripts do set the end points of acceptability on the behavioral continuum, most times these scripts are defined loosely, leaving the observer to fill in the missing gaps (Abelson, 1981; Schank & Abelson, 1977). An example of this might be family scripts that dictate the generic script of placing importance on having intimacy prior to any sexual relationship. Although the adolescent is exposed to this script that includes intimacy, the term "intimacy" is a very vague term. Intimacy means different things to different people. Each person may hold a completely different perception of the word. An adolescent's peer group's interpretation of what intimacy means may be very different from that of the parents, thus leaving the adolescent with multiple messages about any given behavior (see Atwood & Kasindorf, 1991).

Sexual scripts impact on people because they incorporate both physical and mental development as well as the meaning of the exploration of what these changes are and how they feel. With the onset of puberty, boys have a growth spurt both in height and muscularity, development of pubic hair, and an increase in the size of the genitalia. This is accompanied by the deepening of the voice, possible skin problems, and a first ejaculation. Girls' hormonal influences trigger the growth of pubic hair, the development of breasts, and the onset of menarche (Weinstein & Rosen, 1991). Once these biological changes begin to emerge, the socially scripted messages about what these changes mean are multiple and can be quite confusing for the adolescent.

It is not a new phenomenon that the media's portrayal of style can raise havoc on the development of a body image for an adolescent. The images of "perfection" of sexual attractiveness are everywhere. Television, music videos, magazines, and the current store fashions dictate what sexual attractiveness is. Peer groups perpetuate the myths. The message though is loud and clear: sexual attractiveness is manifested in terms of physical appearance. While the adolescent's body is changing and maturing, he or she generally compares his or her body image to those around him or her and those in the media. So that while parents are teaching their children to love themselves unconditionally, their peer groups and society are teaching them how to mold themselves into the current sexy fad in order to be attractive. For most, the impact of the pressures from the peer group and the media far outweigh the family messages. During adolescence especially, the pressure to belong to the larger social group of peers is tremendous.

Sexual scripts also may contain age appropriate messages. A typical family script is that sexual activity is for adults. Adolescents living in families where this message is prevalent may incorporate sexual activity as a statement of proving his or her maturity. This may be interpreted by parents as a rebellious behavior because their family script does not include sexual activity at early adolescent age.

Generally, by the time individuals have reached the age of 12 or 13, they have been exposed to a multitude of the prevailing sexual scripts of their families and of society. From very early on, boys and girls are socialized into the double standard: female sexual behavior should be more restricted than that of male sexual behavior (Safilios-Rothschild, 1977). Besides sexual scripts being less restrictive for males, role prescriptions for males appear to be more clear cut than for females (Atwood & Gagnon, 1987; Carns, 1973; Gagnon & Simon, 1973; Gilgun, 1984). Men are more pressured than females by same sex peers to engage in intercourse and are given much more social approval when they do so. Occasionally females report same sex pressure to lose their virginity as a way of gaining adult status, but this is generally not the case. To add to the multiplicity of social messages, the adolescent's own family messages may be incongruous. Young women may be taught to believe that sexual behavior is dirty or bad, while boys may be encouraged to feel proud of their masculinity and to flaunt it.

Parents may be verbally and nonverbally more accepting of masturbation and premarital sexual activity for boys than for girls (Atwood & Gagnon, 1987; Roberts, Kline, & Gagnon, 1978; Ross, 1979). There may be different scripts for the males in families than for the females. Adolescent males who are sexually active generally are not perceived as rebellious as are the females who are sexually active at the same age. On the other hand, if during adolescence the young man is not actively pursuing female sexual relationships, indicating little to no interest in girls or if he is discovering a sexual attraction to males, he might be considered a script-breaker.

For some adolescents, the message content may be given that sex is beautiful, or dirty, or that men need sex more than women, or that sex is to be saved for marriage, or that sex is appropriate under certain situations, or a combination of rules is given; for some, no information is given at all. For all people, though, the period of exploring our rapidly changing own bodies and incorporating an identity as a sexual person involves dealing with multiple messages about how to behave and what it all means. Questions about feelings, intimacy, desires, consequences, and the morality of behavior are uppermost in adolescents' minds. The current social norms may be in conflict with a person's meaning system or with his or her family script. The pressure to perform or to withhold sex; how far to go with someone; how to handle the issue of birth and disease control; what feels good; what hurts; the feelings before, during, and after; did you do it right; whom to tell, what will your partner think about you after; what will friends and parents think; and where and when to have sex are loaded issues for adolescents.

The majority of adolescents receive their sex education from homosocial peer groups. In general, adolescent boys learn how to provide pleasure for their own bodies and possibly those of partners, whereas girls learn about being attractive, falling in love, and intimacy (Gagnon, 1977; Gagnon & Greenblatt, 1978). Cassell (1984) found that young females much more than young males report "being in love" as a primary reason to become sexually active. Girls learn to link sex with love (Gordon & Gilgun, 1987). One could hypothesize then that courtship or adolescent dating involves a tradeoff: boys teach girls about sexuality and girls teach boys about intimacy and love.

There are times when a family will present with an adolescent sexual issue and what has occurred is that the covert messages given may have become more of the rule than the overt messages. An example of this would be a family who presents with a sexually acting out girl adolescent. As they begin to story about their problem verbally, you can almost practically hear the covert, subliminal messages that one parent or both are giving the daughter that they are living vicariously through her. Their sexual fantasies of their adolescence are being played out by their child. It may have been that for them in their family of origin scripts that sexual behavior was so restricted and closely monitored that having a sexually active and/or permissive daughter is being encouraged by them and is helping to edit their own family of origin sexual scripts. The modification of the script to allow more flexibility in sexual roles, attitudes, and behaviors may be the purpose of the covert, unspoken messages.

No discussion of sexuality can conclude without the mention of adolescent pregnancy and sexually transmitted diseases. The parental fears of these have been incorporated into family scripts generating rules concerning sexual activity; however, their possibilities have not substantially influenced the way families communicate about sexual matters to their adolescents, until AIDS. The onset of AIDS added to the confusion. Parents tend to be afraid that if they provide appropriate information about safer sex, especially condom use, they are promoting or encouraging their adolescent's sexual activity. It is possible that the AIDS health crisis is so frightening that it eventually will supersede family belief systems in determining what adolescents will be told about sexual behavior and prevention. With the outbreak of HIV into the heterosexual population, there has been an increase in parental awareness and concern, resulting in the need to rewrite the family scripts for adolescent sexuality to include the discussion of protection. Unfortunately, many families are not responding to the urgency fast enough. The impact of AIDS on adolescent sexual scripts will continue to be a factor in the development of adolescent sexual beliefs and behaviors in the future.

## ADOLESCENT SCRIPT #3: THE FUTURE

Adolescents frequently report that they feel as if all eyes are upon them, waiting for them to decide what they are going to with their lives. This focus encompasses educational directions, career choices and options, moral development, and a decision regarding when and whom to marry. The numbers of decisions adolescents make during this transitional period are staggering. For many, the pressures from the family, peer groups, and society become quite overwhelming. While the two life scripts presented earlier in this chapter (autonomy and sexuality) led to an increase in adult status, this life script for the future may become the area that creates the desire for the adolescent to return to childhood when the decisions were so much easier. Some adolescents do make this choice—they choose not to choose. Some opt to escape through drug use, parenthood, or marriage. Some choose delinquency while others choose to pursue education and college or work. In so doing, they simply put off the inevitable.

Golombeck and Kutcher (1990) described the adolescent routes in terms of three directions: the clear stable route, the fluctuating route, and the unstable disturbed route. The first path, the *clear stable route*, encompasses those adolescents who develop without showing any evidence of an upheaval. They are described as being cooperative, being optimistic, approving, capable of showing affection, having a good self-image, and feeling competent about mastering their environment. Their family relationships are generally positive, and they enjoy satisfying peer relationships. In general, they appear rather well-adjusted.

The second route, called the *fluctuating route*, describes adolescents that at times appear emotionally stable and well-adapted and at other times are distressed and have difficulties coping with everyday challenges. They have intermittent serious complaints about interpersonal relationships and tend to have periods in which they feel uncooperative and unaffectionate. They are occasionally impulsive and show considerable variation in self-esteem. The third route, the *unstable disturbed route*, includes adolescents who demonstrate clear and multiple disturbances not only in their functioning but throughout their development. These are the youths that often are described as having psychiatric disorders and often require hospitalization.

It is not surprising that the first two categories housed the greatest number of adolescents of the study, equaling approximately 75% of those studied. These findings follow suit with a longitudinal study of adolescents and their "normality" done by Offer, Ostrov, Howard, and Atkinson (1990). Their research yielded results that indicated that 80% of adolescents are normal and functioning well. All too often, though, our research on adolescents is guided by the other 20% of the adolescents whom we consider troubled or delinquent or following that disturbed route. Due to the vast research on this sect of the overall group, the impression transmitted about the stage of adolescence is that it is a period that represents the storm and stress model of constant turmoil and distress. This is absolutely not to mean that stress, indecision, and overwhelming pressures are not part of that "normal" experience but instead to remark that they are a part, not the whole, of the adolescent existence.

The three sub-script tasks involved in the development of the overall future script are the development of morals and values, the development of a career path, and the development of the direction of one's personal and interpersonal relationships.

## Adolescent Moral and Value Development

The strongest influence on moral scripts are those of the family and the social environment. From birth, the child learns the belief systems of the family regarding religion, mores, norms of behavior, attitudes, and values, which are passed down from generation to generation. Individuals learn their previous generations' morals, beliefs, and values through interpersonal interactions, socialization, and story and legend telling. As the norms of society shift, notions of right and wrong are questioned (Elder, 1975; Riley, 1976). Looking back at the period of social upheaval in the 1960s and 1970s, both the youth culture and the mass media placed emphasis on the rejection of traditional values and socially accepted traditions. Adolescents in the 1980s were viewed as more practical, more interested in financial security, and perhaps less moral than their predecessors (Perlmutter & Shapiro, 1987). The legacy for adolescence in the 1990s is still to be written. Every generation of adolescents establishes some balance and integration of the continuity granted by established values of the previous generation within the creative discontinuity of finding their own way in the world. Because there are so many social and generational changes that take place so quickly, adolescents often may feel confused about what morals are right for them. Perlmutter (1985) reported the following passage written by a 17-year-old girl. It is offered to highlight the difficulty of developing one's individual values.

> My mother's generation had it much easier in terms of values and what is expected of a person—a teenager. My mom tells me she did not sleep with any man before she got married; she was 23 years old then. She didn't even sleep with my father before marriage, and she loved him. But nice girls didn't. And it was just like that! With us, you have all these different things—someone like my mom would be weird. Sometimes I wish I knew what I should do and not do. I can't listen to how

my mother was; it does not help me. But when I listen to my
friends, I'm also confused.

Changes in society such as an increase in women in the work force, a
more flexible set of sexual standards and acceptable behaviors, the AIDS
epidemic, the lessening of the nuclear family influence, the expansion of the
media, and the financial climate cause difficulty for adolescents in establishing continuity with the morals and values of their parents' lives. Without
the connection to the traditions of the previous generation, the options
available to adolescents can become overwhelming (Perlmutter & Shapiro,
1987). It is perhaps true that the increased social flexibility of morals and
values of the 1960s and 1970s was necessary for social growth; however, it
is perhaps also necessary that in the AIDS era, society needs to place
stronger emphasis on the adherence of stricter or more defined socially
acceptable rules. The challenge for adolescents is the balancing of the discovery of new sexual values for the self while maintaining some congruence
with family values.

**Establishing a Career Path**

The scripting related to this sub-task includes the family, the social
environment of the community, school, current work experience, educational opportunities, prejudice, and gender factors. The 1980s ushered in
an increase in the number of adolescents in the work force and in the
number of career and educational opportunities available to adolescents.
Although some changes have taken place, there are still different career
opportunities for different sects of our society. White, upper-class men are
still more occupationally mobile throughout life and have more opportunities than lower-class men or women in general. Men still earn higher wages
and achieve higher positions than women. These factors weigh heavily on
the decisions adolescents make regarding their employment choices.

The past two decades have seen vast changes in all areas of education
(Bottoms & Coppa, 1983). The pressures to receive at least a college education are increasing. If they choose the educational path, adolescents need
to decide between two-year and four-year schools, neighborhood schools
vs. going away to college, and state schools vs. private schools. Familial,
financial, and community influences impact on these decisions because for
some families and for some communities, education and career are not as
highly valued as is working in the community. The choice whether or not to
follow in the communal adherence regarding the college/work route may

depend upon the adolescent's family scripts and/or the adolescent's writing of his or her own autonomy scripts.

### Developing a Future Personal/Interpersonal Script

This sub-task really encompasses the culmination of the other tasks set before the adolescent. As adolescents begins to be bombarded with the various scripts described above, they begin to work out who they are as individuals. As their identity becomes more stable, the scripts for the future are written. Peer groups are established, identity is formulated, sexualities are explored, sex roles and adherence to a sexual preference occurs, career and educational choices are made, and the person's morals and values are solidified.

While this is happening, the adolescent is interacting continually with others, sifting through who and what feels right and who or what fits with his or her developing belief systems. All these tasks, explorations, and pressures pave the way toward adulthood. It is difficult to try to identify where adolescence ends and adulthood begins. According to life cycle literature, the beginning of adulthood includes those individuals in their twenties who are

- physically separate (although possible short-term returns to the nest may occur);
- post college and/or military or (if under 21) working and living apart from the parental home; and
- largely financially independent (although this may be an evolving issue). It includes individuals who married young and divorced a year or two later, as well as those who are living together without marriage. It does not, however, include children of any age who never have left home (Aylmer, 1989).

The need for further research in this area is apparent because there are increasing numbers of exceptions or questions arising concerning whether certain groups of people are adolescents or adults, i.e., an individual who chooses to further his or her graduate education. Master's degrees or doctorates may take anywhere from 2 to 10 years to complete depending on the university. This means that persons may be in their mid- to late-20s or 30s before finishing school. And some never leave! At what point do we refer to them as adults? Many either stay in or return to the parental home due to financial necessities.

The issues of marriage and child rearing also play a major role in this stage of the life cycle. For an increasing number of adolescents, the decisions they make about marriage include "new" choices such as to not marry, to put off getting married for years, or to live with somebody of the same or opposite sex in a romantic setting with or without the intention of marrying. Also, with the increases in technology and women in the work force, more opportunities are afforded to people to have children outside of marriage.

# A MODEL OF THERAPY

## Environment Setting

Underlying the beginning of any therapy is the importance of joining or constructing a workable reality. Cimmarustu and Lappin (1985) believed that the dynamic interplay of joining and constructing a workable reality initiates the process of change. The construction of workable realities is defined as the process in which the view of the problem is transformed from a paradigm of individual causality to a paradigm of interaction. It is a process analogous to socializing by which an empathic rapport is developed with the clients. The therapist's reflections serve to create an environment conducive to change. In this environment, the therapist listens to the family's language, learns it, and uses it to create a comfortable and safe environment. Sensitivity to client's preferred language is very important. Clinicians risk alienating clients by using unexpected or uncomfortable language (McCormick, 1987). If an atmosphere of intimacy is provided and modeled for the family, they will feel more at ease discussing their family life, joys and pains. The safety provides the family with an opportunity to do something different. The basic assumption is that the family, not the therapist, is the expert in knowing what is best for them. The role of the therapist is that of a curious observer—interested in learning about the family's story. The therapist interacts with the family, selectively interacting with only selected parts of the family system (Atwood & Dershowitz, 1992).

## Exploring the Family Scripts with the Family

As was discussed earlier in this chapter, adolescents experience external as well as internal pressures. It is therefore helpful to include in therapy a discussion of the pressures weighing on the adolescent and his or her family. A more intimate tone for therapy is achieved if the adolescent member and

## A MODEL OF THERAPY FOR THE ADOLESCENT AND FAMILY

### ENVIRONMENT

- Provide a safe atmosphere so that the family will feel comfortable and intimate enough to story and restory the family scripts.
- Learn the family's language regarding their scripts.
- Validate all feelings of the family members.

### EXPLORATION OF THE RELEVANT SCRIPTS

- Family Scripts
- Peers
- Sex, STDs, AIDS
- Career/job
- Social Norms
- Self
- School
- Gender
- Religion
- Media

### EXPLORATION WITH THE FAMILY

- Feelings
- Perceptions
- Reactions

### WORKING WITH THE ISSUES

- Role-plays
- Work with Subsystems
- Adolescent Groups
- Reframing
- Metaphors
- Rituals

### EDITING OF FAMILY SCRIPTS

- Incorporation of new scripts

### RESTORYING OF FAMILY SCRIPTS: FUTURE SCRIPTS

- Provide family with opportunity to retell their story, including possible alternatives.

the other family members are provided with the opportunity to fully verbalize the pressures they feel, the emotional roller coaster they experience, and their fears and hopes so that they can feel heard by the other family members.

## Working with the Issues

Once the stage of therapy is set, the adolescent and his or her parents now can learn different ways of communicating with each other about the options available to them. They also can explore the consequences of their actions. One way to accomplish this is to set up role playing activities where the family members can practice different options, exploring the consequences and feelings associated with each. These scenarios can start out with relatively simple issues, leading to more toxic ones as the family becomes comfortable. At this point, they already will have experienced success in previous role playing and decision making activities.

In addition to working with the family as a whole, it may be useful to do therapy with various subsystems separately (Minuchin 1974; Nicholson, 1986; Preto, 1989). Meeting with parents and adolescents separately increases the therapist's ability to support both generations at once while clarifying the boundaries. It also helps the therapist avoid getting caught in power struggles, such as if adolescents become belligerent or refuse to say anything in session. Meeting with adolescents and their siblings, with their peers, or anyone else who is influential in their lives opens up the system to new opportunities and thus to new possibilities.

Group counseling for adolescents, especially around sexuality issues, can be very effective. Due to the influence and attachment to peers, groups may be particularly good for beginning dialogue, for the sharing of information, and for the normalization of issues with other similar adolescents. Groups often can offer support, advice, and communication. Rap groups in schools facilitated by counselors or peers as well as community or religious groups also can offer the adolescent a safe haven to explore his or her issues with others in an intimate and ongoing voluntary basis. Often teenagers may be able to connect with other teenagers who are experiencing similar problems and who can identify with their struggles.

The art of ***reframing*** refers to the "changing of the conceptual and or emotional setting or viewpoint in relation to which a situation is experienced and to place it in another frame that fits the facts of the same situation equally well or even better and thereby changes its meaning" (Watzlawick, 1984, p. 95). Reframing can be very useful and effective for families. Sometimes reframes help families "see" their situation differently. A well-known example of a reframe is that of the "smother mother" who becomes the mother that loves too much (Atwood, 1991). Reframes are not lies or manipulated maneuvers; they are just examples of a different script or a different way of viewing the same idea. Their use is to provide an opportunity for change to occur.

Another helpful way of working with adolescents is through the use of ***metaphors*** (Atwood & Levine, 1990, 1991). Metaphors are analogical representations of reality in which the concreteness of reality is transformed to the abstraction of figurative constructions. As Lakoff and Johnson (1980) point out, metaphors are pervasive in everyday life, not just in language but in thought and in action. Our ordinary conceptual system, in terms of which we both think and act, is metaphorical in nature (Goncalves & Craine, 1990). The use of metaphors for some families may seem quite natural and may work effectively because they can talk about sensitive issues in a gentle way. Communication occurs on a totally different level as families search for new structure and new meanings. In so doing, they create new possibilities (Atwood, 1991).

In our society, there are relatively few rituals that signify adulthood. There are religious rituals such as a bar mitzvah or confirmation, society rituals such as obtaining one's driver's license, and social rituals such as the sweet sixteen party, but in general, there are no discrete rituals that a family prepares for the onset of adolescence or for the entrance into adulthood. Rituals function to reduce anxiety about change. According to Schwartzman (1982), rituals make change manageable, as members experience change as part of their system rather than as a threat to it. Rituals have the capacity to assist in the resolution of conflict (Imber-Black, 1989). Therefore, having the family discuss and plan a ritual for the entrance into adolescence may aid the family in a smoother transition into the future. At the very least, it will aid the family in developing a meaning system that concretely symbolizes their experience.

### Editing of Family Scripts

The family's discussion and exploration of adolescent scripting pressures and options is basically a rewriting or editing of their family script. By editing, they include a more comprehensive or expansive script. Flexibility is the key to success in this process. If newer more effective ways of communication have been incorporated and a deeper relationship has been established, the transition stage of adolescence may be easily rescripted. If done with a mixture of seriousness, sincerity, feeling, flexibility, and humor, the results of the new edition can be both rewarding and joyful.

### Restorying of Family Scripts: A Future Frame

The last phase of therapy includes the opportunity and experience for the family members to actually retell the story and process of their therapy. This helps solidify their success. Time also should be allotted for the family to tell the new family story. Hearing the new scripts will start a fresh baseline from which the family can continue to grow but in a newer, fresher, future oriented direction.

## DISCUSSION

For so long, society has viewed clients from a negative perspective. The medical model dictated that clients had problems and needed an expert to fix them or guide them into resolution. Recently, however, the field of marriage and family therapy has moved away from this model, toward a more experiential therapy. Much of the literature on adolescents really has focused on the delinquency rates, the drug abuse statistics, and the storm and stress notions about adolescents. It is apparent that for many, adolescence can be a difficult time. But looking at adolescence from a social scripting perspective, the notions of choice and possibility are emphasized. The idea of editing, rewriting, or restorying is a much more positive humanistic type of approach, providing a safe environment for families to restory their lives. If Hoffman is accurate in saying that problems are stories people tell themselves, then being there with clients and assisting them in retelling themselves a different story is probably the most beneficial thing therapists can do for their clients.

## BIBLIOGRAPHY

Feixas, G. (1990). Personal construct theory and systemic therapies: Parallel or convergent trends? *Journal of Marriage and Family Therapy, 16*(1), 1–20.

Lambert, B.G., & Mounce, N.B. (1987). Career planning. In V.B. Hasselt & M. Hersen (Eds.), *Handbook of adolescent psychology* (pp. 33–47). New York: Pergamon Press.

Pearl, R., Bryan, T., & Herzog, A. (1990). Resisting or acquiescing to peer pressure to engage in misconduct: Adolescents' expectations of probable consequences. *Journal of Youth and Adolescence, 19*(1), 43–55.

# REFERENCES

Abelson, R.P. (1976). Script processing in attitude formation and decision making. In J.S. Carroll & J.W. Payne (Eds.), *Cognition and social behavior* (pp. 54–64). Hillsdale, NJ: Erlbaum.

Abelson, R.P. (1981). Psychological status of the script concept. *American Psychologist, 36*, 715–729.

Allen, J.P., Aber, L., & Leadbeater, B. (1990). Adolescent problem behaviors: The influence of attachment and autonomy. *Psychiatric Clinics of North America, 13*(3), 455–467.

Anderson, S.A., & Bagarozzi, D.A. (1983). The use of family therapy myths as an aid to strategic therapy. *Journal of Family Therapy, 5*, 145–154.

Atwood, J.D. (1991). *Constructivist marital therapy: Ways to help couples not to leave their lover.* Hempstead, NY: Hofstra University.

Atwood, J.D., & Dershowitz, S. (1992). *Constructing a sex therapy frame: Ways to help couples deconstruct sexual problems.* Hempstead, NY: Hofstra University.

Atwood, J.D., & Gagnon, J.H. (1987). Mastubatory behavior in college youth. *Journal of Sex Education & Therapy, 13*(2), 35–42.

Atwood, J.D., & Kasindorf, S. (1991). A multisystemic approach to adolescent pregnancy. *American Journal of Family Therapy, 20*(4), 341–360.

Atwood, J.D., & Levine, L. (1990). The therapeutic metaphors. *Australian Journal of Clinical Hypnotherapy and Hypnosis, 11*(2), 17–40.

Atwood, J.D., & Levine, L. (1991). Ax murderers, dragons, spiders, and webs: Therapeutic metaphors in couples therapy. *Contemporary Family Therapy: An International Journal, 13*(3), 201–217.

Aylmer, R.C. (1989). The Launching of the single young adult. In B. Carter & M. McGoldrick (Eds.), *The changing family life cycle: A framework for family therapy* (2nd ed.) (pp. 191–208). Boston: Allyn and Bacon.

Bandura, A. (1969). *Principles of behavior modification.* New York: Holt, Rinehart and Winston.

Bandura, A. (1973). *Aggression: A social learning analysis.* Englewood Cliffs, NJ: Prentice Hall.

Bandura, A., & Walters, R.H. (1959). *Adolescent aggression.* New York: Ronald.

Bandura, A., Ross, D., & Ross, S. A. (1963). Imitation of film-mediated aggressive models. *Journal of Abnormal and Social Psychology, 67,* 3011–3020.

Becker, W.C. (1964). Consequences of different kinds of parental discipline. In M.L. Hoffman & L. Hoffman (Eds.), *Review of child development research* (pp. 169–208). Chicago: University of Chicago Press.

Bottoms, G., & Coppa, P. (1983). A perspective on vocational education today. *Phi Delta Kappan, 64,* 348–354.

Bowen, M. (1978). *Family therapy in clinical practice.* New York: Aronson, Inc.

Bray, J., Williamson, D., & Malone, P. (1984). Personal authority in the family system: Development of a questionnaire to measure personal authority in intergenerational family processes. *Journal of Marriage and Family Therapy, 10,* 167–178.

Byng-Hall, J. (1988). Scripts and legends in families and family therapy. *Family Process, 27,* 167–179.

Carns, D.E. (1973). Talking about sex: Notes on first coitus and the double standard. *Journal of Marital and Family Therapy, 35,* 677–688.

Carter, B., & McGoldrick, M. (Eds.). (1989). *The changing family life cycle: A framework for family therapy* (2nd ed.). Boston: Allyn and Bacon.

Cassell, C. (1984). *Swept away: Why women fear their own sexuality.* New York: Simon and Schuster.

Cimmarustu, R.A., & Lappin, J. (1985). Beginning family therapy. *The Family Therapy Collections, 14*, 16–25.

Elder, G. (1975). Adolescence in the life cycle: An introduction. In S. Dragastin & G. Elder (Eds.), *Adolescence in the life cycle: Psychological change and social context.* New York: Wiley.

Ferreira, A.J. (1963). Family myth and homeostasis. *Archives of General Psychiatry, 9*, 457–463.

Fleming, M., & Anderson, S. (1986). Individuation from the family of origin and personal adjustment in late adolescence. *Journal of Marriage and Family Therapy, 12*(3), 311–315.

Gagnon, J.H. (1977). *Human sexualities.* Glenview, IL: Scott Foresman.

Gagnon, J.H., & Greenblatt, C.S. (1978). *Life designs: Individuals, marriages, and families.* Glenview, IL: Scott Foresman.

Gagnon, J.H., & Simon, W. (1973). *Sexual conduct: The social sources of human sexuality.* Chicago: Aldine.

Gergen, K. (1985). The social construction movement in modern psychology. *American Psychologist, 40*, 266–275.

Gergen, K.J., & Gergen, M.M. (1983). The social construction of narrative accounts. In K.J. Gergen & M.M. Gergen (Eds.), *Historical social psychology* (pp. 79–84). Hillsdale, NJ: Erlbaum Associates.

Gilgun, J.F. (1984). Sexual abuse of the young female in life course perspective. *Dissertation/Abstracts International, 45*, 3058.

Golombeck, H., & Kutcher, S. (1990). Feeling states during adolescence. *Psychiatric Clinics of America 13*(3), 443–454.

Goncalves, O.F., & Craine, M.H. (1990). The use of metaphors in cognitive therapy. *Journal of Psychotherapy: An International Quarterly, 4*(2), 135–149.

Gordon, S., & Gilgun, J.F. (1987). Adolescent sexuality. In V.B. Hasselt & M. Hersen (1987). *Handbook of adolescent psychology* (pp. 105–120). New York: Pergamon Press.

Guerin, P., & Guerin, K. (1976). Theoretical aspects and clinical relevance of the multigenerational model of family therapy. In P.J. Guerin (Ed.), *Family therapy and practice* (pp. 72–82). New York: Gardner Press.

Hall, G.S. (1904). *Adolescence: Its psychology and its relations to physiology, anthropology, sociology, sex, crime, religion, and education* (vols. 1 & 2). New York: Appleton-Century Crofts.

Havighurst, R.J. (1972). *Developmental tasks and education* (3rd ed.). New York: David McKay.

Havighurst, R.J., Bowman, P.H., Liddle, G., Matthews, C.V., & Pierce, J.V. (1962). *Growing up in River City.* New York: Wiley.

Hollingshead, A.B. (1949). *Elmstown's youth.* New York: Wiley.

Imber-Black, E. (1989). Idiosyncratic life cycle transitions and therapeutic rituals. In B. Carter & M. McGoldrick (Eds.), *The changing family life cycle: A framework for family therapy* (2nd ed.) (pp. 41–61). Boston: Allyn and Bacon.

Karpel, M. (1976). Individuation: From fusion to dialogue. *Family Process, 15*, 65–82.

Kelly, C., & Goodwin, G.C. (1983). Adolescent perceptions to three styles of parental control. *Adolescence, 28*(7), 567–571.

Lakoff, G., & Johnson, M. (1980). Metaphors we live by. Chicago: The University of Chicago Press. In O.F. Goncalves & M.H. Craine (Eds.), The use of metaphors in cognitive therapy. *Journal of Psychotherapy: An International Quarterly, 4*(2), 135–149.

McCormick, N.B. (1987). Sexual scripts: Social and therapeutic implications. *Sexual and Marital Therapy, 2*(1), 3–26.

Mead, M.(1950). *Coming of age in Samoa.* New York: New American Library.

Mead, M. (1953). *Growing up in New Guinea.* New York: New American Library.

Minuchin, S. (1974). *Families and family therapy.* Cambridge: Harvard University Press.

Nicholson, S. (1986). Family therapy with adolescents: Giving up the struggle. *Family Therapy, 7,* 1–6.

Nisbett, R., & Ross, L. (1980). *Human inference: Strategies and shortcomings of social judgment.* Englewood Cliffs, NJ: Prentice Hall.

Offer, D., Ostrov, E., Howard, K., & Atkinson, R. (1990). Normality and adolescence. *Psychiatric Clinics of North America, 13*(3), 377–388.

Pardeck, S.A., & Pardeck, J.T. (1990). Family factors related to adolescent autonomy. *Adolescence, 25*(98), 311–319.

Perlmutter, R. (1985). *Teenagers and their feelings.* Unpublished Manuscript.

Perlmutter, R., & Shapiro, E.R. (1987). Morals and values in adolescence. In V.B. Hasselt & M. Hersen (Eds.), *Handbook of adolescent psychology* (pp. 90–100). New York: Pergamon Press.

Preto, N.G. (1989). Transformation of the family system in adolescence. In B. Carter & M. McGoldrick (Eds.), *The changing family life cycle: A framework for family therapy* (2nd ed.) (pp. 255–283). Boston: Allyn and Bacon.

Riley, M. (1976). Age strata in social systems. In R. Binstock & E. Shanas (Eds.), *Handbook of aging and the social sciences* (pp. 189–217). New York: Van Nostrand.

Roberts, E.J., Kline, D., & Gagnon, J. (1978). *Family life and sexual learning: A study of the role of parents in the sexual learning of children.* Cambridge, MA: Harvard University Press.

Ross, S. (1979). *The youths values project.* New York: Grune & Stratton.

Safilios-Rothschild, C. (1977). *Love, sex, and sex roles.* Englewood Cliffs, NJ: Prentice Hall/Spectrum.

Schank, R.C., & Abelson, R.P. (1977). *Scripts, plans, goals, and understanding: An inquiry into human knowledge structures.* Hillsdale, NJ: Lawrence Erlbaum.

Schwartzman, J. (1982). Symptoms and rituals: Paradoxical modes and social organization. *Ethos, 10*(1), 2–23.

Simon, W., & Gagnon, J.H. (1986). Sexual scripts: Permanence and change. *Archives of Sexual Behavior, 15*, 97–120.

Sisson, L.A., Hersen, M., & Hasselt, V.B. (1987). Historical perspectives. In V.B. Hasselt & M. Hersen (Eds.), *Handbook of adolescent psychology* (pp. 101–106). New York: Pergamon Press.

Watzlawick, P. (1984). *The invented reality: How do we know what we know? Contributions to constructivism.* New York: W.W. Norton Company.

Weinstein, E., & Rosen, E. (Eds.). (1988). *Sexuality counseling: Issues and implications.* Pacific Grove, CA: Brooks-Cole Publishing.

# Chapter 6

# EXPLORING SHADOW SCRIPTS IN COUPLE THERAPY

*Joan D. Atwood*

This chapter presents the underlying assumptions and theoretical concepts of social constructionism, combines social constructionism with couple therapy, and presents a model of social constructionist couple therapy. The approach to couple therapy presented is based on the belief that we create our own reality. Couples make sense of their ongoing experience, and it is this process of making sense that is the object of this therapy. The therapy takes as its focus couples' meaning systems and scripts, viewed from the past, present, and future—both negative and positive. The initial focus of the past is affective—understanding how meanings and scripts developed and how couples believe these affected them in the past. Once the past is put in perspective, the second focus of the approach is cognitive—on couples' meaning systems and scripts in the present and on their maintenance, helping couples be aware of their processes, and facilitating learning about and amplifying options to the process in order to provide possibilities for new solutions. Future focus enables couples to image how different meanings could affect their relationship in a positive way. Re-visioning the relationship is the last stage of this therapy and emphasizes future visions of the couple relationship without the problem. Thus, this chapter views couple problems as sociocultural symbolic constructs. Inquiry into the sources, processes, and consequences of their construction and organization is the therapy that flows from this view.

Social constructionism places emphasis on social interpretation and the intersubjective influences of language, family, and culture. As Gergen (1985) stated, "From the constructional position the process of understanding is not automatically driven by the forces of nature, but is the result of an active, cooperative enterprise of persons in relationship" (p. 267). Thus, social construction theory proposes that there is an evolving set of meanings that emerges continually from social interactions. These meanings are part of a general flow of constantly changing narratives.

Social constructionist couple therapy explores the meanings that incidents, behaviors, and encounters have for couples and how these affect the couple script. The sociocultural environment equips couples with methods and ways of understanding and making judgments about aspects of being in a couple ranging from how they feel about being in a relationship to what it means to be a man or a woman. These ways of making sense of experiences are embedded in a meaning system that is accepted as reality by the social group and in the scripts (ways of behaving) that are a part of each individual's meaning system. The dialectical relationship between individual realities and the socially constructed meanings around being a couple is one focus of this chapter.

# THEORETICAL CONCEPTS

## Social Construction of Perceptions

Berger and Luckmann (1966) described social constructions as the consensual recognition of the realness and rightness of a constructed reality, plus the socialization process by which people acquire this reality. A social construction includes not only the routines and the mechanisms for socializing the children of the system, but also the means for maintaining the definition of reality on which it is based. Language is one way that a community reaffirms the dominant reality and discredits competing social constructions. What it means to be a couple, which is a social construction, refers to the complex and unique definitions in each individual that influence couple behavior. These meanings were constructed in childhood and are maintained by ongoing socialization. These meanings are created, embedded in, and recognized by the larger social group and thus operate at the social, interpersonal, and intrapersonal levels.

Gergen (1985) used the term "self-narratives" to describe the social psychological process whereby people tell stories about themselves to themselves and others. Gergen characterized self-narratives as the way individuals establish coherent connection among life events. He believed that individuals have a set of schema that they use to understand life events as meaningful and systematically related. In this way, events are rendered understandable and intelligible because they are located in a sequence or as part of an unfolding process. It is this process that enables individuals to make sense out of nonsense and to interpret events in a coherent, consistent manner.

These narratives or belief systems are originally created by and maintained by interactions with significant others. The process begins at birth and continues until death. A person holding a particular belief system will seek out events and persons that are consistent with that belief system. These belief systems in turn lead to belief states, the emotional reaction to the belief system, and belief behaviors, the behaviors that are consistent with the belief system. Therefore, each person brings forth a different reality.

## Constructing a Time Line

The concept of time is an important part of this model (Atwood, 1991; Penn, 1985; White, 1985). For example, by asking questions such as, "How long has this problem been around?" and "When did you first start becoming depressed about your relationship?", the therapist introduces a historical context of a beginning, a middle and, hopefully, an end. These types of questions give couples information about the origins and persistence of problems and how the trends developed over time. This also helps to dispel beliefs that people are born that way or are just like one of their parents. The problem becomes located in time rather than in the couple, and its characteristics are then examinable and observable.

## Collapsing Time—The Rubber Band Backwards and Forward

Asking a couple about what life was like before the problem implies that there was a time when the problem was not there and further implies that perhaps at some point in time it also will not be there. As will be discussed in a later section, the rubber band can also be used (if requested by the client) to stretch back in time to explore the couple's story as children in their families of origin. A future without the problem also can be explored. Here couples are asked, "If I were to take the rubber band and stretch it forward, say three months from now, and the problem was gone, what would your relationship be like?"

Questioning about development over time is an effort that not only draws attention to the fact that the intensity of the experience of the problem varies over time but also identifies that there are times when the problem is absent and presents the possibility that the problem might not be there in the future. This might lay the groundwork for the ideas that the couple at one time had some control over the problem and that at some point the problem will no longer be there. The progressive use of directional description of the time metaphor allows couples to understand their participation in the problem's persistence at different points in time (White, 1986).

**Change**

Watzlawick, Weakland, and Fisch (1974) described two types of change—first and second order change. Simply, first order change is a change that occurs *within* a system, while second order change is a change of the system itself. Second order change is considered a *change of change*. First order change maintains homeostasis, whereas second order change is a change of the premises governing the system as a whole. First order changes are incremental modifications that make sense within an established frame (Watzlawick, 1978; 1984). Second order change changes the frame itself. In order to accomplish second order change, the therapist phases in particular material and phases out other material. Second order change is represented by the approaches of Minuchin and Fishman (1974), Haley (1967), Watzlawick (1978, 1984; Watzlawick et al., 1974), and White (1985, 1986, 1989). "Frame," a word originally used by Bateson (1972), refers to the context of the problem, the definition of the situation, the meaning the problem has for the couple.

Because the focus of intervention is on couples' meaning systems and the resultant behavioral scripts, the change model adhered to in this chapter is a second order change model. It is similar to Epston and White's (1990) recent work wherein the therapist initially assists the couple in learning processes that help them to amplify (be aware of) their couple process, provides techniques that the couple can use to generate new possibilities, and is someone who creates a "safe environment" for the couple to explore their process, generate new possibilities, consider the implications of the possibilities, and negotiate a shared frame around the chosen change. These ways of learning can be used by the couple outside therapy. Over time, as the couple learns to rely on their own self-healing processes, they become more confident in the processes and in their own abilities to generate growth and change. In this case, the result is new structures that are of a higher order—ones that are more connected and integrated than the prior ones. They are more complex, more flexible, and more susceptible to further change and development.

**Role of the Therapist**

Human beings "name" the world, and in naming the world they give meaning to the world around them. Using this view, the therapist sees the couple's problem as a normal part of living—rooted in their language, rather than in personal inadequacies. Problems are not a symbol of a failing relationship but a challenge to seek new and better ways, to create new knowledge. Through joining with the couple in a collaborative manner, a sense of community between the therapist and the couple develops. Pooled ideas and their individual owners become less strange, and the search for new and better ways becomes a collaborative process rather than an isolated or individual effort. This process requires both therapist and couple to stretch their vision, creating a vision that is richer than each could achieve individually. The atmosphere is one of, "Maybe you see something I don't see. What might that be?" In the process, existing ways are challenged and better ways emerge. The inside becomes outside and the outside becomes inside. Both therapist and clients are involved in the process and transformed by it.

## ASSUMPTIONS

The basic assumptions underlying this position are as follows:

1. There are no absolute truths and there are no absolute realities.
2. People co-construct reality through language with another in a continual interaction with the sociocultural environment. Thus, what

is "real" is that which is co-constructed through language and interaction by the couple in continual interplay with the surrounding
sociocultural environment.

3.  Individuals' inner world is a construct, colored by the past and the
    past, is a construction.

4.  Couples tend to re-create an image of their world by noticing be-
    havior in others that confirms their self-definitions and definitions
    of situations and by selectively ignoring disconfirmatory behavior.

5.  How couples "see" problems, how they "see" roles, how they "see"
    couple relationships—all these ideas do not simply reflect or elab-
    orate on biological "givens" but are largely products of sociocul-
    tural processes.

6.  Couples who come for therapy are experiencing problems in their
    relationship. They have tried many solutions, many of which have
    been unsuccessful. The problems they report are not seen as being
    functional in maintaining the system or as a manifestation of un-
    derlying pathology. They are seen as problems—problems that have
    negative effects for the couple. The way that couples language
    about problems is the way they can use language to co-construct a
    new story.

7.  Repetitive knowledge of partner behavior that is discrepant with
    the perceptual view of the partner will result in a change in the
    person's perceptual view. This is accomplished by exploring the
    couple's shadow scripts, those scripts in the background, peripheral
    to their vision (see Chapter 1), and by focusing on and amplifying
    exceptions in the person's description of the world.

Thus, social constructionist couple therapy focuses on exploring the
couple's view of the problem—breaking up or confusing their definition of
the problem and the meaning that the problem holds for them. This can be
facilitated through the use of techniques such as metaphors and reframes
that amplify the couple's process, and then by finding exceptions to it or by
exploring the couple's shadow scripts, thereby providing the seeds (construction) for transformation.

## SOCIAL CONSTRUCTION THERAPY WITH COUPLES

This chapter sees couple problems as sociocultural symbolic constructs.
Inquiry into the sources, processes, and consequences of their construction
and organization is the therapy that flows from this view.

## Joining the Couple's Meaning System

Underlying the beginning of any therapy is the importance of joining the couple's meaning system and constructing a workable reality. Joining is a process analogous to socializing by which an empathic rapport is developed with the clients (Minuchin & Fishman, 1974). The dynamic interplay of joining and constructing a workable reality initiates the process of change. The construction of workable realities can be defined as the process in which the view of the problem is transformed from a paradigm of individual causality to a paradigm of couple interaction. The therapist's reflections serve to create an environment conducive to change. In this environment, the therapist listens to the couple's language, learns it, and uses it to create a comfortable environment. The basic assumption is that clients are experts in knowing what is best for them. The role of the therapist is that of curious observer—interested in learning about the couple's story.

## Proposing the Notion of a Couple Meaning System

Using the above as a background for social construction therapy, couple therapy can be divided into three different stories: the couple's story about their families of origin (how the meaning system developed in the first place), their story about their relationship (how the meaning system is maintained), and their story about what they see for their future (how their meaning system can change). Knowledge of each of these three stories helps the therapist understand the couple's frame of the problem. The telling of these stories helps the couple learn about their frame of the problem. Hoffman (1990) stated that "Problems are stories people have agreed to tell themselves; then we have to persuade them to tell themselves a different, more empowering story, have conversations with them, through the awareness that the findings of their conversations have no other reality than that bestowed by mutual consent" (pp. 3–4).

Thus, clients are asked about what their problems mean to them in their given sociocultural contexts. The problem is seen as emanating from various forms of action or practice within the couple's relational life. The couple relationship and the couple problem are treated as a symbol invested with meaning by society, as all symbols are. The approach to the problem is thus a matter of symbolic analysis and interpretation.

**The Past: Development of the Meaning System.** Berger and Luck-mann (1966) believed that the socially constructed meanings that individuals inherit are "opaque" (p. 55). By this they meant that the ways in which meanings are constructed are invisible, as are the elements that compose them. The social world individuals are born into is experienced by the child as the sole reality. As children, the rules of the world are nonproblematic, they require no explanation, and they are neither challenged nor doubted. Through socialization, the socially constructed meanings are internalized; they are filtered and understood through meaningful symbols. From these socially constructed meanings flow psychological meanings and scripts for behavior. A person attempts to match his or her own experience with the available meanings and scripts. The person learns the language and the appropriate behavior for his or her gender, age, and culture. In this way, a person develops an individual identity, an individual script, and along with it individual meanings—all of which are created by and embedded in the dominant culture. This match is never perfect, and the ensuing gaps provide alternatives to the couple's story.

Using the above as a backdrop for couple therapy, it is helpful to explore what being part of a couple and/or being married means for each individual. In western society, ideas about the nature of reality stem mainly from nineteenth century Cartesian-Newtonian mechanistic and reductionistic be-liefs. These ideas are pervasive in our language in that it generally is believed that there is one truth and that if one "dug deeply" enough, one would discover it. These notions formed the bases for traditional ideas about ther-apy and are well-known in western cultures. As a result, people often come to therapy with the belief that in order to solve their present problem, it is necessary to explore and examine parental hurts from the past. This notion is exemplified in deShazer's (1991) report on the client who came for therapy because she had become a nymphomaniac. "As she saw it, her nymphom-ania was a problem rooted in her infancy that would require deep therapy" (p. 64). deShazer (1991) redefined it as a sleep disturbance and reported that "At this point in the session, the meaning(s) of what was going on was set adrift in a sea of potential meanings" (p. 66).

While it was not necessary for deShazer to dig deeply into the client's past, many times, at the onset of therapy, individuals are prepared to ver-balize all their childhood painful experiences with the hope that this then will alleviate the problem in the present. More cognitively or behaviorally oriented therapists who attempt to focus the client on the here and now often meet with client resistance because clients tend to believe that present oriented therapy is just skimming the surface and that if they do not dig deeply enough they will not get to the root of their problems. Clients who feel this way are doing the only thing that makes sense for them: "Every system is where it is, in a present, in congruence with its medium, and cannot be anywhere else" (Goudsmit, 1989, p. 19). So that with clients who believe that there are past events that are affecting their present behavior, during the initial phases of therapy, a re-creation of these childhood events is often helpful. This exploration is based *not* on the notion that clients need to have a cathartic experience in order to move forward; but rather, that if clients believe that the past is affecting their present behavior, discussing it in therapy often can facilitate rather quickly the letting go of the past or at least putting the past in perspective. In some cases, exploring the client's past is a useful first step in the restorying of the present and the opening up of new possibilities for the future. In many cases, it brings forth the client's new awareness of competencies and strengths.

When therapists feel this exploration would be helpful for the clients (as indicated by the client's request), therapists can use the **rubber band** to help the client move back in time. "If I were to take a rubber band and stretch it back to when you were a little girl/boy, when you also felt how you are feeling now, could you tell me what that was like?" "Could you tell me how you feel it affected you (your relationships) then?" Therapists can elicit a deepening of the clients experience through the use of questioning. "Tell me more about how that was for you. What were the effects of these events for you?" In couple therapy, this occurs with the partner listening, which helps him or her understand more about his or her partner and helps increase feelings of intimacy.

After both partners have re-created their perceptions of their childhoods, which in many cases turns out to be painful, they then are requested to balance their definitions of the past. "If you were to consider the learnings, strengths, and competencies that you received from these experiences, what would they be? What else would they be?" This step facilitates the balancing of the past—the client now understands that he or she received both sadness and strengths in early relationships. The client also is asked to recognize the gifts (e.g., sense of humor, kindness) that he or she received from significant caretakers. This experience also is amplified through the use of *questioning*. "What other positive gifts did they give you? Do you remember more about this positive experience? What effects have these gifts had on you? On your relationships?"

**Putting the Past in Perspective.** After both partners have told their story of the past, the past is put in perspective. This can be facilitated by a ritual. The clients can write down all the important childhood events that related to the explored issue, both negative and positive, and place the paper in a shoe box and bury it (symbolically burying the past). The client could write a letter to his or her significant caretakers from childhood, forgiving them for their mistakes and thanking them for the gifts they gave. This letter could be either mailed or buried. The client could have a ritualistic ceremony whereby he or she symbolically lets go of the pain, and the effects of the pain, by setting a balloon or kite free at the beach. He or she can symbolically show appreciation for caretakers by doing something special for them.

## Exploring the Couple's Present Meaning System

Berger and Kellner (1964) defined marriage as a definitional process. Two separate individuals come together with separate identities and begin to construct a life as a couple. What once were the independent identities of the two individuals are now modified to incorporate the "relationship" identity. Now the two individuals construct a relationship reality where all conversations serve to validate this coupled identity. At this point in therapy, the couple tells their present story, how they negotiated their individual meaning systems and behavioral scripts to co-create a couple script—a sense of "we-ness." Here the therapist attempts to obtain as complete an understanding as possible of the couple's story. That is, their discussion centers around how the problem became scripted into the couple relationship, at both the individual and the couple levels. A therapist can learn about the couple's story by paying careful attention to linguistic symbolizations such as couple myths, couple legends, rites, and metaphors.

An individual's reality is maintained by developing a personal sense of self that is congruent with social constructions. As stated earlier, based on early interactions and ongoing socialization, individuals construct a reality around meanings that includes a preferred way of relating to others. This then becomes the basis for how they view others and how they expect others to view them. In many ways, these perceptual sets determine predictable ways of interacting with others. Here relevant questions might be, "How do you think of the problem? What meaning(s) does the problem hold for you, for your relationship? Do you see any other options? What solutions have you attempted?"

When uncovering the couple's story about the present, both the therapist and the couple learn what information the couple selects out of their environment and how they fit that information into an already existing meaning system so as to reinforce that system. The therapist and the couple learn how the couple's patterned conversations and attempted solutions reflect this meaning system, and they learn how the problem became scripted into the couple relationship.

According to cybernetic theory elaborated by Bateson (1972) and employed by White (1985), circularity is a fundamental phenomenon whereby events in systems feed back on themselves, and causes and effects become indistinguishable. When couples learn their story and hear how their problems affect the relationship, they gather information about how they inadvertently have participated in the perpetuation of the problem.

Applying these concepts, questions also can be asked about the beginnings of the couple story. How did they meet? What did they think about each other when they first met? How did they know "this was it"? How did their relationship evolve? Did they find each other attractive? How did they feel in each other's presence? How was their first encounter? How do they both "see" the beginning of their couple story—similarly or differently? Where is there agreement? Where does the story differ? The therapist, facilitating the couple story, at this point focuses on the themes and metaphors that run through the couple's construction of their meaning system. At this point also, the couple can explore the different facets, the rigidity, the conventionality, and the satisfaction and dissatisfaction of their relationship. The therapist pays close attention to what is not being said—the other parts of the story the couple is presenting. In this way, the shadow scripts begin to emerge.

Once the couple accepts that there are many ways of seeing and responding to reality and that their meaning systems are constructed socially through interactions with others, it then becomes possible to deconstruct it. The process of deconstruction involves breaking up, loosening up, taking apart the couple's meaning system. It is only after the deconstruction of the couple's present meaning system that new, alternative meanings can take hold. Through the process of deconstruction, couples begin to question their entrenched meaning system. The therapist's role at this time is that of balancing: He or she is breaking up the entrenched meaning system while simultaneously planting seeds for new possibilities. Change can occur only when the couple begins to question their old definitions of their relationship. Colloquially stated, if they continue to see their relationship the way they always did and continue to do what they always did, they will get more of what they always got.

The following section elaborates on the processes by which the couple's meaning system can be uncovered and then challenged or deconstructed in order to make room for new experiences. Techniques used to amplify the family's process can be used. These processes often help the couple learn where they are stuck. At this point, the family meaning system is uncovered and the possibility of choice arises in terms of whether to keep the uncovered meaning system or to change it.

When couples learn about their meaning system and connect it to the way they "see" their problems, they gather information about how they inadvertently have participated in the perpetuation of the problem. For many couples, telling their story invokes a revolving door image with no exits, as they begin to see themselves as going around in the same cycle, unable to break out of the pattern. It is here that the couple begins to reflect on the implications of their meaning system. This reflection eventually will lead to reconstructing which is crucial in social constructionist therapy.

### Expanding the Couple's Meaning System

**Loosening Up the Frame.**   Usually when couples come for therapy, the crisis that brought them there in the first place is enough to "loosen up" their entrenched frame. Below are listed additional ways of loosening up the couple's frame.

*Amplifying the Couple's Process.*   Some ways of amplifying the couple's process are tracking, circular and reflexive questioning, exaggeration, word imagery, and sculpting. *Tracking* is a technique where the therapist focuses on the symbols, metaphors, themes, and language of the couple in order to help the couple better understand their transactional process (Minuchin & Fishman, 1974). Sometimes tracking the presenting problem is enough for the couple to see the recursiveness of their language about the problem. It often serves to help the client "see" the redundancy of their interactions. *Circular questioning* is when the therapist invites one member to comment on the relationship of two other members (Boscolo, Cecchin, Hoffman, & Penn, 1987). Through circular questioning, the meaning the problem holds for the couple emerges, which allows both the therapist and the family to appreciate its interconnectedness and circular nature. *Reflexive questions* are questions that enable the family's own healing processes to emerge (Tomm, 1987). Tomm (1987) believed that therapists can ask questions that emphasize a family's healthy patterns and/or stabilize patterns that are still fragile. Tomm (1987) believed that change occurs because of changes that occur in the couple's meaning system. The difference between circular questioning and reflexive questioning is that in circular questioning, the therapist is taking a neutral stance, whereas in reflexive questioning, there is intentionality. An example of a reflexive questions is, "If you made no changes in your relationship, what do you think the consequences would be? What would have to happen in order for you to realize that the problem was getting a little better?"

***Exaggeration*** of a problem often helps couples learn the absurdity of their interactions. The jealous husband who does not want his wife to leave his sight for fear that she will find another man can be tied to her with a rope at the waist. By tying the two together, this aspect of the relationship can be demonstrated visually. The couple can be tied together for the entire therapy session or they can tie themselves together for a full day at home. After the task, the therapist then can ask them to describe how being tied together affected them and their relationship. Another example can be used when one partner blames the other for a failed marriage. The blamee could be asked by the therapist to go back for one week and restate past accounts of blaming episodes. For example, "It was my fault that you spilled the water from the coffee pot on the floor, because I was standing next to you and made you nervous." "It was my fault that you backed into the tree in the back yard because I'm always critical of your driving." "It is my fault that we don't have sex anymore because it takes me so long to have an orgasm and you get tired of waiting." Often this list helps the couple see or be aware of their linear notions of cause and effect and also the redundancy of their interactions. Haley (1967) presented a case whereby he encouraged a woman who was cleaning the house all day and night to scrub the kitchen floor with a toothbrush.

***Word imagery*** is asking the clients to give color, shape, and/or form to their words in order to explore the consequences or effects of the words. "What do the words do?" "What are the effects of the words?" Here the therapist can ask each client what image he or she would give his or her partner's words around a particular interaction. Clients have verbalized, "The words made me shrink. I felt inadequate." "They felt like cotton balls, so I didn't pay attention to them." "They made me feel invisible; I felt like no matter what I did, no one paid attention to me." "They made me feel soft and warm." "They made me feel like I was hit over the head with a bowling ball." "The words were like sharp little darts coming at me; I felt like I had to defend myself." Therapists can then ask the partners, "How could you use your words differently (or different words) to create different effects or meanings for yourself, for your partner?"

***Sculpting*** is a technique used mainly by therapists who practice psychodrama and by experiential couple therapists. It can be used to amplify process. Here the couple is asked to position their bodies so as to sculpt themselves in terms of how they see the problem. One adolescent daughter sculpted her mother as standing behind her with her arm around her neck in a stranglehold amplifying her feelings of being suffocated. One husband sculpted his wife standing over him with a stern look on her face and pointing finger. When he sculpted himself, he positioned himself cowering on the floor.

The use of hypnosis, humor, paradox, telling stories, and making "crazy" or ridiculous statements also provide the context for change. Erikson (Haley, 1967) described a situation where he instructed a "bed wetter" to purposefully urinate in bed before going to sleep for six nights. Here the therapist facilitates the process unfolding, thereby producing a *reductio ad absurdum*. Sometimes the awareness the couple achieves through the amplification of their process is profound enough to help the system evolve toward a new structure for maintaining its organization. The direction of this change is unpredictable. Maturana (1988) applied Heisenberg's uncertainty principle to living systems in his belief that the person always will make changes in his or her best interest, determined by the system's coherence. "But the psychotherapist does not know the final answer either, so they face the problem together" (Maturana, 1988, p. 229).

*Confusion Techniques.*  Confusion techniques have been used to play with reality for centuries by Zen masters through the use of koans (paradoxes to be meditated upon) (Lao Tsu, 1972). Erikson (Haley, 1967) also used these techniques often when working with individuals. The confusion is uncomfortable, and the client moves to eliminate it. The introduction of confusion and the resultant search for new meaning loosens up the frame. Whitaker's (1975) "psychotherapy of the absurd" also discussed the relation between prescribing the symptom and reducing to absurdity the couple's dilemma, generally producing confusion in his clients. Trommel (1989) described how confusion techniques can be used by therapists in working with couples who do not understand each other's language. Confusion helps loosen up the client's frame thereby making it more permeable to new meanings and new possibilities for change.

*Instant Replay.*  Another method for loosening up the couple's frame is to ask them to do an instant replay. Often couples come into therapy reporting on an argument they had during the week. Here the therapist asks each member of the couple to describe the argument in detail, asking many questions to help them clarify their definitions around the quarrel. After each member has described the argument to the therapist in great detail, the therapist then asks the couple to reenact the argument but to give it a different ending. In this way, the couple learns that things could be different—events do not always have to end in one way. They learn that they have control over the effects of their arguments and that there are other possibilities.

*Philosophy of "As If."* German philosopher Vaihinger (1966) presented the "Philosophy of As If." This philosophy can be applied to working with couples. Basically, the couple is asked to behave "as if." The situation presented is one that provides a new possibility for the couple. To a couple who said they were miserable, the therapist might say, "behave 'as if' you were a happily married couple on Monday, Wednesday, and Friday. Tuesday, Thursday, and Saturday, behave the way you typically do—miserably. On Sunday, rest." This "as if" directive forces the couple to (1) image reality as a happily married couple and (2) behave as though they were that couple. Even if it is a temporary image, it is an image different than the one the couple came into therapy with. Further, asking the couple to behave as if they were miserable often has the effect of the prescription "be spontaneous." Once it is verbalized, it is impossible to do. Couples often report that when they behaved as if they were miserable (their more typical behavior), they burst out laughing. Ultimately, the use of the "as if" philosophy helps clients conceptualize new meanings for their relationship, helps them place the new meaning in an action context, and ultimately helps them understand that they have control over some outcomes in their life.

*Guessing Game.* The guessing game also helps loosen up the couple's frame in that it provides the couple with a re-imaging of their partner. The couple is told that over the course of the next week, they should do three nice things for each other—things that each partner would like. However, neither should not tell his or her partner what the three things are. Each has to guess. In therapy the following week, the couple then tells each other what the nice things were and they learn if they guessed correctly. This exercise helps each member of the couple first place himself or herself into his or her partner's shoes as he or she tries to figure out what nice thing he or she could do for the partner. Next, it helps each focus on the positive things that his or her partner does for him or her. This usually helps them notice that partners do many more nice things than they originally thought. Many couples guess incorrectly and are surprised at how often the partner does positive things. This helps them to re-image each other.

**Parts and Wholes.** At this point, after the couple's frame or definition of the problem has loosened, the therapist has the option of intervening at the level of construction, the meaning system, either by focusing on a part of the meaning system or by concentrating on the whole. Here the therapist can move into finding and amplifying exceptions to the presented problem (see later sections), working on a "part" of the couple frame or on the couple's belief system as a "whole." Both ways of working eventually will result in change. Working with a "part" is like chipping away at a brick wall, piece by piece. Eventually the wall is down. Working with the "whole," with metaphors and reframes, is more like going in with a bulldozer—the wall falls away with one sweep. This might be because working with a "part" of the frame means working through a problem entrenched in language. Working with metaphors or the "whole" bypasses this entrenched language system, going directly to right brain processes that give new definitions to whole frames. Both ways of working give rise to new frames—ones containing emergent possibilities. The above methods primarily address meaning systems, but in addition, the therapist can work at the level of action by prescribing tasks or rituals, thereby offering a framework at both the meaning and behavioral levels.

**Explore the Effects of the Problem.** It is useful for the couple to focus on the effects of the relationship problems rather than specifically focusing on the content of the each problem (Durrant, 1991). In so doing, the problem begins to be located external to the couple. They begin to see themselves not as having a relationship problem, but rather, as the problem having negative effects for the relationship. "How has the problem influenced your relationship? How has it influenced your relationship with your children? Friends? What was it like before the problem was there? How was your relationship different? What was different about your relationship when the problem was not there?" The therapist uses language that presupposes change.

**Therapeutic Frame: Working with the Whole.** Since the therapist only can make constructions of the couple system (of which he or she is a part), there are no correct views, only ones that "fit" the system and are acceptable to it (Speed, 1991). Using this therapeutic frame, the therapist focuses on second order changes—those that promote changes of the frame itself (Watzlawick, 1984). Ways of promoting second order change involve the use of reframe or metaphor.

*Reframe.* *"Though gold dust is precious, in the eyes it obscures the vision"* (Lao Tsu, 1972). Watzlawick (1978) developed the constructivist

concept of reframing: "reframing, to change the conceptual and or emotional setting or viewpoint in relation to which a situation is experienced
and to place it in another frame which fits the 'facts' of the same situation
equally well or even better and thereby changes its meaning" (p. 95). Here
the couple presents their story to the therapist. The therapist takes the same
story and, using the clients' language, gives it a new meaning, one which is
equally believable to the couple. Examples of reframes are the well-known
"smother mother" who becomes the mother who loves so much. Questions
then can be asked that emphasize moving the problem out of a "problem
frame" and moving into a "change frame." "What would worry you the
most if Johnny became more independent?"

Restructuring works similarly. The therapist could say to the same
mother, "When did you divorce your husband and marry your son?" Or to
a remarried father whose daughter from the first marriage cooked for him
and whose new wife was complaining and feeling jealous—"How is it that
you have two wives?" Both these restructurings have the dramatic effect of
shaking the foundation of the old frame. The couple's response is also
usually dramatic and change tends to happen in a global way.

*Use of Metaphor.*   Our concepts of reality are influenced by our language, and our language is grounded in metaphor. A metaphor also can be
seen as a model for changing the way we look at the world. Metaphors are
intended to help couples elicit an unconscious search for alternatives and
new meanings. Developmentally, we learn the written and unwritten rules
of our society. When these unwritten or unconscious rules are broken, we
are left in an uncomfortable place; we simply do not know how to behave.
Witness the reaction to the person who gets on an elevator facing the rear
or the reaction of the salesperson if you offer to pay more than the quoted
price for any item in a store. You will have broken unwritten or unconscious
rules. Metaphors work in similar ways. Just as people struggle to create new
rules in the above situations, couples struggle to create new rules around
their problems when faced with good metaphors. Couples experience this
transformation in typical ways. Psychologically, when the metaphor is first
presented, they express curiosity. They feel some dissonance (Festinger,
1957) or anomie (Durkheim, 1951); the way they used to look at the problem
does not quite seem relevant to them anymore. Yet they feel unsure about
new ways. They may ask for clarification: "Wait, what are you saying?"
Their cognitive structure has been pulled out from under them, and until
they create a new structure, they feel as though they are in an in-between
place. Physiologically, they feel uncomfortable. They feel as though things
are not totally "right" with them. They may leave the therapist's office and

ask themselves, "What just happened to me?" They will struggle to find new meaning around their issue because the old meaning is not "right" for them anymore; it just does not seem to make as much sense as it used to. These, then, are the seeds of transformation. The condition for second order change is ripe. The direction of the change is unknown. Couples will struggle with the new seeds and eventually will incorporate new meanings that ultimately will lead to new possibilities.

***Couples choreography***, as defined by Papp (1982), is an excellent method for using metaphor to get to the core of the couple's struggle. Using imagery, the couple is asked to visually depict themselves and the struggles of their relationship in a nonhuman form. The imagery that each develops eliminates the description of the problem in the language most typically used (and most typically stuck in) and replaces it with images. It is then easier for the couple to accept the images depicted in the metaphor because each spouse is viewed as "playing a particular role" not as "being" a certain kind of person. This indirectness allows the couple to see the reciprocal relationship in a gentle way and each person's participation in its maintenance without the usual resistance.

One example of a metaphor given by a client is the following: "There were two cats, one big one and one smaller one. The big cat was nasty and mean and the smaller one was afraid every time the big cat came close. Then the big cat came up to the smaller cat and went inside the smaller cat's mouth and started eating the smaller cat from the inside out." A second client imaged herself in plant form: "I was a little chubby bush, and he was a tall tree standing next to me. I was dying because I had no food or water so I couldn't grow. The big tree was taking all the sun and eating up all the food and water with its big roots so that there was nothing left over for me." A third client stated, "I was a small, black, mean little fly with sharp teeth in a square sealed container. I couldn't get out and kept banging my head against the sides of the container." These metaphors are ripe with substance about core issues and provide couples with many new avenues for problem-solving possibilities. Using the metaphor, the individual and the couple meaning systems, the sequence of activities, and the future of the couple are explored in detail. Through the exploration, discussion, and the consequential expansion and rewriting of the metaphor, the couple then can begin to reconstruct a new metaphorical image of their relationship—one that incorporates a meaning system without the problem.

**Therapeutic Frame: Working with a Part—Looking for Competing Meanings (Exceptions).** Once the notion of a couple meaning system is accepted, and the individual and couple meaning systems are uncovered, a competing meaning system can be introduced. It is not apparent to most individuals that there are alternative ways of behaving at each encounter. Our meaning systems make areas outside the dominant ones appear invisible. This invisibility serves to maintain and foster adherence to the dominant definitions. In fact, the function of socialization and of the sanctions against moving outside the dominant script is to keep individuals within it (Simon & Gagnon, 1977). To find, name, focus on, and help couples experience alternative meanings is the intention of this section.

The view expressed in this paper is that change is normal and that people have a choice in change. Knowledge about how to behave is learned by social definitions of appropriate and inappropriate ways of behaving; however, individuals can choose to develop their own personal attitudes and concepts which differ from the traditional ones. Numerous ways of being are available to us for examination. Here the role of the therapist is to notice competing constructions or exceptions in the couple's meaning system. Change requires a two sided perspective and a therapist may seek to construct a relational definition by developing two (or complementary) descriptions of the problem (White, 1986). Complementary questions are derived and introduced to challenge or help to deconstruct the dominant explanation and to assist couples in achieving a relational or double description of the problem. This double description then provides the source of new responses (Atwood and Levine, 1991; White, 1986). The couple's explanation, or frame, begins to overlap the frame offered by the therapist (like two overlapping Venn diagrams), and it is in this overlap that there is the possibility for change.

White's (1989) notion of "subjugated knowledge" was originally based in Bateson's idea of restraints—those ideas, events, experiences that are less likely to be noticed by people because they are dissonant with individuals' description of the problem. Subjugated knowledge is paying attention to what the couple is leaving out. Shadow scripts are based on subjugated knowledge concepts. For example shadow scripts contain the flip side of the coin, the ideas the couple holds which represent the opposite of their current story of the problem. White (1989) believes that as a couple's view of reality is challenged through questioning about these experiences, they ultimately recognize other aspects of their reality that do not involve the problem. In so doing they create another story (narrative), a second story, about their lives which does not include the problem.

deShazer's (1991) notion of "exceptions" refers to times in the client's life when the problem was not happening. Here the therapist "seeks to find the element in the system studied (their conversation about the client's complaint, goals, etc.) which is alogical, the thread . . . which will unravel it all, or the loose stone which will pull down the whole building" (deShazer, 1991). The therapist reinforces alternatives to the dominant description of the problem—helping to make visible areas outside the dominant meaning system. In so doing, he or she begins to undermine what previously had been specifying and justifying the couple's reality (Amundson, 1990). Anderson and Goolishian (1988) stated

> . . . to deconstruct means to take apart the interpretive assumption of the system of meaning that you are examining, to challenge the interpretive system in such a manner that you reveal the assumptions on which the model is based. At the same time as these are revealed, you open the space for alternative understanding. (p. 11)

The therapist now begins to plant new seeds as the old frame begins to break up. The old frame breaking up is the basis of a different level of order. "Are there ever times when the problem is not there?" The receipt of news of difference is essential for the revelation of new ideas and a triggering of new responses for the discovery of new solutions. An exception is found. Now it must be amplified. A piece has been found that does not fit the overall puzzle. This piece has the possibility to grow, beginning with the deconstruction of the old frame (definition of the problem) and through amplification and activation of the new construction into the new frame.

**Amplifying the New Meaning System**

The amplification of the exception is essential for the triggering of the new construction that holds the possibility of new solutions (Bateson, 1972). "When the problem is not there, how is your relationship? If you were to enjoy the relationship more frequently, how would you notice? What would be different?" By helping the couple to deepen the experience of a more positive relationship, the therapist is facilitating a new construction, that of a more positive relationship. This new construction holds new meaning for the couple.

Prigogine and Stengers (1984) described the building of the termites nest whereby a small fluctuation (slightly more hormone) caused more termites to drop their pieces of dirt on the hormone, eventually resulting in the building of a pillar. This analogy can be applied here, showing how a small exception (fluctuation) can create one more positive meaning in the couple relationship, which can result in a more positive definition of the relationship.

**Creating Intimacy through Meaning-Making.**   At this point, members of the couple have altered their view of each other through listening to each other's stories. They have learned that they may speak with similar words and mannerisms that quite often have different meanings attached to them. They have further learned that such differences in their language have been derived through familial contexts and personal experiential worlds that were originally unknown to one another. They have learned what the other's language means. This new knowledge can have significant impact upon their relationship, with the potential of enhancing it. This helps the couple increase their intimacy.

Weingarten's (1991) notions of intimacy have relevance here. She pointed out that the ways in which people define intimacy often interfere in their creation of it. She believed that the usual ways that people define intimacy involve global assessments of the capacity of individuals to experience intimacy or assessments of the quality of relationships. Instead, she defined intimacy as repeated "single" intimate interactions. Weingarten's ideas fit in with the ideas for therapy presented in this chapter, for if the therapist can locate single intimate interaction exceptions in a nonintimate (as defined by them) couple relationship, then these exceptions can be amplified through the use of questions. In so doing, the couple's definition of their relationship as being nonintimate is deconstructed as the new construction of intimacy takes hold.

**Appreciation Frame.**   "When the earth is fertile, the eggplants are large." Included in this therapy is the appreciation frame. At the end of each session, the couple is asked to each tell the other what they each appreciated about each other that day. The therapist then helps the couple deepen this experience by asking them, "Today, when did you feel that you appreciated your partner? What did he or she say or do that reminded you about how much you appreciated him or her? When did you feel that your partner appreciated you? How did you feel when your partner showed you that he or she cared, loved, etc. you?" This helps the couple re-image each other and their relationship in a more positive frame.

### Stabilizing the New Meaning System

At this point, alternative meaning systems are available to the couple, and what once was invisible now holds potential for new solutions. The original meaning system that held the problem has been deconstructed and replaced by a new description. Here a version of deShazer's (1991) "miracle question" can be used: "If a miracle were to happen tonight while you were asleep and tomorrow morning you awoke to find that this problem were no longer a part of your life, what would be different? How would you know that this miracle had taken place? How could others tell without your telling them?" The couple now begins to focus on the future. By asking questions around future trends and choices, the therapist is making that future more real and more stable. As Penn (1985) suggested, when faced with questions about the future—even if that future really only has the status of the hypothetical—"the system is free to create a new map" (p. 300). A questions such as, "How will your future without the problem be different from the future with the problem?" requires speculation about difference and helps consolidate the emerging new meaning system for the couple. Often rehearsal precedes performance. Figure 6.1 summarizes social construction therapy with couples.

**The Future: New Possibilities.**  *Future focus* enables the couple to visualize their relationship without the problem. Questions like, "If you could stretch the rubber band three years into the future and the problem

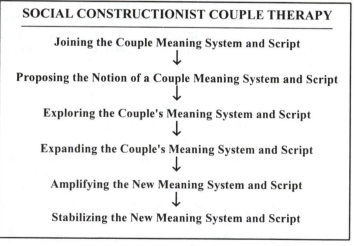

**Figure 6.1.**    Summary of social constructionist couple therapy.

were gone, what would that look like? How would your relationship be different? How else would it be different?" These questions also encourage couples to generate different scenarios in the future but without the problem. Here the questions generate an assortment of possibilities—safely imagined in the present.

**The End of Therapy: Tying It All Up and Rituals for Fresh Starts.** Epston and White (1990) discussed how they invite persons to a special meeting where, through questioning, they discuss the person's story of their therapy adventure. In so doing, the couple is asked to recount how they became aware of their problem and what steps they took to solve it. They recount how and which resources they mobilized as they generated solutions to their problems. Epston and White (1990) believed that here the therapist can ask the couple to give an account of their transition from a problematic status to a resolved one. In addition, the therapist also can provide his or her story of the persons' therapy adventure, and they then can discuss their collaborative efforts.

At the end of therapy, a ritual for a fresh start may be in order. At this time, couples can choose a date when they will redo their marriage or relationship vows. They can do this alone or with their children, friends, and relatives attending. Some couples prefer to rewrite their marriage vows or their script for their relationship, signifying the beginning of a new chapter in their relationship. They often discuss the type of new relationship they want. Others rekindle positive feelings by restating their original vows. Along with redoing their commitment to each other and to the relationship, they can write down their future vision. This then becomes their future image, their future template for their relationship. Now they have seen that they can write and rewrite their own future story.

## SUMMARY

This chapter presented basic assumptions and theoretical concepts of social constructionism and proposed a model for social constructionist couple therapy. In sum, couples seek therapy because they are having a problem. First, the couple and therapist learn about the problem through languaging about the couple's frame. The therapist then brings in his or her own frame, which is orthogonal to the couple's frame. The therapist's frame must be different enough to cause the couple's frame to be expanded. This is accomplished by use reframe, use of metaphors, exploring shadow scripts, or finding exceptions to the dominant story. After the therapist explores the shadow script with the couple, a new story emerges, modified in the languaging process. Eventually, this co-created story results in a new synthesis—one which is not predictable from past frames. This new synthesis is co-created through languaging between therapist and the couple. A re-visioning of the relationship without the problem in the future is explored, including rituals for "fresh starts." Changes in the narratives that couples hold about their couple scripts can lead to change in their meaning systems. This ultimately can reorganize the way they "see" both their individual and couple realities.

# BIBLIOGRAPHY

Atwood, J. (1992). *Family therapy: A systemic behavioral approach*. Chicago: Nelson Hall.

Berger, P., & Kellner, H. (1979). Marriage and the social construction of reality. In H. Bobboy, S. Greenblatt, & C. Clark (Eds.), *Social interaction: Introductory readings in sociology* (pp. 308–322). New York: St. Martin's Press.

Capra, F. (1982). *The Tao of physics*. New York: Bantam.

Cooley, C. (1902). *Human nature and the social order.* New York: Free Press.

Dell, P. F. (1982). Beyond homeostasis: Toward a concept of coherence. *Family Process, 21*, 21–24.

Gagnon, J.H. (1990). Scripting in sex research. *Annual Review of Sex Research, 1*, 1–39.

Gagnon, J.H., & Simon, W. (1977). *Sexual conduct*. Chicago: Aldine.

Gergen, K.J., & Gergen, M.M. (1983). The social construction of narrative accounts. In K.J. Gergen & M.M. Gergen (Eds.), *Historical social psychology* (pp. 267–288). Hillsdale, NJ: Erlbaum Associates.

Heisenberg, W. (1958). *Physics and philosophy.* New York: Harper Torch-books.

Hoffman, L. (1989). Toward a second order family systems therapy. *Family Systems Medicine, 3*(4), 381–386.

Hume, R.E. (1934). *The thirteen principal upanishas.* New York: Oxford University Press.

Keeney, B. (1983). *Aesthetics of change.* New York: Guilford Press.

Keeney, B., & Ross, J. (1985). *Mind in therapy: Constructing systemic family therapies.* New York: Basic Books.

Kelly, G. (1969). Man's construction of his alternatives. In R. Maher (Ed.), *Clinical psychology and personality: The second papers of George Kelly* (p. 90). New York: Wiley.

Kuhn, T. (1970). *The structure of scientific revolutions* (second edition). Chicago: Chicago University Press.

Maturana, H., & Valera, F. (1980). *Autopoeisis and cognition.* Boston: Reidel.

Maturana, H., & Varela, F. (1987). *The tree of knowledge.* Boston: New Science Library.

Mead, G. H. (1934). *Mind, self, and society.* Chicago: University of Chicago Press.

Nathanson, M. (1963). *The philosophy of the social sciences.* New York: Random House.

Piaget, J. (1951). *Play, dreams and imitation in childhood.* London: Routledge and Kegan Paul.

Reiss, D. (1981). *The family's construction of reality.* Cambridge, MA: Harvard University Press.

Varela, F. (1979). *Principles of biological autonomy.* New York: Elsevier.

von Foerster, H. (1981). *Observing systems.* Seaside, CA: Intersystems Publications.

von Foerster, H. (1984). On constructing a reality. In P. Watzlawick (Ed.), *The invented reality* (pp. 41–61). New York: Norton.

von Glaserfeld, E. (1979). An introduction to radical constructivism. In P. Watzlawick (Ed.), *The invented reality* (pp. 17–40). New York: Norton.

Zukav, G. (1979). *The dancing wuli masters: An overview of the new physics.* New York: William Morrow.

# REFERENCES

Amundson, J. (1990). In defense of minimalism: Making the least out of depression. *Family Therapy Case Studies, 5*(1), 15–19.

Anderson, H., & Goolishian, H. (1988). Human systems as linguistic systems: Preliminary and evolving ideas about the implication for clinical theory. *Family Process, 27,* 371–393.

Atwood, J. (1991). *Constructivist marital therapy: Ways to help couples not to leave their lover.* Hempstead, NY: Hofstra University.

Atwood, J., & Levine, L. (1991). Killing two slumpos with one stone. *Family Therapy Case Studies, 5*(2), 43–50.

Bateson, G. (1972). *Steps to an ecology of mind.* New York: Ballantine Books.

Berger, P., & Kellner, H. (1964). Marriage and the construction of reality. *Diogenes, 46,* 1–23.

Berger, P., & Luckmann, T. (1966). *The social construction of reality.* New York: Irvington.

Boscolo, L., Cecchin, G., Hoffman, L., & Penn, P. (1987). *Milan systemic therapy: Conversations in theory and practice.* New York: Basic Books.

deShazer, S. (1991). *Putting difference to work*. New York: Norton.

Durkheim, E. (1951). *Suicide: A study in sociology*. New York: Norton.

Durrant, M. (1991). *Ideas for therapy with sexual abuse*. Australia: Dulwich Centre Publications.

Epston, D., & White, M. (1990). Consulting your consultants: The documentation of alternative knowledges. *Dulwich Centre Newsletter*, 4.

Festinger, L. (1957). *Theory of cognitive dissonance*. Evanston, IL: Row and Peterson.

Gergen, K. (1985). The social constructionist movement in modern psychology. *American Psychologist, 40*, 266–275.

Goudsmit, A. (Ed.). (1989). *Self-organization in psychotherapy: Demarcation of a new perspective*. New York: Springer Verlag.

Haley, J. (1967). Toward a theory of pathological systems. In G. H. Zuk & I. Boszormenyi-Nagy (Eds.), *Family therapy and disturbed families* (pp. 11–27). Palo Alto, CA: Science and Behavior Books.

Hoffman, L. (1990). Constructing realities: An art of lenses. *Family Process, 29*(1), 1–12.

Lao Tsu. (1972). *Tao te ching*. London: Wildwood House.

Maturana, H. (1988). Reality: The search for objectivity or the quest for a compelling argument. In V. Kenny (Ed.), *Irish Journal of Psychology, Special Issue on 'Radical Constructivism,' Autopoeisis and Psychotherapy, 9*(1), 25–55.

Minuchin, S., & Fishman, C. (1974). *Family therapy techniques*. Cambridge, MA: Harvard University Press.

Papp, P. (1982). Staging reciprocal metaphors in couples group. *Family Process, 21*, 453–467.

Penn, P. (1985). Feed forward: Future questions, future maps. *Family Process, 24*, 299–311.

Prigogine, I., & Stengers, I. (1984). *Order out of chaos: Man's new dialogue with nature.* New York: Bantam.

Simon, W., & Gagnon, J. (1977). Sexual scripts: Permanance and change. *Archives of Sexual Behavior, 15,* 97–120.

Speed, B. (1991). Reality exists, ok? An argument against constructivism and social constructionism. *Journal of Family Therapy, 13*(4), 395–410.

Tomm, K. (1987). Interventive interviewing: Part I. Strategizing as a fourth guideline for the therapist. *Family Process, 26,* 3–13.

Trommel, M. (1989). The use of oneself as an instrument. In A. Goudsmit (Ed.), *Self organization in psychology* (pp. 157–167). New York: Springer-Verlag.

Vaihinger, H. (1966). *The philosophy of as if: A system of the theoretical, practical, and religious fictions of mankind.* New York: Routledge & Kegan.

Watzlawick, P. (1978). *The language of change: Elements of therapeutic communication.* New York: Basic Books.

Watzlawick, P. (1984). *The invented reality.* New York: Norton.

Watzlawick, P., Weakland, J.H., & Fisch, R. (1974). *Change: Principles of problem formation and problem resolution.* New York: Norton.

Weingarten, K. (1991). The discourses of intimacy: Adding a social constructivist and feminist view. *Family Process, 30*(3), 285–306.

Whitaker, C. (1975). Psychotherapy of the absurd. *Family Process, 14,* 1–16.

White, M. (1985). Fear busting and monster taming: An approach to the fears of young children. *Dulwich Centre Review*, 29–34.

White, M. (1986). Negative explanation, restraint and double description: A template for family therapy. *Family Process, 25*(2), 169–184.

White, M. (1989, Summer). The externalizing of the problem. *Dulwich Centre Newsletter.*

# Chapter 7

# THE CHEMICALLY DEPENDENT "CHILD" SCRIPT: WILL PETER PAN EVER GROW UP?

*Audrey Freshman*

We all know the "happily ever after" script—we fall in love, *forever*. We get married and have children. We parent successfully. Our children become independent, happy adults who leave home and fall in love *forever*.

Although the origin of the above-mentioned script may appear to have its roots in the "happily-ever-afterness" of fairy tales, it has derived its empirical validation from the entire spectrum of systems of thought that collectively comprise the field of mental health. In discussing the patholog-izing effects of psychotherapy upon the American psyche, psychologist James Hillman and journalist Michael Ventura (1992) believed that most people think of themselves as dysfunctional essentially as a result of their inability to "fit" into the ideal family. ". . . to tout the ideal family is a way of *making* ourselves dysfunctional, because that ideal makes anything out-side it, by definition, not ideal, i.e., dysfunctional. . . . the ideal family makes us feel crazy" (p. 16). In a society where the rate of divorce has approximated 50%, the remaining 50% of families are left clinging to the ideal, in spite of their fair share of infidelity, abuse, and alcoholism to name but a few of the more common familial skeletons. If even half, i.e., only

**179**

25%, of the "intact" families in society are considered "functional" as defined by the anachronistic standards of mental health, it stands to reason that the remaining 75% of Americans now are fueling the talk show circuits and the Recovery Movement.

What happens to chemically dependent families as they digress from this "ideal" script? How do they incorporate the deviation without feeling deviant? One way to cope is simply to deny the existence of a problem. In fact, denial is the defense mechanism most closely associated with the chemically dependent person and his or her family. Paradoxically, it is often the case that as the chemical dependency worsens, the denial on the part of the addict and significant others intensifies. This denial results in the rigid implementation of coping strategies that the family relentlessly and unsuccessfully employs in an effort to return to "normal" (i.e., ideal).

There emerges a subtle interplay between the ever-changing reality presented by the progression of chemical dependency and the resultant individual and familial response to changes in self-definition that constantly revise the family's script. In this chapter, case material, formulated from a composite picture of virtually hundreds of families presenting for treatment in an outpatient substance abuse clinic, is presented to track the changes in script as changes occur over the progression of the family's life cycle transitions. We will meet Bob and Jane Pan and their 15-year-old son Peter at the emergence of Peter's problem with chemicals. We will revisit the family at several key interval points as Peter matures into "adulthood." Although the impact of the problem is experienced on a familial as well as individual level, it is important to recognize first the sociocultural context that lies as the backdrop to the internalized meaning system of the family.

## SOCIOCULTURAL CONTEXT

According to social construction theory, how individuals and families interpret the world is not in an exact duplicative form, but rather in a subjective confirmation of the reality they construct and subsequently seek to confirm (Gergen, 1985, 1989). In much the same way, the myopic view of therapy, with its focus upon the individual and the family, excludes the social context of the symptom, in this case chemical dependency, by localizing the problem within the psyche. Hillman and Ventura (1992) argued that the therapeurizing of the individual creates a passive acceptance of cultural ills.

Stein (1985), in exploring the societal meaning of addiction, viewed alcoholism as a cultural disorder and the drinking behavior itself an attempt to remedy culturally based ailments. Barrett (1992) expanded upon the use of substance as a metaphor of exhaustion, disconnectedness, and spiritual isolation in response to demands for perfectionism and excessive material consumption in society. Similarly, Peele, (1985) in a more radical view of chemical dependency, argued that addiction itself can be understood best as an adaptation to the social environment.

In a very real sense, the messages that abound within society around chemical usage are at best ambiguous. Consequently, the very society that condemns the addict spends billions of dollars annually in fostering the use of "legal" chemicals such as alcohol, nicotine, caffeine, and prescription tranquilizers. In a society that has come to view alcohol as a prescriptive for stress management (e.g., "This Bud's for you, for all you do."), it becomes difficult to differentiate when the use of a substance is unacceptable, not to mention problematic. The marketing correlation of beer and sports/concerts to young audiences seeks to inextricably link and elevate alcohol consumption to the equivalent pairing of America and apple pie. We are taught to cope with pain through pills—"why suffer?"—and transform our personalities in the era "Beyond Prozac" (Begley, 1994, February 7).

Likewise, as the use of marijuana and alcohol rises among teenagers (Treaster, 1993, April 14), we have constructed a new social reality in which "experimental" drug use among adolescents is accepted as a normative rite of passage (Treadway, 1989). According to a National Institute of Alcoholism and Alcohol Abuse (NIAAA) 1987 report, in this country, the mean age of an adolescent's first drink is 12 years and 3 months. The mean age of the first use of marijuana is 13 years and 4 months. Alcohol continues to be the most popular drug among adolescents (MacDonald, 1987; Bell, 1990). These statistics reflect the "normal" population, not adolescents in treatment (Bell, 1990).

One in six teenagers in the United States suffers from a severe addiction problem (Thorne & DeBlassie, 1985). Unfortunately, it is difficult to distinguish use from abuse and to intervene in a timely manner. Even if one is certain about the need for intervention,

> . . . our attempts to cure, eradicate, prevent, and heal the problems of drug and alcohol abuse involve many different methods and philosophies, often with radical differences between them. We seek solutions through genetics and biology;

> with law enforcement and criminal prosecution; by attempts
> to teach our children to resist temptation, experimentation,
> and peer pressure; through inpatient and outpatient treatment
> programs with varying methodologies; and with academic and
> "popular" investigations of addicts and the families that they
> come from and live in. (Barrett, 1992, p. 33)

In this manner, chemical dependency and its concomitant denial system is easily mirrored and reinforced by the larger social context. In treating the chemically dependent family, we must be mindful of this awareness if we are to successfully challenge the social meaning system that fuels the addiction formation. When the family retrospectively wonders why the person uses chemicals in the first place, they often finish the story with a negative script, e.g., problems with low self-esteem or parenting style or the family's skeletons. It is the therapist's task to amplify the context if the family is to understand that in this society, their child is expected to use substances. He or she is acting in an all-American way.

The recovery process then requires the co-creation of a new script: how to be sober in American society. The addict and family must be taught to find and utilize the supporting structure for abstinence. Shifting focus to new role models and heightening awareness of nonchemical forms of recreation such as sober clubs, retreats, exercise, and meditation, to name a few, are steps in the process. Of course this goal is facilitated by participation in 12-step recovery such as Alcoholics Anonymous (AA), AL-Anon, Narcotics Anonymous (NA), Nar-Anon, or alternatives such as Rational Recovery or Woman for Sobriety.

## EARLY ADOLESCENT YEARS SCRIPT: "IS HE OR SHE OR ISN'T HE OR SHE?"

There are known risk factors that can predispose and/or exacerbate chemical dependency such as genetic predisposition, early age of onset of chemical usage, negative parenting style (inconsistent and/or too rigid), change in peer relationship, and downward school performance (Archambault, 1989). In addition to those indicators already cited, other known predictors include onset of antisocial behavior in early adolescence and being reared by an alcoholic parent (Zarek, Hawkins, & Rogers, 1987). According to Mooney, Eisenberg, and Eisenberg (1992), some of the clues to substance use in the adolescent are rather subtle while some are more obvious. These are listed as follows:

1.  increasing hours spent alone in room, particularly in a child that was not previously a loner;
2.  increased secretiveness;
3.  negative change in attitude at school, with friends, in hygiene, in dress;
4.  changing peer group;
5.  pronounced mood swings;
6.  lying, shoplifting, stealing (money from home);
7.  abandonment of extracurricular activities: sports, clubs, religious services, etc.;
8.  unpredictable rebellious behavior;
9.  curfew breaking;
10. alcohol on breath;
11. discovery of drug paraphernalia; and
12. obvious hangovers, blackouts, drugged behavior.

However, most families tend to negate these early signs and symptoms in favor of a more normative view. Parents frequently frame their child's changed behavior as emanating from the disease of "adolescence" rather than from the disease of addiction.

In a 1984 Johnson Institute survey of Minnesota teenagers (Zarek et al., 1987, p. 484), it was found that parents underestimated the proportion of children who drank regularly by the staggering ratio of 10 to 1. In this same study, parents thought that only 2.5% of the teens drank every 2 weeks, while in reality, 29% were drinking every 2 weeks. Likewise, the teenagers who were abusing alcohol heavily also were found to be abusing other drugs. This helps to dispel the myth that adolescents who are drinkers are not drug users. Even if families do seek treatment at this time, it often will be for other problems such as conduct disorders or attention deficit disorders. Families often believe that the child is primarily depressed—not secondary to the use of chemicals that might be creating the mood disorder. Morrison and Smith (1987) discussed the ramifications of misdiagnosis particularly as a failure to recognize pathology as emanating from intoxication. Misdiagnosis, unfortunately, can lead to inappropriate treatment for psychiatric disorders that generally clear up as the intoxication subsides.

## Case Illustration

Let us now meet Bob, Jane, and Peter Pan at the outset of their encounter with substance abuse in their family.

Bob and Jane are the parents of 15-year-old Peter who recently was caught smoking marijuana on school grounds. Over the course of the past year, Bob and Jane have observed an increased moodiness on the part of their son and a tendency for him to isolate himself from family events. They believe this behavior to be "normal for a kid his age." Although they no longer approve of Peter's friends, some of whom they barely know, Bob and Jane believe Peter's claim that "these kids are just more fun." Bob and Jane are aware that Peter has been drinking beer on weekends, but "so does everyone his age." Peter maintains he would "never use any hard drugs." His grades have begun to deteriorate, and his parents have responded by providing him with tutors. Bob and Jane continue to give Peter his weekly allowance "for lunch money." In response to this latest event, they believe that Peter is becoming scapegoated at school and have begun to investigate placing him in a prestigious private school. Bob and Jane, having both grown up in the 1960s, do not believe there is any significance to Peter's use of marijuana.

One way to reconstruct the interpretation of the familial denial, so salient to the progression of chemical dependency, is to understand the desperate attempt on the part of the addict and his or her family to cling to the original "happily ever after" script even at the expense of reality. Clearly, Bob and Jane both believe that they are doing their best to keep Peter on track towards adulthood. Though their actions obviously are understood as enabling, the therapist must remain attuned to not prematurely labeling their behavior as dysfunctional and, thus, part of the inevitable disease process of codependency. To join effectively with Bob and Jane is to understand that their quest to meet the successive challenges of parenting Peter places them in direct opposition to some of their core beliefs. One can assume that many of these beliefs have been formulated in their own respective adolescent experiences and have been adhered to stubbornly despite these beliefs' inappropriateness to the current situation of caretaking an adolescent son in the 1990s.

On a societal level, parents of the 60s, currently parenting the adolescents of the 90s, need to be helped to recognize the changing cultural context for drug usage. The "love" generation has dissipated to a society riddled with high risks of random violence, AIDS, and addiction. As the number of HIV carriers increases, the lifestyle practices of adolescents and their concomitant drug usage patterns will place them at significantly higher risk. Already, approximately 21% of AIDS cases occur in the 20- through 29-year-old population, with the age of contraction believed to be often during adolescence (Petosa, 1992).

Parents who have failed to update their scripts to accommodate the changing context of substance use may inadvertently tolerate the very behavior they hope their child will outgrow. Age of onset is increasingly becoming earlier, thereby resetting the norm despite its negative consequences. Earlier onset is not only known to be a prime indicator of addictive disorder (Archambault, 1989; Zarek et al., 1987), but it also is correlated with poorer prognosis. Parents frequently are naive to the developmental implications of earlier age of substance use when comparing their child's to their own experiences. Parents may be equally naive to the knowledge that the potency of marijuana is now 20 times stronger than it was 20 years ago (*The New York Times*, 1994, February 6). Parents' messages regarding substance use may be fraught with ambivalence and inconsistency with respect to their own former and/or current patterns of usage. Yet it is known that parental permissiveness toward drinking and drug use is positively correlated with adolescent substance abuse (Johnson, Shontz, & Locke, 1984). Adolescent substance abuse not only results from the imitation of parental substance use but also from the modeling of attitudes toward use, established norms, and standards of behavior (Howard, 1992).

Again, most families do not present for treatment at this early phase. The cognitively dissonant information (Festinger, 1957) that suggests "all is not well" is relegated to the background. What we have are the early traces of the pattern of parental rescuing—a pattern that becomes firmly entrenched over time as the script subtly begins to alter to accommodate chemical dependency. We begin to see changes in the family's ability to process contradictory information through the use of secondary defenses such as rationalization, ("The behavior is normal for a kid."), minimization ("Everyone is doing it."), and externalization of the blame ("It is the school's fault."). An almost imperceptible shift in the collective familial resources to defend against the awareness of a substance abuse problem occurs. Even in moments of confrontation, it becomes reassuring to surrender to false protestations ("No, I do not have a problem." or "Those drugs are not mine; I am holding them for a friend.") than to maintain a reality-based focus that would lead to heightened anxiety. We have the emergence of the dichotomy in individual family members absorbing the blame for the problem, e.g., "Maybe we are just overreacting." Ironically, the family invites the betrayal and then becomes enraged with the addict for being dishonest.


### Family Intervention with the Early Adolescent

The dilemma for the family becomes one in which the very act of seeking help becomes a confirmation of a problem. If they do present for therapy, it is often at the strong suggestion/mandate of a secondary party such as the school-based guidance counselor. Peter has begun to show several of the warning signs associated with substance use. Yet, based on the above information, it would be most difficult and arguably inappropriate to label him as having a disease called addiction at this juncture. Early labeling often creates panic and increases the likelihood of the family fleeing treatment. This can further reinforce the denial of the substance user.

On the other hand, the therapist must absolutely never enter into collusion with the denial system of the family. It is important not to negate the significance of the substance usage or to treat it as a secondary symptom of a larger problem. This is a frequent error easily fallen into when both the therapist and family align in discussions around the "larger issues," hoping that the substance usage will subside merely as a result. This is magical thinking on the part of the therapist and it arguably could be stated that the therapist is utilizing a mental health script to deal with a substance abuse drama.

Through the use of *therapeutic languaging* (Atwood & Zebertsky, 1993; Gergen, 1985), intervention at this juncture requires redefining the frame from one of problem to that of prevention. A further distinction must be made between primary and secondary prevention. Primary prevention is intended to stop the disorder before its onset and can take the from of information dissemination or therapy. Primary prevention also can include parenting skills training, education, and media programming. It is an attempt to alter the script before it has been written. On the other hand, secondary prevention is the attempt to disrupt a process that has already begun, (an early revision of the script). Carroll (Archambault, 1989) believed secondary prevention to be the more realistic alternative since primary prevention strategies designed to stop adolescents from experimenting with usage have thus far been unrealistic.

The strategy of secondary prevention, revising the script to effect a more positive future outcome, becomes the goal of intervention at this time. The therapist can help the family recognize that in the case above, Peter is beginning to have difficulty in the process of meeting his age-appropriate developmental tasks. The family can be helped substantially to be motivated for change through their participation in psychoeducational support groups designed essentially to teach the family what the completion of the script will look like if they fail to intervene at this time. This is concretized through the participation of other group members coping with substance abuse at often more advanced stages. The family is exposed to the realities of the impaired development created and fostered by the progression of chemical dependency. Likewise, they can heed the admonishments of other parents who regretfully feel they failed to intervene sooner, usually as a result of their own denial.

The essential task becomes one of joining with the family to reduce as many of the risk factors (as delineated above) as possible. The intention is to offset the inevitability of family members becoming further entrapped in the stereotypical roles (which will be described at length in the remainder of the chapter) of the chemical dependency script.

To this end, the therapist must seek to become allied with the family in negotiating the significant systems that impact upon the problem. Downhill school performance can be seen as a harbinger of an emergent chemical dependency problem. As such, the interaction between the family and the school must take on significance in the treatment of the family. The therapist must be cautious, however, not to connect to the resistance of the family regarding the outside systems (e.g., Peter's family's view of the school as "scapegoating" Peter), particularly if those systems can be used to maintain leverage for treatment. Instead, the therapist can assist in brokering a cooperative relationship between the family and the school that is needed to facilitate improved school performance. Improved school performance can enhance self-esteem, which can mediate against the use of chemicals to make oneself feel better artificially.

**The Adolescent**

The adolescent must be engaged in the process of co-creating a new definition of self. To that end, a commitment to abstinence is essential and must be contracted for the entire duration of treatment. Of course the goal would be to extend this commitment into the future. In fact, focusing upon the future is one way to assist in the visualization of a future without the problem (Atwood & Zebertsky, 1993). Projecting into the future allows the adolescent to envision and plan a life without the use of drugs. At a minimum, however, the adolescent must be made aware of the need to reestablish a new sober baseline against which he or she later can measure his or her own respective behavior. Should the adolescent return to substance usage at another stage in life, he or she has a reference point of comparison upon which any behavioral changes can reflect.

Clearly, commitment to abstinence is not always easily accomplished, and the operationalization of this goal often forms the central task of the initial phase of family treatment (Usher, 1991). In their discussion of neurolinguistic programming of belief change, Davis and Davis (1991) felt that the "truths" as we see them are the result of conscious or unconscious imprinting experiences. The task is to re-imprint new beliefs by challenging the former process of understanding the universe through the confirmation of the old belief system. The adolescent must be helped in changing the emergent and increasingly pervasive construction of the negative self script. A competing re-imprint of a positive self must be reintroduced to challenge the formation of the destructive belief system. As Baab (1992) noted, the therapist's first step is to help the adolescent distinguish between the self-destructive part (the drug using self, "scapegoat," "patient," or "addict") and the self-nurturing part ("natural child," "inquisitive student," "brother," "sister," or "friend"). If the adolescent can be re-armed with a new script, even if time-limited, for how to interact in the world without chemical alteration, he or she stands a better chance of consolidating developmental gains that bring him or her closer towards maturational goals.

**The Parents**

There are known correlates between parental style and increased risk of chemical dependency. Again, if the therapist is to join with the family in a cooperative venture of eradicating as many risk factors as possible with the goal of "problem prevention," it is important to engage the parents in an exploration of the possible scenarios that exacerbate substance abuse. Lawson, Peterson, and Lawson (1983) have described four parental types most closely associated with increased risk of substance abuse in an adolescent. These are as follows:

1.  "alcoholic parent" script
    The correlation between alcoholism in a parent and the high risk

of alcoholism in the offspring has been well documented over the years through adoption studies (Cotton, 1979; Goodwin, 1983) and longitudinal studies (Chafetz, Blane, & Hill, 1977; Miller & Jang; 1978) that have directed attention to genetic predisposition. A multitude of other studies have sought to examine the interrelationship between family dynamics and the creation of substance abuse in the offspring. These studies range from the impact of parental chemical dependency upon the children (Woititz, 1983; Black, 1982), to the association between the disruption of family rituals and increased substance use in offspring (Wolin & Bennet, 1984), to the significance of cultural patterning (Ablon, 1980; Kaufman & Borders 1984).

In attempting to create an alternative script in which the family is able to address the alcoholic parent, it is necessary to shift the focus of the problem from the adolescent while being careful not to disempower the parent. This is a complex act that requires joining with the parent in the first place, learning and entering his or her respective meaning system regarding chemical usage, and attempting to engage him or her in the possibility of co-creating a new script. This is a complicated process and not without its own set of treatment risks. As Treadway (1989) so clearly pointed out regarding the shift in focus, "The drinker may not be ready to address the alcohol abuse in a motivated manner; the family members may be unable or unwilling to confront the drinking; and the child may 'rescue' the family by creating a distracting crisis" (p. 124). Obviously the task of assisting the parent toward his or her own recovery is quite complex. If successfully achieved, it is profoundly destabilizing; in a sense it renders the individual and the family temporarily "scriptless."

2.  "teetotaler parent" script
    This scenario is marked by parents who adopt an excessively rigid, moralistic, intolerant stance towards substance abuse, not only with regard to themselves but to others as well. Teetotaling parents attempt to instill a dualistic approach to life (right/wrong, good/evil, black/white), leaving their child ill-equipped to deal with all the shades of gray. The child cannot adaptively utilize the rules that are inconsistent with human need. The child therefore can respond contemptuously through the use of substances as a statement of defiance and a means of coping.

3.  "overly demanding parent" script
    In this script, the parent clearly sets forth his or her expectations for the child. Unfortunately, the expectation level itself is not com-

mensurate with the realistic abilities of the child, and as a result the child's self-esteem falters. The parent creates a competitive environment among siblings by frequently drawing comparisons between them. The child often is compared to the child who the parent himself or herself used to be. The overly demanding parent may be modeling an unattainably high level of success as a result of his or her own position in life. Conversely, an alternative is that the parent may be living vicariously through the child in expecting the child to compensate for areas in the parent's own life in which the parent wished he or she had succeeded.

4. "overly protective parent" script
   The overly protective parent conveys to the child his or her lack of faith in the child's ability to negotiate the world. The child fails to master his or her own environment. As a consequence, the child's restricted ability to self-actualize manifests in a compromised definition of self and future capacity. This can be an outgrowth of two dynamic styles that may not necessarily be mutually exclusive. In the first style, the parent can be viewed as narcissistically involved with the child in a way that uses the child to gratify the parent's own ego needs "to be needed." In this way, the parent attains and maintains his or her own measure of self-worth. In the second style, the parent can be defending against subconscious hostile and unwanted negative feelings toward the child and in turn compensating through the use of reaction formation.

In social construction therapy, the therapist assists families in recreating their respective stories through their families of origin " . . . (the origination of the development of the meaning system) and the story of their present family (the maintenance of the meaning system)" (Atwood & Zebertsky, 1993, p. 16). In enabling the teetotaler parent, the overly demanding parent, and the overly protective parent to accept their respective meaning systems as socially constructed, it then becomes possible to facilitate the deconstruction of these scripts to make room for the growth of their respective adolescents' self-esteem. This is accomplished through the expansion of the parents perspectives, descriptions, and explanations for social patterns that previously they have sought to exclude in order to preserve their original meaning system. For example, in working with the teetotaler parent, it becomes necessary for the therapist to challenge the black/white thinking of the parent in order to create space for the gray areas. The use of an artistic metaphor might signal the need for the family to allow the adolescent (and themselves) to add "color" to their life without having to resort to the use of chemicals. The family even can be invited to engage in a ritual that concretizes the metaphor while signalling the expansion into a new level of awareness. As such, the family can be encouraged to participate creatively with each other in painting a new family pattern. The family can be freed up to experiment with the nuance of shade or design as it appears in art and ultimately is reflected in their changing social interactions.

The underlying theme for the adolescent that appears to place him or her at higher risk for substance abuse as he or she develops vis a vis the above-mentioned parental scripts is *the muted growth of his or her internal self-esteem*. It is as if the seeds get planted in a container that is too small. The parental scripts appear to be inhibiting growth. Archambault (1989) poignantly noted that in our society we often ask the wrong questions: What is so addicting and reinforcing about drug usage? Why do drugs make you feel good? Instead, Archambault believed we should be asking this question: Why is the rest of the adolescent's life so unreinforcing, so unpleasurable, that he or she is willing to sacrifice so much in order to use substances?

A basic assumption of social construction family therapy theorists such as Lax (Atwood & Zebertsky, 1993, p. 12) is that people cannot change under a negative connotation. Emphasis is therefore placed upon positive connotations. The approach utilizes the strengths of the family to facilitate change rather than remaining problem-centered. This is supported by basic learning theory that suggests that organisms are more responsive to positive reinforcement than to negative reinforcement. In a most relevant article, Coombs, Santana, and Fawzy (1984) asserted that drug use is a learned behavior that occurs within varied family contexts. They designed a parent training model that teaches parents in single/multiple family sessions to interact constructively with their children. Positive interactional patterns, including more praise, encouragement, and positive involvement were incorporated while parental criticism, complaining, and punishment were diminished. Their hypothesis was based on the reconstructive philosophy of the social learning model: Adolescent behavior is instigated and consequated within the family and the peer system. It is a derivative of social interaction. They asserted that by educating the parents to increase positive reinforcement rather than negative response to adolescent rebelliousness, the self-esteem of the adolescent could be enhanced within the family. In turn, this would make it unnecessary (or at least less likely) for the adolescent to seek approval from drug using peers.

Again, let us return to the image of the seeds in the small container. We help the seeds (the adolescent) become life affirming in seeking nurturance—to put down the destructive use of chemicals. In turn, we work with the family (the container) to expand and to maximize the blossoming of the individual, i.e., the adolescent's self-esteem. In so doing, a significant step forward is taken to reduce the likelihood of the full-blown chemical dependent script taking root.

It can be difficult for a family to know whether or not their early adolescent has a substance abuse problem. In a society that legitimizes substance usage, compounded by parents who themselves were raised at a time when use of chemicals was often acceptable, the assessment becomes far too sophisticated. It is easier to "stick to the script"—deny—and hope that it will all blow over as the adolescent matures. As demonstrated in the case illustration of Peter, the family, in their inability to mobilize in a new direction, loses an opportunity to participate actively in engineering a new course. In so doing, the irony is that they increase the likelihood of following the chemical dependency script instead of the happily ever after script, which is their intention.

# LATE ADOLESCENCE/EARLY ADULTHOOD SCRIPT: "THE HARDER WE RUN, THE LESS DISTANCE WE GO"

## "Normal" Script

The socioculturally determined script for transition between late adolescence and early adulthood in Western society calls for a resolution of the major tasks of this developmental period, i.e., *identity* and *separation*. The period between the ages of 18 and 21 is known to be a time of reduced restlessness and of increased integration of self. At this time, the adolescent is able to handle the tasks and responsibilities of adulthood. The adolescent has become a separate entity from the family and therefore does not need to engage in an oppositional stance in order to maintain self-definition. Adolescents no longer are as preoccupied with body image concerns. By ages 16 to 19, most adolescents have adjusted emotionally to their sexual capabilities. "They are comfortable with their bodies by now, even if not completely satisfied" (Bell, 1990, p. 63). The peer group values become less important as the late adolescent is better able to differentiate and maintain his or her own set of values.

With regard to identity development, Neinstein (1984) characterized four steps of ego development as follows:

1. The development of a rational and realistic conscience.
2. The development of a sense of perspective, with the abilities to delay, to compromise, and to set limits.
3. The development of practical vocational goals and the beginning of financial independence.
4. Further refinement of moral, religious, and sexual values. (p. 38)

Furthermore, in the cognitive sphere, Bell (1990) noted that the mental development of the adolescent has reached its highest level of abstract thinking according to the Piagetian model. By age 19, the adolescent has developed *formal operational thinking* that involves the ability to formulate complex ideas and concepts, cause/effect reasoning, and hypothesis/deductive thinking. Additionally, the adolescent now has a sense of time perspective, a sense of his or her place in time, and a concept of future. The adolescent gains mastery over the expression of impulses, not merely in terms of repression of drive, but in the rechannelment and appropriate expression befitting adaptation (Group for the Advancement of Psychiatry [GAP], 1968).

In Western culture, the enjoyment of adult prerogatives usually is attained during this period. By the completion of this stage, the adolescent is allowed to drive a car, vote, earn wages, and even drink and smoke. As the adolescent increasingly demands the rights to autonomous functioning, he or she decreasingly accepts the limits and restrictions placed upon him or her by adult society. The interplay between the adolescent and his or her family is at its most heightened fluidity with respect to the boundary dividing one generation from the next at this stage. It is precisely on this boundary that cultural change takes place, as one generation yields to the next.

Parents as well can be going through their own respective life cycle transitions. Parenthood itself can be viewed as a developmental process. According to the GAP report (1968), the intrapsychic behavioral determinants impacting upon parents of late stage adolescents are as follows:

> (1) the continued and dynamically significant existence in the parent (at a conscious or unconscious level or both) of unresolved conflicts from their own childhood experiences; (2) the omnipresent wish for solution of these conflicts in order to gain relief from tension; and (3) the opportunity for attempt at solution by reliving one's one childhood vicariously through identification with the child. (p. 99)

As the family enters the "leaving home stage" of the family life cycle, parents also have to renegotiate the status transition from being primarily a parenting team to that of a couple (Treadway, 1989). They may each experience the anxiety accompanying the empty nest as it manifests in their own respective midlife identity crises. Likewise, they may each be facing increased caretaking responsibilities with regard to their own aging parents and must negotiate the division of labor presented by this new demand.

## Chemical Dependency Script

In the case of the older adolescent who continues to use drugs abusively, there can become a deepening of the commitment to a lifestyle pattern that is inclusive of chemical usage. For those adolescents, the disruption in the completion of age-appropriate developmental tasks becomes proportional to the substance abuse and consequently, more readily apparent than in early adolescence. The greater the maturational damage, the more effort needs to be expended to maintain the belief that "all is well." The denial system must be expanded. The earlier efforts of minimization, rationalization, and externalization of blame are no longer sufficient to maintain the happily ever after script. Reality needs to be altered to accommodate what now begins to appear as delusional thinking. The shared meaning system of the family subtly adapts to the deviation from the norm. Even when the family no longer can believe that "all is well," they redouble their intense efforts to rectify the situation. The goal becomes "getting back to normal" so that life can continue according to "plan."

During late adolescence and into early adulthood, the progression of chemical use often involves an escalation in the level of experimentation and abuse of substances beyond the gateway drugs of alcohol and marijuana. Switching to "harder" substances such as depressants and stimulants further accelerates the progression of chemical dependency. For example, The National Survey on Drug Abuse in 1979 revealed a prevalence of 3.2% in 12- through 17-year-olds and 17% in 18- through 25-year-olds of barbiturate use. According to the 1980 survey, the prevalence of cocaine use by 12- through 17-year-olds was 5.4% when compared to 27.5% in 18- through 25-year-olds. Heroin was not found to be a commonly used drug among adolescents. Less than .5% used it, though there still was a slight increase between the 12- through 17-year-olds (.5%) and the 18- through 25-year olds (3.5%) in trying it (Neinstein, 1984). Accompanying the change in chemical use are concomitant changes that manifest behaviorally.

## Case Illustration

Let us return to visit with the Pan family 6 years later in order to highlight some of these behavioral changes. There has been no attempt at therapeutic intervention since our last encounter with the family.

Peter is now 21 years old. He has since graduated from a prestigious private high school although his grades remained average. His first move away from home occurred 3 years ago at the age of 18 when his parents sent him to a private college. Peter quickly became involved in the "party" scene at the university, attending keg parties on weekends and smoking marijuana daily.

He began to use barbiturates "to get to sleep" and amphetamines "to keep going" for exams. He experimented with cocaine "but only on occasion and with friends." He doesn't believe drugs have caused him any problems; to the contrary, he feels drugs have helped him "make friends," "study better," and "get by."

In his junior year, Peter no longer was able to maintain his C grade point average and was asked to leave school. His parents were very distressed to learn of his plans to return home. They "always knew" he was a poor student who "got into trouble" at school. Peter contends that he "never really liked school anyway and was happy to be able to get out and make some real money."

As a couple, Peter's parents share the belief that Peter is simply immature and "needs more time" than the average teen to develop. However, as individuals, they have started to have serious disagreements as to the proper course of action. Bob believes that Peter could use some "toughening up." Bob is in favor of placing "serious restrictions" upon Peter, "or else he can just get out." Jane believes that Peter is troubled by Bob's lack of empathy for his son and therefore refuses to go along with Bob's discipline plans. She is worried that Peter "cannot find himself." She does not believe he should take "just any job" and instead convinces her husband that Peter should go to work for him in the family business. She believes this not only will improve the father/son relationship but also will make Peter more responsible if he has a "good paying job." She also secretly hopes that Peter will not use drugs "as often" if he knows his father is watching.

At this time it becomes more difficult for the Pan family to cling to the happily ever after script without seriously compromising their own sense of reality testing. There is a distortion in thinking that is necessary to accommodate the false belief that all is well in spite of the use of chemicals. Twerski (1990) referred to this as ***addictiologia*** (addictive thinking). In discussing the self-deception involved in addictiologia, Twerski stated, "Everyone gets 'taken in' by addictive thinking, but the person most affected by it is the one who is doing the deceptive thinking, the addict" (p. 22). In order for Peter to believe that all is well, he has to continue to deny any cause/effect consequences to his use of substances. He believes he is happier now that he has failed out of school. His meaning system alters to adapt to the continued use of substances.

In a sense, Peter cognitively reframes the negative consequences of his usage through his ongoing focus upon the positive attributes of the effects of drugs. He is reconstructing a new reality . . . a never-never land in which drug use becomes the solution to, rather than the source of, problems. The "cognitive" part of the cognitive social learning theory of alcohol abuse suggests that Peter uses because of what he believes the chemical will do for him, i.e., increase self-esteem, power, license, emotional range (Nathan, 1985). So Peter believes that drugs "help him make friends," "study better," and "get by." It is important to note that he is still in pursuit of the happily ever after script; he simply is expediting (from his point of view) the means by which he achieves it.

One can appreciate the complications of substance use upon the chemically abusing adolescent's ability to master the developmental milestones discussed previously. The profound disturbance in addictive thinking that stands in marked contrast to the "high level of abstract thinking" that is necessary to undertake adult tasks is readily apparent. With increasingly impaired judgment, the adult prerogatives (such as driving a car) become possible licenses for further destruction of self and others. Other developmental tasks such as time perspective, future orientation, impulse mastery, and rechannelment of drive also are warped by the "addictive thinker's" concept of time (Twerski, 1990). The addictive thinker measures time in minutes or even seconds. Drug addiction depends on impulse gratification at the expense of long-term consequences and goals. The ability to develop the rational and realistic conscience is impeded by the self-deception necessary to engage in continued drug use in spite of the consequences. Instead of the usual decreased preoccupation with body image at this age, Coleman (1986) reported a very strong preoccupation with body image on the part of the addict, with bodily concern evidenced by a higher degree of somatization.

The moral, sexual, and religious value system of the family does not get revised, updated, and incorporated into that of the addicted emerging adult. Instead, it gets discarded as the person adapts to the competing demands in the role of addict in the chemical dependency script. As Coleman, Kaplan, and Downing (1986) noted, the concrete value system of addicts

> . . . characterizes their central adolescent-like quality. They are not yet ready to encompass society's goals and values, as they are still locked into the incomplete task of growing up and leaving home. . . . To go beyond the family system to embrace the larger system is a step they are not ready to take. (p. 21)

**Separation/Individuation: "I Won't Grow Up"**

Although the extent of developmental damage is mediated by age, frequency of use, type of drug and underlying genetic and personality variables, we can see the title of Peter's song beginning to shift from, "I Won't Grow Up" to "I Can't Grow Up." The central tasks of the late stage adolescent, identity formation and separation, become impaired. The impact of this dynamic upon the family has been well documented in the field of family treatment. Classic among the theorists are Stanton and Todd (1982), who conceptualized drug taking as a homeostatic device to prevent the separation of the adolescent thereby preserving the stability of the family. In this model, the drug taking itself becomes an expression of and resolution to the underlying conflict. The addict can be within the family while emotionally removed on drugs. The addict gives the illusion of independence and rebelliousness while simultaneously maintaining a very dependent stance vis a vis his or her family. Furthermore, even when the addict appears to separate, Stanton and Todd refer to this as ***pseudoindividuation***—a state that is easily revoked by the return to drug taking, i.e., relapse.

For Peter, this dichotomous behavior is evidenced by his return to the family home and entrance into his father's business. In a sense, the family continues to supply the props for Peter's performance in the "normal" script. As his progression into chemical usage causes him to "outgrow" his costumes, the family responds by providing even larger costumes to cover him up. In the chemical dependency treatment world, this is referred to as **enabling**, and the family role is labeled **codependency** (Cermak, 1986; Beattie, 1987). Family members must work harder to split off the growing awareness of addictive behavior. Again, the belief is in the false notion that if they can keep the chemical dependency script from becoming manifest, then it will not exist. They refuse to recognize Peter's involvement in never-never land and work harder and harder to cover up for his absences. Of course, underlying this behavior pattern is the growing fear that one day he will not return. Coleman et al. (1986) further refined the association between drug use and inability to separate by associating the link to unresolved grief within the family system. In this study, chemical (in this case heroin) use becomes the metaphor in which the family repeatedly reenacts the death scene in a repetition/compulsion style.

Finally, Noone and Reddig (1976) offered a relabeling of the separation/individuation fixation of the family as a way of maintaining loyalty. The tales of the "dramatic episodes of drug abuse, law violations, and destructive behaviors" offer the family an opportunity to demonstrate a host of subtle family loyalties and heightened interactions. The mock separations created by hospitalization, institutionalization, or incarceration provide a sense of drama and urgency for the renewal of family ties. In Noone and Reddig's model, the family definition of the problem never is seen as the separation; it only is viewed as the drugs.

**Dueling Scripts**

As the progression of substance abuse accelerates, the family is involved in competing constructions. One scenario follows the all is well script with its emphasis on the continued functionality of the addict. In this case, Peter can be viewed simply as an adolescent who did not like school, dropped out, and now is going to work for his father. Functionality always becomes a circuitous way of reconfirming denial (for example, the oft heard statement, "He [or she] can't be an addict because he [or she] goes to work every day."). Of course, in the competing dialogue of the chemical dependency script, Peter appears to have already suffered substantial developmental damage. He continues to utilize substances, perhaps even accelerating the need to self-medicate (Khantzian, 1989). In this script, his life choices arise from the consequences of his usage.

The feeling states in the family clearly will be mediated by the operative script.

Again, the reassurance and ease accompanying the all is well script abound even if the family becomes responsible for the manufacturing and maintenance (albeit an ever-demanding task) of the functioning level of the addict (e.g., giving Peter the high paying job). Of course, this behavior is driven by the defense against the feelings of anxiety and despair invoked by the chemical dependency script. When acting in the chemical dependency script, parents feel grief, loss, shame, anger, and uncertainty about the future. They may question their parenting skills and tend to ruminate about perceived mistakes. Guilt abounds and oftentimes is accompanied by angry outbursts projected at the adolescent for having caused the pain. It is far more clear that the enabling behavior of the codependent in the all is well script is not the result of a primary disease as is often suggested but rather is a defensive posture (Cermak, 1986).

The duality in scripts usually gets "acted out" in the parental unit. The parents themselves become polarized in their response to the adolescent/young adult. Treadway (1989) noted that parents split on the debate between firmness/discipline and nurturance/understanding. However, one can see that the appropriateness of each side of the split would be congruent with the competing scripts relative to the family meaning system. The typical split between two parents (i.e., that of good/bad parent) can be reinterpreted through a social constructionistic frame. The parent adhering to the "good" approach is more likely to feel that the child will benefit from greater nurturance. The "good" parent's tendency is to minimize the problem, fix it, nurture, and hope that "all will be well." In contrast, the "bad" parent will become the disciplinarian and limit setter. He or she may wish to adopt a "tough love" approach to the adolescent. Yet in adopting the no-nonsense role, the limit setter often sets unrealistic punishments. His or her view of the developmental impairment caused by chemical dependency is just as unrealistic as that of the "good" parent. The "bad" parent may see the use of substances as "willful" behavior and the co-occurring failure to grow up as "laziness" that can be corrected through the use of punishment.

The good/bad parents often are involved in an elaborate game of seesaw. Either parent can sabotage the efforts of the other one regardless of which approach happens to be the more appropriate to use in the moment. The erosion in the parental unit, with its ramifications for the marital relationship, fertilizes the climate in which chemical dependency flourishes. Yet each parent simply is responding to the Dr. Jekyll/Mr. Hyde nature of coexisting scripts.

## Family Intervention

Gergen (1985, p. 268) believed that the properties of social patterns are formed of the self-selected descriptions and explanations that are chosen to support the patterns to the exclusion of a competing understanding. Family treatment, using a constructionist model, more typically moves to effect change by offering a complementary meaning system that cannot coexist with the former system. This is achieved through the introduction of a competing meaning system that forces a change in the perspective of the original definition of "problem." In so doing, the therapist would help the family expand their awareness of themselves without "the problem."

In dealing with the chemical dependency script, however, what ironically is presented by the family is not necessarily "the problem" to which a competing framework needs to be designed. In fact, as was described in the section on dueling scripts, the family already coexists in a state where two competing scripts remain operative. Conversely, the family does not need help by the therapist to describe themselves from a "new and non-problem-saturated perspective" (White, 1989, p. 5, as cited in Atwood, 1993, p. 20). They already have denial of the problem even in the face of ample evidence to the contrary. One could argue that they could benefit more from the amplification necessary to help them understand that they do have a problem, namely chemical dependency.

What seems most indicated in dealing with the chemical dependent individual and family members alike is the synthesis of competing scripts. Thus, the adolescent needs to be helped in deconstructing the addictiologia—the addictive reality in which two competing and mutually exclusive concepts of self coexist. This is evidenced in the statements or behavior of Peter that suggest, "I use drugs/I have no problem"; "I failed school/I am happy"; "I am an independent young adult/I cannot function without my parents." In other words, "I cannot complete the normal developmental tasks of adolescence while simultaneously impairing all functions necessary to complete my normal development."

Likewise, the family must be helped to reintegrate their own dichotomous thinking. In seeking to preserve the all is well script, they enable the chemical dependency script to flourish. They must also be helped to understand that the constructs, "My child is an independent adult/My child needs me to function" cannot exist simultaneously without resulting in a constantly fluctuating reality. They cannot continue to problem solve and rescue on behalf of their adolescent and think that will lead to development of adult skills. In other words, the parent who carries the baby cannot believe simultaneously that the child is learning how to walk.

It is in a parallel process that the parents need to reconcile their own divergent thinking and styles. The good/bad parent styles must become unified in response to the Dr. Jekyll/Mr. Hyde personas of the chemically dependent adolescent. It is far better to create limits that both parents can adhere to than for either to cancel out the other's efforts. An integration of style helps implement more realistic limits on a consistent basis. Treadway (1989) noted the following:

> With adolescents 17 and older, parents need to stop trying to control and direct the adolescent and learn how to negotiate with the child as an adult. At this age, parents cannot legislate behavior; however, they can decide what they will and will not support. They cannot order a child to go to school, come home at a certain time, or abstain from drugs, but they can withhold financial support, forbid him from living at home, or insist he pay room and board. The message to the child is that with adult freedom comes adult responsibility. (p. 147)

Ultimately, the therapist needs to join with the family in the reintegration of their competing social meaning systems to create a new script in which the adolescent can be helped to "grow up." Again, this requires the honest awareness that this process has become impeded by chemical dependency. The family has to stop working so hard to pretend otherwise. Once again, they must be helped to recognize the irony that the harder they work to make it all better, the more distance they must travel in reaching the goal. To continue on the same path is to remain stuck on a treadmill of illusion.

## ADULT "CHILD" SCRIPT: "FOREVER YOUNG"

In a society that has placed an inordinate value upon youth, it is a perverse truth that becoming chemically dependent provides a vehicle for staying young. We use chemical solutions to retard and camouflage the aging process. Psychoactive drugs use, while perhaps originally a playful venture of the adolescent, becomes the emotional crippler of the addict.

In this final section, we briefly will return to look at the Pan family now that Peter is chronologically an adult. Predictably, what we will find is that without intervention, the family has remained fixated at the life cycle stage of the late adolescent. This holds true regardless of whether or not the adult "child" actually resides in the parental home or is separated by vast geographic distance. Stanton and Todd (1982) found that the preponderance of addicts in their 20s and 30s had greater frequency of contact with their family of origin than other groups (both psychiatric and normal). Stanton and Todd further cited a study by Perzel and Lamon who found that 64% of heroin addicts were in daily telephone contact with at least one parent, compared to 51% of polydrug abusers and 9% of normals (p. 9). Even in skid row populations, it was found that many homeless alcoholics still are involved in ongoing relationships with one or more significant other family members (Steinglass, 1987). In a study by Chein, Gerard, Lee, and Rosenfeld (1984), it was noted that the married addict often leaves his spouse and returns home to his parent(s).

### Case Illustration

Peter is now 33 years old. He has been married to his wife, Wendy, for the past 5 years, and together they have a 2-year-old son. Peter continues to be employed by his father as a "top" sales representative in the company.

Peter's drug abuse became more pronounced 2 1/2 years ago when he began to use cocaine more regularly. This coincided with his wife's progression to her third trimester of pregnancy and his father's contemplation of retirement.

Peter concedes that ". . . things got a little stressful" and he "got a little out of control" but still feels he "can stop any time" he wants. Lately, Wendy has been telling Peter to "just go back home to your parents" because she does not "need another 'child' around the house." On two occasions, she has "permanently" locked him out only to change her mind several days later.

Peter's parents know that Peter is having "marriage problems." They are also aware of his financial difficulties but cannot quite understand where the couple "spends all the money." Peter's mother often finds herself buying "a little extra groceries and clothes" for the family. She does not see this as a "major problem" because she can "afford" to help out her son and his family.

Peter's father is aware of Peter's erratic work performance but cannot "fire [his] own son." Besides, he worries who will then take care of Wendy and his grandson. Peter's father also fears that he cannot sell out his business to another outside party because he knows that Peter will become unemployed shortly thereafter. As a result he feels he must delay his plans for retirement until Peter becomes more responsible. Although many of their contemporaries have moved to retirement communities, Bob and Jane Pan realize they must wait.

What exactly is it that the family needs to wait to have happen? Any one individual can become unstuck. Wendy can move to terminate the marriage. Peter's parents also can decide to retire in spite of the situation, thereby declaring their willingness to get on with their life cycle tasks. Peter can choose to begin the recovery process. Yet collectively, they remain interlaced, each one looking toward the other as the reason for their entrapment.

It is highly improbable that Peter independently would seek counseling for his substance abuse problem, primarily because he still does not believe fully that he has a problem. From his point of view, he is right. He still has all the ingredients in place for the pretense of the happily ever after script (a wife, a child, a job, and a family).

For any one of the family members to become unstuck, he or she would need to risk scrapping the above script. The stakes get higher and higher as the responsibilities of the "pseudo" adult become more complex. Family members fear they have more to lose by letting go of the props that enable the show to go on.

Yet because of the cyclical nature of the substance abuse, with the on-off periods of intoxication varying with sobriety, the family must adapt to the duality in their interactional behavior patterns as well. Steinglass (1987) noted that the sharp contrast in behavior of the addict is as striking as the manic depressive cycle of bipolar disorder. He believed this results in an off-on cycle replication in the family. As we have seen previously, the duality in the "happily ever after script" vacillates with that of the "chemical dependency script" in an ever more predictable fashion. Yet the constructs fail to integrate.

Now the behavioral patterns accompanying the chemical dependency are firmly entrenched. The roles become increasingly predictable and rigidified. The stereotypical behavior is now subjected to professional labeling, and a new language has emerged to describe chemical dependency. The disparaging descriptions of the marriage partner by Whalen in 1953 (cited in Steinglass, 1987, p. 7) of "Suffering Susan," "Controlling Catherine," "Wavering Winifred," and "Punitive Polly" have been redubbed "codependent," "enabler," "co-alcoholic," and "provacatrix," respectively (Kellerman, 1980) in the 1990s. There are also roles for different family members: "hero," "scapegoat," "mascot," and "lone child" (Wegsheider, 1981). If the family does not stage a "planned intervention" (Johnson, 1973), they must wait for Peter "to hit bottom."

In the moments of "hitting bottom," family members individually or collectively finally come to acknowledge that "all is not well." They now can pursue a new direction into recovery. In so doing, they finally become free to grow.

## SCRIPTLESS IN RECOVERY

There is an interesting expression known to people in "the Program" (12-step), and it is as follows: "There are two types of people in the world—those who are in recovery and those who haven't gotten there yet."

But what exactly does everyone in society need to be in recovery from? What is the social context fueling this movement? Is it the mass alienation, rampant materialism, or excessive pressure to have instantly the perfect life/wife/body? Is the addiction to chemicals such as insecticides, aerosols, cosmetics, electromagnetic waves, and lawn growers—to name but a few of our favorites—the substances we cannot live without?

Hillman and Ventura (1992) noted the following:

> . . . each week, 200 types of 12-step recovery groups such as Alcoholics Anonymous or Overeaters Anonymous draw 15 million Americans to 500,00 meetings across the nation. . . . On one given day in Santa Fe, there were groups meeting for ". . . Debtors Anonymous, Incest Survivors Anonymous, Adult Children of Alcoholics, Survivors of Suicide, Narcotics Anonymous, Co-Ed Incest Therapy Group, manic-depressive

and mood disorder group, . . . Support Group for Persons
with Environmental Illnesses . . . " and so on. (p. 134)

The only requirement for the feeling of community is the willingness to
recognize oneself as a victim. The selection of the grouping depends upon
the symptom cluster that best represents what we feel most victimized by—
be it our own illnesses or someone else's. It is a new way to form an identity.

Yet, when we reexamine the arrested development of Peter, it is not
true that he failed to form an identity. What is more true is that he could
not accept the identity he was forming, i.e., that of an addict. Neither could
his family. Therein was the struggle. In the final analysis, it is the acknowledgment and acceptance of the unacceptable script that provides relief to
the individual and family members as well. There is the surrender to the
recognition that there was a coexisting script all along. It has a name, and
it is called chemical dependency. The family finally can understand the story.
The family does not need to construct an alternative story to enable them
to perform new meanings (Atwood & Zebertsky, 1993). Rather, they need
to accept the story as it fully exists.

Much has been written about the destabilization that occurs when the
family enters recovery and the addict becomes abstinent (Treadway, 1989;
Steinglass, 1987). The family no longer knowing how to act and must be
helped to redevelop skills in a process that can take several years (Usher,
1991). They are scriptless. They flounder. Their major fear is that of the
relapse. Yet relapse can be understood simply as a return to the former
confusion of the coexisting scripts. It is not even necessary to resume chemical use in order for this to happen. Rather, it is the return to the duality of
thinking—the simultaneous state of knowing and not knowing. As uncomfortable as the former script may be, it is predictably unpredictable. It is
known.

Generally, the unknown is even more frightening than the known. The
return to the familiar (relapse) can become alluring. It is in recovery that
the therapist can join with the family in the expansion of their story. The
starting point is in the confirmation of the duality of the roles that have
existed all along. The script for "normal" is already in place. What they
need help in accepting is their coexisting script for the deviation from the
norm. In broadening their self-definition to include the labels of "addict"
and "codependent," they begin to become whole. It is the final irony, that
in accepting the very script the family and child refused to acknowledge all
along, the "happily ever after" script can begin.

# REFERENCES

Ablon, J. (1980). The significance of cultural patterning for the alcoholic family. *Family Process*, 19, 127–144.

Archambault, D. (1989). Adolescence: A physiological, cultural, and psychological no man's land. In G. Lawson & A. Lawson (Eds.), *Alcoholism and substance abuse in special populations* (pp. 223–245). Gaithersburg, MD: Aspen Publications.

Atwood, J., & Dobkin, S. (1992, October). Storm clouds are coming: Ways to help couples reconstruct the crisis of infertility. *Contemporary Family Therapy*, 385–402.

Atwood, J., & Zebertsky, R. (1993). *Using social construction with the REM family: The real father*. Reprint requests to Hofstra University, Hempstead, NY.

Baab, K. (1992). Neurolinguistic programming and hypnosis during intervention with substance-abusing adolescents. In G. Lawson & A. Lawson (Eds.), *Adolescent substance abuse: Etiology, treatment, and prevention* (pp. 197–206). Gaithersburg, MD: Aspen Publications.

Barrett, K. (1992, July). Addictions treatment. *Family Dynamics of Addiction Quarterly*, 33–43.

Beattie, M. (1987). *Codependent no more*. Center City, MN: Hazeldon Foundation.

Begley, S. (1994, February 7). Beyond Prozac. *Newsweek*, 36–43.

Bell, T. (1990). *Preventing adolescent relapse*. Independence, MO: Herald House.

Black, C. (1982). *It will never happen to me!* Denver, CO: MAC Publishing.

Cermak, T. (1986). *Diagnosing and treating codependence*. Edina, MN: Johnson Institute.

Chafetz, M., Blane, H., & Hill, M. (1977). Children of alcoholics: Observations in a child guidance clinic. *Quarterly Journal of Studies on Alcohol*, 32, 687–698.

Chein, I., Gerard, D., Lee, R., & Rosenfeld, E. (1964). *The road to H.* New York: Basic Books.

Coleman, S., Kaplan, J. & Downing, R. (1986). Life cycle & loss: The spiritual vacuum of heroin addiction. *Family Process, Inc., 25*, 5–23.

Coombs, R., Santana, F., & Fawzy, F. (1984). Parent training to prevent adolescent drug use: An educational model. *Journal of Drug Issues, 14*, 393–402.

Cotton, N. (1979). The familial incidence of alcoholism: A review. *Journal of Studies on Alcohol, 40*, 89–116.

Davis, D., & Davis, S. (1991). Belief change and neurolinguistic programming. In G. Lawson & A. Lawson (Eds.), *Family Dynamics of Addiction Quarterly, 1*(2), 34–44.

Festinger, L. (1957). *A theory of cognitive dissonance*. Stanford, CA: Stanford University Press.

Gergen, K. (1985, March). The social constuctionist movement in modern psychology. *American Psychologist*, 266–275.

Gergen, K. (1989). Social psychology and the wrong revolution. *European Journal of Social Psychology, 19*, 463–484.

Group for the Advancement of Psychiatry (GAP). (1968). *Normal adolescence*. New York: The Scribner Library.

Goodwin, D.W. (1983). Familial alcoholism: A separate entity? *Substance and Alcohol Addictions, 4*, 129–136.

Hillman, J., & Ventura, M. (1992). *We've had a hundred years of psychotherapy and the world's getting worse*. San Francisco: HarperCollins.

Howard, M. (1992). Adolescent substance abuse: A social learning theory perspective. In G. Lawson & A. Lawson (Eds.), *Adolescent substance abuse* (pp. 29–40). Gaithersburg, MD: Aspen Publications.

Johnson, G., Shontz, F., & Locke, T. (1984). Relationships between adolescent drug use and parental drug behavior. *Adolescence, 19*(74), 295–298.

Johnson, V. (1973). *I'll quit tomorrow*. New York: Harper & Row.

Kaufman, E., & Borders, L. (1984). Adolescent substance abuse in Anglo-American families. *Journal of Drug Issues, 14*, 365–377.

Kellerman, J. (1980). *Alcoholism: A merry-go-round named denial*. Center City, MN: Hazeldon Foundation.

Khantzian, E.J. (1989). Addiction: Self-destruction or self-repair. *Journal of Substance Abuse Treatment, 6*(2), 75.

Lawson, G., Peterson, J., & Lawson, A. (1983). *Alcoholism & the family: A guide to treatment and prevention*. Gaithersburg, MD: Aspen Publications.

MacDonald, D. (1987). Patterns of alcohol and drug use among adolescents. *Chemical Dependency: The Pediatric Clinics of North America, 34*(2), 275–288.

Miller, D., & Jang, M. (1978). Children of alcoholics: A 20-year longitudinal study. *Social Work Research and Abstracts, 13*, 23–29.

Mooney, A., & Eisenberg, A., & Eisenberg, H. (1992). *The recovery book*. New York: Workman Publishing Company.

Morrison, M.; & Smith, Q. (1987). Psychiatric issues of adolescent dependence. *Chemical Dependency: The Pediatric Clinics of North America, 34*(2), 461–480.

Nathan, P. (1985). Alcoholism: A cognitive social learning approach—The Bond Symposium. *Journal of Substance Abuse Treatment, 2*, 169–173.

Neinstein, L. (1984). *Adolescent health care: A practical guide*. Baltimore: Urban & Schwarzenberg.

*The New York Times*. (1994, February 6). Pot surges back, but it's like a whole new world. The New York Times, The Week in Review.

Noone, R., & Reddig, R. (1976). Case studies in the family treatment of drug abuse. *Family Process, 15*, 325–332.

Peele, S. (1985). *The meaning of addiction*. Lexington, KY: Lexington Books.

Petosa, R. (1992). Designing effective AIDS prevention programs for adolescents. In G. Lawson & A. Lawson (Eds.), *Adolescent substance abuse: Etiology, treatment, and prevention* (pp. 463–480). Gaithersburg, MD: Aspen Publications.

Stanton, M.D., & Todd, T.C. (1982). *The family therapy of drug abuse and addiction*. New York: Guilford Press.

Stein, H. (1985). Alcoholism as metaphor in American culture: Ritual desecration as social integration. *Ethos, 13*, 3.

Steinglass, P. (1987). *The alcoholic family*. New York: Basic Books.

Thorne, B., & DeBlassie, R. (1985). Adolescent substance abuse. *Adolescence, 20*, 341–346.

Treadway, D. (1989). *Before it's too late: Working with substance abuse in the family*. New York: Norton.

Treaster, J. (1993, April 14). Eighth grade habits among the youngest: A rise in marijuana, cocaine & LSD. *The New York Times*, A1.

Twerski, A. (1990). *Addictive thinking*. Center City, MN: Hazeldon Foundation.

Usher, M. (1991). From identification to consolidation: A treatment model for couples and families complicated by alcoholism. In G. Lawson & A. Lawson (Eds.), *Family Dynamics of Addiction Quarterly, 1*(2), 45–58.

Wegsheider, S. (1981). *Another chance*. Palo Alto, CA: Science & Behavior Books.

Woititz, J. (1983). *Adult children of alcoholics*. Hollywood, FL: Health Communications.

Wolin, S., & Bennet, L. (1984). Family rituals. *Family Process, 23*, 401–420.

Zarek, D., Hawkins, D., & Rogers, P. (1987). Risk factors for adolescent substance abuse: Implications for pediatric practice. *Chemical Dependency: The Pediatric Clinics of North America, 34*(2), 481–494.

# Chapter 8

# PRE-SCRIPTS AND POST-SCRIPTS: FAMILIES, LIFE SCRIPTS, AND AIDS

*Nancy Cohan*

As families construct their own narratives about what is occurring in the here and now, it is likely that these constructions co-created by family members color and shade their remembrances of the past as well as alter their plans for the future. Yet a diagnosis of Acquired Immune Deficiency Syndrome (AIDS) in a family member challenges the family's understanding of itself in the past and the present. It therefore can render their meaning systems inappropriate and life scripts inadequate for the future. Byng-Hall (1988) conceptualized the family script as "used to explain the mechanism that enables families to repeat particular family scenarios when similar contexts are encountered" (p. 130). However, learning that a partner, child, or sibling has AIDS may stop the automatic utilization of the family's script and necessitates the development of a new script at a time when the family, in many ways, is depleted and vulnerable.

Historically, there may be little or no correlation between long-standing family beliefs and the family's reaction to the AIDS diagnosis; however, current events may alter or obscure the clarity of memories or beliefs about the past. Recollections may become confused or inappropriately poignant as the family tries to integrate the AIDS diagnosis into a coherent, cohesive self-understanding. Learning that a loved one has AIDS may prompt the family to question the validity of the life script on which it previously had relied and the credibility of the meaning system upon which that script was developed.

## AIDS AND THE FAMILY'S FORMER LIFE SCRIPT

For many families, the revelation of an AIDS diagnosis in a family member is a dual one in that the disclosure of the illness may be the first time the family learns that an adult child is gay or has been involved in IV drug use (Dane, 1991, 1989; Garrett, 1988; Kelly & Skyes, 1989; Lamendola & Wells, 1991; Land & Harangody, 1990; Lovejoy, 1990; Stulberg & Buckingham, 1988; Weiss, 1989). Similar to other studies (Cramer & Roach, 1988; Savin-Williams, 1989), Cain (1991) found that one half of the gay men in his sample had concealed their homosexuality from parents. However, for many of these men, an AIDS diagnosis necessitated disclosure to parents and other members of the family. Such a discovery may force families to confront issues they previously had avoided or denied, thereby forcing them to confront illusions they may have maintained about the individual with AIDS or the family as a whole (Dane, 1991). For those families with tacit agreements not to discuss or ask questions about a son's (daughter's) sexuality, learning that he or she has AIDS may require that they relinquish that specific area of denial from their script. Similarly, a family's beliefs about their closeness, their cohesiveness, and the openness of their communication may be challenged by the knowledge that a significant part of a family member's life has been kept secret from them (Stulberg & Buckingham, 1988). This realization may bring into question the parent's beliefs about the nature of the parent-child relationship as it existed prior to the AIDS diagnosis and the son's (daughter's) coming out to the family.

Despite the ongoing debate among researchers concerning the origins of homosexuality, for many parents the culturally popular notion that the roots of homosexuality can be traced to an incorrect pattern of early parenting continues to prevail (Hersch, 1991; Gelman, Foote, Barrett, & Talbot, 1992). As Hersch (1991) reported, "Many young lesbians and gays are made to feel not only that they have failed their parents, but that they have also made their parents feel like failures" (pp. 41–42). Parents, therefore, may feel personally responsible for somehow influencing their child's initiation into a lifestyle that they believe resulted in the grown child's contracting a life-threatening disease (Dane, 1991; Lovejoy, 1990).

Parents who thought they had fostered an atmosphere of honesty and open communication with their son (daughter) may find that they review past interactions differently in light of the new information obtained via the AIDS diagnosis. Recollections of mundane discussions of possible marriage and potential grandchildren may be recalled later as incidents of evasiveness and deception (Cain, 1991). A brother or sister who had considered the sibling a close friend and had confided in him or her (Cain, 1991) may find that the friendship has been compromised by the discovery that the sibling withheld the information that he or she is gay.

Issues of trust and loyalty often accompany the discovery that some members of the family had known of an individual's gay lifestyle or drug use and others had not (Stulberg & Buckingham, 1988; Tiblier, Walker, & Rolland, 1989). Long-standing covert alliances may become overt, indicating the inclusion of some siblings in the secret and the exclusion of others. Parents may be dismayed to find that not only is a son (daughter) gay but that he or she has shared this information with a sibling who in turn actively participated in keeping the secret from the parents (Cain, 1991; Tiblier et al., 1989). Cain (1991) found that the siblings of some gay men in his sample played roles "facilitating or impeding disclosure within the family. For instance, parents sometimes approached a brother or sister for 'inside information' on the respondents" (p. 348). For some of these parents, learning their son (daughter) is gay also implicates a second child in the deception and may be experienced as an additional betrayal. A sibling, whose customary role had been to protect parents from adverse information or to shield siblings from parental disapproval, may find that the AIDS diagnosis has altered or eradicated his or her role in the usual family drama. Similarly, other role assignments in the family may require change to accommodate AIDS. A son who previously had held a distant position in the family's configuration may find that illness dictates that he solicit caretaking from the family from which he previously was estranged. Or as Tiblier et al. (1989) reported, "A person with AIDS, for instance may designate a sibling who seems more tolerant of his or her lifestyle to replace the mother as caregiver, thus upsetting the normal family hierarchy" (pp. 89–90).

Married siblings of people with AIDS may have difficulties reconciling loyalty to their family of origin with loyalty to their own nuclear family. This can be particularly problematic if the family of origin's script maintains that although they may marry and move on, the primary allegiance of individual family members must remain with the family of origin. Conflict and resentment from the spouse of the sibling of the AIDS patient may arise if that spouse finds more and more of his or her partner's time and energy redirected toward a sick in-law.

Similarly, the anticipation of the loss of a child or a close sibling may precipitate a reexamination of a tenuous marital relationship and could result in the family's reorganization (Walker, 1991). Walker (1991) cited the example of a sister who, after the diagnosis of her brother, "realized that her closeness to him had made staying in a loveless marriage for the sake of her children bearable" (p. 180). After her divorce and a subsequent remarriage, "the long-standing coalition of brother and sister against the rest of the family weakened; the mother, who had always felt herself to be in an outside position in the family, was able to meet with her son in a therapy session and discuss her feelings about his being gay" (Walker, 1991, p. 180).

A family may be gratified to find that their son has developed a close network of friends but simultaneously disappointed to find that he has come to consider these friends, and not the family, his primary system of support (Lamendola & Wells, 1991; Levine, 1991a; Land & Harangody, 1990; Tiblier et al., 1989). Lamendola & Wells (1991) cited, for example, a couple who four days before their son's death were met by his friend who "took them aside when they arrived at the hospital and said, 'Jim is gay and he has AIDS. You need to go into his room and tell him you know he is gay and has AIDS and that you love him and you need to use all these words'" (p. 24). This type of scenario could be particularly problematic to a family with tightly closed boundaries who believe that blood ties are the only connections to be relied on in times of trouble.

A family whose script requires that they anticipate or mourn their losses privately and who are acutely aware of any boundary encroachments might feel resentful or displaced to arrive at a hospital room and find it overflowing with the patient's friends. These friends are likely to be viewed by the family as intrusive, and in the case of a partner, may be blamed for the illness (Dane, 1989; Land & Harangody, 1990; Tiblier et al., 1989). If the family's previous experiences with life-threatening illnesses have lead them to construct a script that calls for bringing the patient home for care, they may be dismayed to hear that he or she has made prior arrangements to be cared for by people the family may not even know.

The scripts of some families do not recognize full adult status in any grown child unless he or she has married. As a result, the gay young adult may linger in a prolonged state of adolescence in the family system. To many gay men, a move away from home facilitates the establishment of a career, often coincides with involvement in the gay community, and helps solidify their sense of adulthood (Walker, 1991). For the gay man who must leave his job and rely on parents for caretaking as his illness progresses, Walker (1991) commented that "as he returns home, it is as a son or sibling, with the makers of his adult gay identity left behind" (p. 14).

Conflicts between the script of the family and the script of the patient's partner can arise if the family's script invalidates or disqualifies the spousal role that the partner has assumed in the life of the person with AIDS (Dane, 1991; Levine, 1991a; Lovejoy, 1990; Walker, 1991). Walker (1991) cited the difficulties some families may encounter accepting the role of the gay partner "without having had the ritual of a marriage to mark the transfer of power from the parents as principal caregivers and decision-makers to a spouse" (p. 16). Similarly, the gay partner involved in a committed, long-term relationship and who has supported his partner with AIDS throughout the early and protracted stages of the illness, may be disheartened to find that the biological family intends now to assume total responsibility for his partner's care (Lamendola & Wells, 1991; Stulberg & Buckingham, 1988; Tiblier, 1987; Tiblier et al., 1989). As there exists little or no legal consideration for the role played by the gay life partner, disputes between the parents and partner may persist after the patient's death and become vehicles for unresolved anger over the common loss (Lamendola & Wells, 1991; Levine, 1991a; Lovejoy, 1990; Nungesser, 1986; Weiss, 1989).

In many ways AIDS has brought into question the traditional definition of family and, quite often, the constructs of biological families and larger social system differ from those of the AIDS patient, his partner, and others in the gay community (Levine, 1991a). A family of origin, after losing their son to AIDS, may attempt to claim property and belongings acquired by their son and his partner despite the many years the couple lived together. Levine (1991a) discussed the difficulty a partner living in a city may encounter when a person named on a lease dies and both the surviving partner and the family claim the right to remain as a tenant in a rent-controlled or rent stabilized apartment (p. 60). Lamendola and Wells (1991) offered the example of a man with AIDS whose prearrangement for cremation and a nonreligious funeral was overturned by his parents who, after his death, opted for a funeral mass and excluded his gay friends from attending. In these cases, the functional construction of family was superseded by the more traditional definition that tends to define the family in terms of biological connections (Levine, 1991a).

For families who have derived their life scripts from scripture, an AIDS diagnosis may compel either the reassessment of one or more religious doctrines or perhaps the abandonment of the person with AIDS. As Moynihan, Christ, and Silver (1988) have reported, "Although many clergy and religious groups have responded with compassion to AIDS patients, others feel they are limited by strict interpretation of religious law" (p. 386). Some families may experience difficulty reconciling their feelings of love for the member with AIDS with the tenants of a church that adheres to a strict or literal interpretation of biblical doctrine (Lovejoy, 1990; Moynihan et al., 1988; Round, 1988; Schaper, 1987; Urwin, 1988). Families who have depended on what Urwin (1988) described as "the rules of religion in living and dying" may find these rules inappropriate to their experience of coping with AIDS, particularly if these rules depict a dying son as a recipient of God's wrath against homosexuals (Schaper, 1987; Urwin, 1988, p. 157). Or an individual who has witnessed a loved one undergoing extensive physical and psychological suffering may find that the AIDS experience has precipitated a questioning, or in some cases a loss, of faith. Compounding the potential pain of a spiritual severance from the church is the lack of social support a family may encounter if they abruptly leave the church community (Round, 1988). The church can be a predominant support system in times of crisis for many families, particularly those in rural or African American communities (Round, 1988; Walker, 1991). For these families, alienation from the church can result in feelings of isolation and inadequacy when facing the innumerable stresses accompanying AIDS.

The family of an HIV infected drug abuser also may need to revise their life script when AIDS is diagnosed. For some families, the inability to reconnect with the AIDS patient may be related not to the illness, but to the drug abusing behaviors that preceded it (Drucker, 1991; Walker, 1991). As Walker (1991) stated, "families of drug users share community anger at their deviant members" (p. 280). Long-standing family conflicts such as difficulty with separation, problems establishing boundaries, and a history of unresolved loss often predate the AIDS diagnosis in the substance abuser's family of origin (Coleman, 1991; Drucker, 1991; Walker, 1991). Families may continue to harbor deep-seated resentments resulting from the adverse effects the drug abuse have had on their lives and, therefore, may be reluctant to care for the drug abuser with AIDS. Those families resolved to no longer offering assistance to the child who continues to abuse drugs may have difficulty maintaining this stance if that individual becomes hospitalized with an opportunistic infection (Bartlett & Finkbeiner, 1991).

Coleman (1991) has found that issues of unresolved loss abound in the meaning systems and scripts of many families of drug abusers. She reported that, as a result, "any type of separation is particularly difficult for addict families" (Coleman, 1991, p. 265). Families scripted to continuously rescue the drug abuser may feel guilty for not preventing that individual from engaging in the behaviors that resulted in his or her contracting the AIDS virus (Tiblier, 1987; Walker, 1991). A family that had utilized a cutoff as a means of coping with the individual's drug abuse, when faced with his or her impending death, may feel guilty over the estrangement or regret the time together that was lost.

Similar to the conflicts that may occur within the families of some gay men with AIDS, the drug abuser's family may blame a partner for the abuser's continued substance abuse (Walker, 1991). Or the partner or spouse of the drug user may assert that the abuser's parents or siblings are in some ways responsible for the addiction (Walker, 1991). Conflict between partner and parents may result, for example, in the caring of an ill daughter and her children by her family being contingent upon her promise to have no further contact with her husband who also may be dying of AIDS (Walker, 1991). And, as it is less likely for the drug abuser with AIDS to have access to the level of community support that the gay man with AIDS may find available, the drug abusing AIDS patient is more apt to look to family for caretaking and support throughout the course of his or her illness.

A spouse in a bisexual couple whose partner becomes infected with the AIDS virus as a result of sexual contact outside the marriage must reexamine his or her beliefs and reevaluate his or her script of the couple relationship. For some couples, a husband's bisexuality is framed as having occurred prior to the couple relationship and as an event of the past, not considered part of the marital script (Maloney, 1988; Walker, 1991). Maloney (1988), however, suggested that when a husband is diagnosed with AIDS, "the wife, after the initial crisis, begins to wonder about her husband's former lifestyle; knowing he was bisexual does not necessarily indicate sophistication about gay sexual practices. Did he frequent bathhouses? Was he promiscuous aside from the lovers she knew about?" (p. 146).

In other couples, a wife might suspect that her husband had or is having a sexual relationship with another man but believes that a pursuit of her suspicion could compromise her marriage or, at least, her beliefs about that marriage (Walker, 1991). Some women construe a husband's bisexual behavior as their own personal failure (Walker, 1991). Some couples are likely to try to utilize scripts that dictate that sexual secrets must be protected, and a husband's bisexuality is tolerated by his wife only within the context of the appearance of a traditional marriage. Lastly, there are some women who, prior to learning of their husbands' diagnosis with AIDS, were completely unaware that their husbands had any sexual involvement with men (Maloney, 1988; Walker, 1991).

Often the couple will avoid sharing information concerning the husband's illness with friends or extended family, as disclosing the illness may jeopardize the couple's public persona of the typical American family (Maloney, 1988; Walker, 1991). Maloney (1988), however, has found the following:

> . . . when AIDS families lie, vaguely implying that they have cancer, they do not get the support they need. People respond to a definite reality, but they do not respond well to an anonymous illness with no predictable course, specific therapy, or clear-cut symptoms. Some people, friends as well as family, are lost along the way. (p. 146)

The family of the bisexual person with AIDS, therefore, is apt to be further isolated by the illness as they often are unwilling or not able to elicit adequate support from either the heterosexual or the gay community.

Hemophiliacs and other blood product recipients must reorganize their life scripts to accommodate the realization that they have contracted the AIDS virus from the miracle of modern medicine that they previously held responsible for their survival (Bayer, 1989; DiMarzo, 1989; Tiblier et al., 1989; Walker 1991). "Because the management of hemophilia has been achieved by carefully controlling much of their environment, infection with HIV may destroy hemophiliacs' fundamental trust in their ability to control their fate" (Tiblier et al., 1989, p. 100). Bayer (1989), a hemophilia infected with the virus, said the following:

> After more than 30 years of enduring one miserable disease, hemophilia, my life now was shaken by another. More than that, the very treatment that had at last given me an almost normal life was responsible for infecting me with the most dreaded and despised affliction of the century. (p. 50)

Families often utilize denial as an effective means of managing hemophilia. Somewhat based in this denial, a reality is constructed by the families that, when augmented by the use of the clotting factor, offers the hemophiliac the opportunity to lead a normal life and develop a positive script for the future (Bayer, 1989; DiMarzo, 1989; Walker, 1991). However, when faced with the spectre of HIV infection, a script based on denial can result in not seeking early treatment for the HIV infection and potentially infecting others with the virus (DiMarzo, 1989; Walker, 1991). Seroconversion also may alter the hemophiliac and his or her partner's scripts for intimacy (Bayer, 1989; DiMarzo, 1989; Walker, 1991). Bayer (1989) stated that as a result of testing positive for the HIV virus, he has come to believe that "a virus has assumed primary control of my romantic life" (p. 55).

For families who once had emphasized the importance of leading a "normal life," the stress of the AIDS diagnosis may be compounded by the stigmatization of the groups with which the disease has been associated. Bosk and Frader (1991) reported that hemophiliac patients in hospitals often emphasize how they contracted the disease. Bosk and Frader found that "these patients 'display' wives and children to differentiate themselves from homosexual patients" as they believed they would be afforded better treatment by the hospital staff than gay or drug abusing patients infected with the virus (Bosk & Frader, 1991, p. 164). This was reinforced in some hospitals where staff members designated AIDS patients exposed to the virus through blood products the "innocent victims" of the disease (Bosk & Frader, 1991).

## FAMILIES AND AIDS: DEVISING AND REVISING LIFE SCRIPTS FOR LIVING WITH THE VIRUS

Although family scripts rely on the family's past behaviors as guidelines for dealing with new experiences, it is unlikely that families have had many previous experiences that will prepare them for the many challenges of living with AIDS. Walker (1991) stated that "the combination of illness, actual or potential loss of family members, and the powerful stigma of AIDS creates an AIDS family, with new coalitions, structures, secrets, and boundaries" (p. 179). The family must compose a life script that incorporates AIDS into their lives without permitting the prevailing negative social constructions to permeate their meaning systems and hinder their ability to cope with the disease (Tiblier et al., 1989). The adequacy of the family's revised script, as well as their ability to meet the needs of the person with AIDS and other members of the family, may be contingent upon the rigidity of the former life script and the course taken by the illness itself.

The family who is aware that their son is gay and that he has tested positive for the AIDS virus before he becomes symptomatic is likely to find more latitude for revising their life script than the family who rushes to the hospital when notified their son is critically ill with an opportunistic infection such as pneumocystis carinii pneumonia. For the latter family, the demands of the medical crisis, combined with their reactions to the startling often unsolicited news about the patient's sexuality or drug use, may diminish their ability to competently meet the demands of the disease (Walker, 1991).

The family's attempt to equip themselves to cope with a chronic, life-threatening disease can be complicated further by the "roller coaster-like" nature of AIDS (Dane, 1991; Stulberg & Buckingham, 1988; Tiblier, 1987; Walker, 1991). Frequently there are alternating periods of acute illness and times when the person with AIDS appears to have improved (Dane, 1991; Moynihan et al., 1988; Walker, 1991). This can require that the family not only abandon its pre-illness script but also, at times, rewrite the recently constructed one as well.

The family may find that they repeatedly must shift from a primarily caretaking role to one in which they permit the individual with AIDS an opportunity to partially return to a level of pre-illness functioning (Moyni-han et al., 1988; Walker, 1991). Partners and family members, prepared to care for a dying patient, may have difficulty accepting the patient's decision to return to work or to participate in other activities that do not fit the family frame for serious illness (Moynihan et al., 1988). Equally proble-matic, however, is the family whose denial of the illness encourages them to place "unrealistic demands on the patient to function independently and fail to provide comfort, support, and practical help" (Moynihan et al., 1988, p. 382). Tiblier et al. (1989) wrote that "family identity following an AIDS diagnosis will never be the same" (p. 118). As a result, the person with AIDS, his or her partner, family, and friends will be required to compose life scripts based on those meaning systems and identities irrevocably altered by AIDS (Walker, 1991).

The newly constructed script of the individual infected with the AIDS virus, however, may not necessarily replicate the scripts created by the people who love him or her. A similarity of scripts for the AIDS experience is somewhat contingent upon a concurrence of the meanings the individual family members ascribe to AIDS. This can include how each individual defines the illness, his or her pre-illness relationship with the person with AIDS, the extent to which the illness impinges upon his or her life, as well as the influence of the individual's sociocultural milieu.

The person with AIDS might wish to frame the disease as a chronic condition and concentrate on the unpredictability of his or her life expectancy in lieu of focusing on the inevitability of an early death. Nevertheless, he or she still will reconsider former life goals and need to make adjustments for the disease.

> The fact that individuals are likely to become HIV infected at an early age in the life cycle has important implications. A young man of 25, recently diagnosed with HIV, who is now drug free after an adolescent phase of drug abuse, suddenly finds that such normal life goals as marriage and children are closed to him. The life decisions he must now make are distinctly different than if he were to become ill at a later stage in life after he had accomplished more of his life goals. (Tiblier et al., 1989, p. 118)

The individual who tests positive for the HIV virus but whose symptoms remain manageable may be more prone to addressing the ways in which he or she can continue to enhance the quality of life than to planning for his death from the disease (Moynihan et al., 1988). However, as the individual attempts to manage the progression of the disease and to lead a meaningful life, he or she may find his or her endeavors undermined by continuous media attention emphasizing the rise in AIDS mortality or, perhaps, by those losses from AIDS that he or she has experienced personally (Moynihan et al., 1988). Sustaining a balance between hope and a realistic appraisal of the AIDS crisis may be difficult for a person with AIDS in the gay community. Helquist (1989) suggested that "with so much uncertainty and fear overshadowing their days, gay men must find their own ways to cope, to not sink into a constant demoralized state that robs them of a present as well as a future" (p. 292). A similar, albeit less optimistic script for balancing an AIDS diagnosis and hope is offered by Holleran (1989) who wrote that "One has to have two programs, two set of responses, ready at all times: (a) Life, (b) Death. The switch from one category to the other can come at any moment, in the most casual way" (p. 42).

Walker (1991) has found that the "initial experience of hospitalization can be a framing event for the family" (p. 162). The first, and subsequent, hospitalizations of the person with AIDS may require that the individual and other members of the family quickly become accustomed to dealing with the health care system. As the immune system becomes increasingly compromised, AIDS patients become susceptible to different opportunistic infections that assault various parts of the body and that require various types of treatment (Walker, 1991). A patient's hospital stay may last for many weeks and involve a seemingly never ending parade of medical professionals. As Lovejoy (1990) has found, "Family members who have not dealt with the health care system since 'my son was born' or 'I needed shots for school' find medical terminology, cost of care, and the complex health care system shocking" (p. 288). Ironically health care providers, particularly in hospitals that are short staffed and strained by the demands of the AIDS crisis, may look to the families of patients as auxiliary resources of care for the patient within and outside of the hospital (Walker, 1991). It is not unusual for a person with AIDS to receive a significant percentage of his care outside of the hospital (Walker, 1991). Very often, the family of the AIDS patient find they must revise their script to accommodate the need for home care.

AIDS is incongruous to the life cycle as aging parents are asked to tend to the health care and ultimately the death of an adult child. Carter (1989) wrote

> Given that persons with AIDS are likely to be adults, a variety of outcomes are foreseeable. Adult parents of persons with AIDS may find income saved for retirement spent on their ill children, families and couples may lose their primary bread-winner or may devote all their available funds to care for the ill family member, and single individuals may find themselves financially devastated as a result of the cost of treating AIDS. (p. 166)

Older parents who had developed a life script that organized their lives in such a way that they worked hard and saved throughout their lives so that they could comfortably enjoy their later years may experience difficulty adjusting to the many requirements of their adult child's illness. They may have further difficulties if they view the disease as a result of behaviors they do not condone. The strain of caring for the AIDS patient may compound preexisting stresses; conceivably the parents of the AIDS patient who returns home for care may already be responsible for the care of their own elderly or infirmed parent. Dissention among family members can result from conflicting individual scripts concerning the extent to which the family is responsible for caring for the individual with AIDS (Kelly & Skyes, 1989). Family members directly involved in daily patient caretaking may become resentful of others who, they believe, have reneged on a family responsibility. For many patients and their families, revising a script to contend with AIDS may mean relinquishing a sense of control (Bartlett & Finkbeiner,

1991; Stulberg & Buckingham, 1988). Families will find that AIDS is a formidable opponent to a script that insists on order and stability as the course of the illness is unpredictable and medical treatment can be, essentially, one crisis intervention after another.

The person with AIDS and his parents, who may have instilled in their children a strong sense of self-reliance, might have difficulty adjusting to his or her increasing dependence as the illness progresses (Bartlett & Finkbeiner, 1991). Couples may lose equilibrium as the well partner is asked to assume more and more caretaking responsibilities (Bartlett & Finkbeiner, 1991; Walker, 1991). For some couples, when the individual who before his or her illness was the predominate caretaker comes to require nursing and nurturing from his or her partner, AIDS can precipitate a major role shift in the relationship (Walker, 1991). One wife of a person with AIDS said that "the more she took out the garbage, paid the bills, and mowed the lawn, the more her husband felt he was losing control, and the unhappier he became; sometimes he was grateful, she said, and sometimes he just screamed" (Bartlett & Finkbeiner, 1991, p. 93).

Levine (1991a) stated, "Traditional families that already have developed internal ways of coping may be totally unprepared for the stress created by external pressures such as stigma" (p. 52). The stigmatization of many of the groups associated with AIDS and the constructs society has adopted for HIV disease may hinder the family's ability to develop an acceptable script for the illness (Tiblier et al, 1989). Stigmatization, be it actual or perceived by the family, challenges the family's constructs about the external world and brings into question how they should operate in relation to that world. For many traditional families, instantaneous admittance into a community that their friends, relatives, and clergy have designated as immoral and deviant can be disconcerting and unsettling.

The approach of some families to disclosure of their son's AIDS diagnosis is often not dissimilar to his secrecy or openness about being gay, as they are likely to have adhered to relatively similar scripts. The family may replicate his coming out process or choose to continue preserving the secret. As "one mother explained, 'When your child comes out, the family goes into the closet'" (Hersch, 1991, pp. 41–42). Opting to contain information concerning the AIDS diagnosis within the nuclear family may lead to a new family script developed specifically to protect the secret. The stress of coping with the illness then becomes further compounded by the additional stress created from the many requirements needed to maintain the secret.

Conflict between family members occasionally will arise if some members, particularly the individual with AIDS, do not agree to operate within the auspices of a secrecy script and wish to be more candid about the diagnosis than others (Stulberg & Buckingham, 1988). Those family members who fear rejection and insist on secrecy must worry over whom to tell and who does or does not know about the AIDS diagnosis, as well as maintain a consistent, plausible story that will explain changes in their behavior (Kelly & Skyes, 1989; Stulberg & Buckingham, 1988). As secrecy and deception become more and more embedded in the family's illness script, the family is apt to feel alienated from friends, neighbors, and coworkers (Kelly & Skyes, 1989). The individual who begins to believe that he or she will be ostracized by others when they learn that a family member has AIDS may begin to reevaluate the nature of those relationships and question the validity of those friendships. That individual may begin to systematically isolate himself or herself, thereby diminishing potential sources of support (Dane, 1991).

Byng-Hall (1991) stated that "the most powerful way to maintain self-deception is to remain surrounded by those who see things in a similar light" (p. 16). As the family systematically severs community ties to hide the AIDS diagnosis, the ensuing isolation places additional pressure on the family system (Tiblier et al., 1989). As extrafamilial influences on the family's developing AIDS script decrease, the likelihood of problematic interaction within the nuclear family may increase. As Tiblier et al. (1989) found, "the smaller the relationship arena, the more intense the pressure on that system" (p. 105). The many stresses resulting from the day-to-day management of AIDS may reactivate long-standing family difficulties and conflicts (Kelly & Skyes, 1989). Individuals may return to the family and reassume roles they had abandoned while living on their own or reenter triangles with parents or siblings. If the secrecy surrounding the diagnosis has isolated the family sufficiently, they may find little respite from the physical or psychological strains of caring for a person living with AIDS.

Gay and heterosexual couples with an infected partner may need to reevaluate their scripts to successfully accommodate intimacy and the AIDS virus. Developing an intimacy script appropriate to AIDS may lead to a reappraisal of current or future relationships and encounters. As Kantrowitz (1986) stated, "I stopped partying as soon as I realized that my survival was at stake, and I settled down in a relationship" (p. 16). Couples living with AIDS may find that they are unable to differentiate their feelings about sexuality from their adverse feelings about the virus (Bartlett & Finkbeiner,

1991; Walker, 1991). As Bartlett and Finkbeiner (1991) have found, "some people equate making love with getting sick" (p. 97).

A family member with AIDS can directly challenge the family's notion that the future can be even marginally predictable. For those families who have been overly reliant on a life script as a means of mastering fear or as an attempt at gaining some control over the future, this lack of predictability can be overwhelming. Families may become frustrated when unable to receive definitive answers from medical professionals about what to expect from the illness or discouraged to find that overcoming one life-threatening opportunistic infection does not preclude the immediate development of a second one. Lovejoy (1990) has found that "Occasionally, a family member may adapt the actress or actor role, pretending that the patient will get well or that a vaccine will be developed in time to save the patient's life. The pretense is difficult to maintain and inhibits the patient from discussing death-related concerns" (p. 303). The timetables of individual family members may no longer be coordinated, with one individual undergoing anticipatory bereavement and another frantically searching for a new drug protocol with the hope of extending the patient's life.

As the illness progresses, the family integrates the demands of the illness into their script so that they can provide adequate care for the person with AIDS. In addition, they also must continue fulfilling many of the basic requirements of their own lives. They must work towards the development of a future script that simultaneously will take into account the loss of the AIDS patient but still be appropriate for surviving family members (Tiblier et al., 1989). Given that there is no absolute schedule for the progression of AIDS and that many families are unaware that an individual is ill until the last stages of the disease, some families may find that these separate scripts for past, present, and future converge throughout the course of the illness. For example, a wife may find that she must combine the tasks of caring for a terminally ill husband with those of working, maintaining a home, and raising children. While continuing to perform many of the functions of her previous roles, it is likely that during her husband's illness, she has assumed many of his as well. And, if she has resisted sharing her husband's condition with others, she may not have an adequate support system. Concurrent with her attempts to manage the constant stresses of living with AIDS is the necessity that she begin to make appropriate plans for her children and herself in anticipation of the impending death of her spouse.

Tiblier et al. (1989) found that in "a couple where one person is sero-positive and the other is not, each person may have a different time frame for life" (p. 108). Whereas the partner with AIDS may feel a need to address unresolved issues or reconcile with the family of origin, the other may not experience the same sense of immediacy. The pressing needs of a medical crisis or the underlying realization that the life of the person with AIDS may be prematurely curtailed can result in the family's belief that there is insufficient time to complete unfinished business with the AIDS patient. However, families may be unwilling to address negative feelings or express anger at the individual, as they believe the person with AIDS already has experienced excessive suffering as a result of the disease. Often the family's AIDS script will lag behind the progressive stages of the illness and compromise the patient's ability to manage the later stage of the illness and anticipate or plan for his or her death.

Families with rules that prohibit the discussion of painful topics such as death, much like those families who prohibit discussions of homosexuality or drug use, may find that these rules compel them to relinquish the opportunity to repair or restore relationships with the family member who is dying of AIDS. Terminal patients may find that their families attempt to prevent or discourage conversations concerning the extent of the disease or certain medical interventions as the family insists on proceeding as if the patient will soon recover. The denial, utilized by the family before AIDS, may not be discarded with the onset of the illness; but rather, it may become reworked into a script that now denies anticipating the death of the patient in many of the same ways that it denied aspects of his or her life.

## SETTING THE STAGE: AIDS AND THE FAMILY'S LIFE SCRIPT FOR THE FUTURE

Rolland (1989) wrote that patients with a disease such as AIDS and their families experience

> an undercurrent of anticipatory grief and separation that per-
> meates all phases of adaptation. Families are often caught
> between a desire for intimacy and a pull to let go, emotionally,
> of the ill member. The future expectation of loss can make it
> extremely difficult for a family to maintain a balanced per-
> spective. (p. 463)

As the expectation of the loss expands into the family's illness script, they begin to revise that script for the future, making adjustments for the eventual loss of the person with AIDS.

The individual patient with AIDS may require a reconnection to key relationships, as well as a reconciliation of his self-definition and self-esteem with the suffering incurred as a result of the illness (Moynihan et al., 1988; Walker, 1991). He or she may want to make explicit his or her plans or hopes for the futures of the survivors, fulfilling obligations or tending to those responsibilities that he or she anticipates continuing after his or her death (Moynihan et al., 1988). Adequate provisions for the custody of children will be a crucial issue for parents with AIDS (Bartlett & Finkbeiner, 1991; Drucker, 1991; Walker, 1991). Unable to sufficiently complete the tasks of parenting, the parent with AIDS may wish to structure a script that secures a future for his or her children after his or her death.

Lovejoy (1990) stated that the anticipatory grief of the families of terminally ill patients "begins when the patient begins to withdraw his emotional investment in others" (p. 307). For some AIDS patients, this withdrawal may coincide with the completion of unfinished business or may be related to progressive neurological impairment resulting from the illness itself. The patient may retreat from the family, turning instead to the medical professionals for palliative care and the management of increased pain (Reiss, Gonzalez, & Kramer, 1986; Walker, 1991). The family's response to this initial separation from the dying patient can be a precursor of the ways in which they will integrate loss and bereavement into the script they are currently constructing for use after the death of the person with AIDS.

Dane (1991) discussed the detachment process that the family of the AIDS patient may undergo during the later stages of the illness as the limitations for treatment of the illness become increasingly apparent. Caregivers begin to anticipate, and perhaps hope for, the end of the illness nightmare (Land & Harangody, 1990). Dane (1991) reported that during this process, "Hospital personnel sometimes complain about families' callous behavior or lack of interest in the PWA [person with AIDS]" (p. 114). However, this stage actually may be a rehearsal of the script that the family soon will find they must reenact. They therefore begin partially to reinvest in their relationships with each other and begin the reassignment of roles and functions to compensate for the decreasing involvement of the terminally ill patient (Dane, 1991; Grief & Porembski, 1988; Macklin, 1988). Yet this initial period of detachment does not guarantee the family's transition to a future-oriented script or eradicate the influences of the scripts that were utilized before the family experienced the loss of a loved one to AIDS.

Walker (1991) stated that "the meanings that family members give to AIDS will define their participation with the patient and the healing of their own system throughout illness after the patient dies" (p. 10). It is unlikely that any family's script can sufficiently prepare them for the devastation presented by the death of a family member from AIDS. However, it would seem that those families who insist on a rigid adherence to the pre-illness script, or whose belief systems deny the inclusion of the AIDS experience, will have greater difficulty integrating that experience into the family's narrative.

Byng-Hall (1991) stated, "Coping with threatened loss for any indeterminate period makes it much harder for a family to define present and future structural and emotional boundaries" (p. 149). Although this is apt to hold true in the case of any chronic, terminal illness, there are restructuring dilemmas that in some ways are unique to a loss from AIDS (Tiblier et al., 1989; Walker, 1991; Weiss, 1989). As families confront AIDS bereavement, they may find accomplishing the tasks of reorganization after the loss hindered by many of the same obstacles they faced during the patient's illness.

Families of people who have died from AIDS embark upon the bereavement process depleted and, in some ways, diminished by the experience of having cared for someone dying of the disease. Long-term vigilance to the needs of the patient (and for many families the relentless requirements of caring for a dying person at home) combines physical exhaustion with emotional fatigue (Kelly & Skyes, 1989). The death of the patient, however, does not offer the family respite as they must then meet the adjustment demands of bereavement. This can be especially difficult for the partner or other family member who, once directly involved in the patient's care, must, after the death, relinquish the caretaking role assumed during the stages of illness. This caretaking role may have served as a buffer to many of the stresses associated with anticipating a life devoid of the person with AIDS, and the loss of that person constitutes the ensuing loss of that role. Compounding the loss of the person with AIDS, bereaved spouses or partners contend with what Lovejoy (1990) described as "secondary losses" (p. 308). These losses may be comprised of the lack of social support, the loss of the couple identity, a possible decrease in economic stability, and the loss of a sexual relationship (Lovejoy, 1990).

The loss of a partner may bring the arrival of previously unaddressed concerns about the status of one's own health or that of a child (Land & Harangody, 1990; Oerlemans-Bunn, 1988; Walker, 1991; Weiss, 1989). Many of the somatic responses to bereavement, such as chills, shortness of breath, and muscle weakness, may appear to the survivor to be the harbingers of early HIV disease. And the individual, whose caretaking of the partner has left himself or herself attuned to noticing any minute physical changes, may begin to anticipate undergoing a similar medical crisis and an equally untimely death (Weiss, 1989). As Oerlemans-Bunn (1988) has found, "Among bereaved lovers of men who have died from AIDS, the fear of developing the disease is both acute and very painful. And, in view of our current knowledge of transmission, it is painfully realistic" (p. 474). The bereaved partner who is infected with the AIDS virus may face the prospect of his own declining health without the same level of support he was able to provide to his deceased mate—worrying that "there will be no one to take care of me when I need it" (Land & Harangody, 1990, p. 477). The surviving partner may feel guilty for not having saved the patient, or for subjecting him to what often were painful and ultimately ineffective medical procedures (Oerlemans-Bunn, 1988). If both members of the couple were seropositive for the HIV virus, the remaining partner may be concerned that he brought the virus into the relationship and feel culpability for the death of his mate (Lamendola & Wells, 1991; Land & Harangody, 1990; Oerlemans-Bunn, 1988; Walker, 1991). The seropositive individual also will become susceptible to the taxing effects that the psychological strain of bereavement may place upon his health (Oerlemans-Bunn, 1988; Walker, 1991). Walker (1991) reported that the stress accompanying loss and grief can compromise the immune functioning of the bereaved, noting that "to a person who is immuno-compromised or already ill with AIDS, the death of a partner constitutes a serious threat" (p. 250).

Single women with children may find that the impact of losing their spouse is obscured by overwhelming economic, housing, and child care issues, as well as their own infection with the virus (Levine, 1991b). These substantial issues, which may need to be addressed with immediacy in the midst of mourning, can divert the family's focus away from constructing a script that adequately incorporates the loss of the husband or father.

Many gay and heterosexual families experience losses from AIDS while devoid of their accustomed support systems. As the result of self-imposed isolation or fear of stigmatization, they may not look to extended family, their church, or friends for assistance in navigating the bereavement process (Lovejoy, 1990; Oerlemans-Bunn, 1988; Walker, 1991; Weiss, 1989).

If the family devised a secrecy script at the onset of the AIDS experience, this secrecy may permeate the script that the family adopts for mourning and reorganization after death. Families who were unable to differentiate their negative feelings about the AIDS-inducing behaviors from their feelings of love for the person with AIDS while he or she was ill, may find that disclosure impinges upon their ability to retain the memory of their loved one in a positive frame or is construed as posthumous disloyalty to the deceased.

Bereaved gay life partners may have already experienced multiple losses to AIDS and may find their support system depleted by the epidemic (Helquist, 1989; Lamendola & Wells, 1991; Oerlemans-Bunn, 1988; Walker, 1991; Weiss, 1989). This may be particularly problematic for the gay partner who, furthermore, may be cut off from his own family of origin and unwilling or unable to elicit their support (Oerlemans-Bunn, 1988). Reluctant to open up discussions of his own sexuality, the bereaved gay lover may return to work and refrain from discussing his experience with coworkers or colleagues. Or, as Oerlemans-Bunn (1988) reported, many gay men "only publicly demonstrate grief appropriate to the death of a good friend but not to the loss of a long-term partner" (p. 474).

Future-oriented scripts founded in shame and secrecy surrounding the AIDS death may present special difficulties for children in families with AIDS (Tiblier et al., 1989; Walker, 1991). Denial and confusion concerning the death of a parent may permeate the scripts of these children beyond the bereavement stage, for "it is hard to grieve when one cannot openly discuss the cause of death" (Tiblier et al., 1989, p. 114). Issues of trust and/or deception may become predominant themes for children who have been prohibited from understanding the nature of a parent's death. These issues may remain an influential part of their meaning system and the development of their own scripts for years after the death of the parent. Byng-Hall (1991) stated that at a "fundamental level, the way that the members of the family normally manage all their separations and losses determines the way that the distress of grieving is handled" (p. 131). In this way, the earlier scripts of separation are played out in the script the family constructs for loss and bereavement.

However, for some AIDS families, there may be a history of an inability to contend with losses in previous generations, as is often the case in the families of substance abusers (Stanton & Thomas, 1992). Or there may be an aversion by the family to acknowledging differences, as in the case of those families who disown a gay son or a drug abusing daughter. For these families to integrate the loss of a member from AIDS, it would seem that their former life scripts would require revision so that the AIDS death would not become another unacceptable difference or unresolved loss. Difficulty developing a post-AIDS narrative may arise precisely because the family has experienced an enormous shift and yet continues to try to perceive itself as if the shift has not occurred. Because of the negative cultural implications of AIDS, the family may remain reluctant to identify with the disease or the ensuing AIDS death. This reluctance, coupled with an attempt to diminish the pain of the loss, may encourage family members to identify instead with distorted roles from the illness and dying script (Byng-Hall, 1991). Byng-Hall (1991) categorized these distorted roles as "the dying person; good caregivers who attempt to help, or in the imagination, may even manage to prevent death; failed caregivers who are often held responsible for deaths; or killers who take an active role in promoting the death" (1991, pp. 132–133). The opportunity for overidentification with the deceased permeates the mourning stage of the gay partner, who may be infected with the same virus as the lover who died (Byng-Hall, 1991; Oerlemans-Bunn, 1988; Walker, 1991). However, this identification is not necessarily limited to the partners of the person who died. Members of the family, perhaps as a function of a shared sense of difference from the others in the family system, may incorporate this particular feeling of camaraderie into a "replicative script" (Byng-Hall, 1991, p. 133). This script can be potentially dangerous if it precludes the seropositive partner from attending to his own medical care; if it is motivation for a family member to engage in self-destructive activities, such as drug use; or if it results in the individual phobically curtailing his or her life to avoid "all contexts similar to that in which the death occurred" (Byng-Hall, 1991, p. 133).

The permanent stance of either a successful or thwarted caregiver may be a natural post-AIDS script for the individual who already may have participated as a caregiver to the deceased for years. And, as previously noted, the role of the ineffective rescuer may have been operable in the drug abusing family before the introduction of AIDS into the family script (Byng-Hall, 1991; Tiblier et al., 1989). Discouragement caused by the caregiver's inability to save the person who died of AIDS may result in the composing of a script in which the surviving individual seeks out those circumstances where he or she may prevail at the successful, or conversely, the repeated failure of, saving others (Byng-Hall, 1991).

Identifying with a perpetrating role can be harmful to others as well as to the survivor, if the individual engages in harmful behaviors as a result of the role assumption (Byng-hall, 1991). This is especially salient in the case of those survivors infected with the virus whose sexual behavior in the role may be potentially fatal to new partners who they may infect. An overly corrective adaptation of this role, designed to manage fears about death's unpredictability, may result in a script that calls for the individual excessively restricting or curtailing any activity deemed dangerous (Byng-Hall, 1991).

## CO-SCRIPTING AN AFTERLIFE: IMPLICATIONS FOR INTERVENTION FOR FAMILIES WITH AIDS

Bereavement offers a family an opportunity for change stating: "One of the advantages of grieving work is that the intensity and urgency of the emotions that are generated can be used to get people together and to alter the family structure" (Byng-Hall, 1991, p. 135). If bereavement offers the chance to alter family structure, it follows that it will be a time when the family's script will be readjusted as well. Intervention, therefore, should be aimed at assisting the family as they integrate the AIDS diagnosis, the stages of the illness, and ultimately, the death into the family's meaning system in such a way that they can competently manage the health care requirements presented by AIDS, but also so that they can eventually redirect their energies to new experiences and relationships after the person with AIDS has died (Walker, 1991; Walsh & McGoldrick, 1991).

Families can be encouraged to reconnect by exploring shared experience or by focusing on those aspects of the person with AIDS that do not reflect the virus-contracting behaviors (Walker, 1991). Meeting on common ground can be the impetus the family requires to eventually address and accept differences. For example, a family's constructions about homosexuality can be revised to accommodate new information. Describing this as a "template for recognition and growth," Walker (1991) stated the following:

> . . . the experience of learning about their child's life, his friendship network, the meaning that being gay has had for him, and of caring for him within this context can be transformative, deeply enriching their lives, their sense of themselves as a family. It may even transform their politics. (p. 17)

To counteract feelings of stigmatization and isolation, patients and their families can access services or support from organizations such as The Gay Men's Health Crisis or local peer support groups for People with AIDS and the Families of People with AIDS (Walker, 1991). Bereavement groups specifically designed for those who have lost loved ones to AIDS can present families with safe, nonjudgmental environments in which they can address the loss without fears of rejection or reprisal.

Families can be directed toward developing new rituals that will serve to memorialize the person who died with AIDS and that add to their comfort. One family, in memory of their son, joins his friends in a yearly march to raise money for research directed at finding a cure for the AIDS virus. Therapeutic intervention can assist the family who rejects sharing their grief publicly by helping them develop memorial practices or rituals that are better tailored to fit their particular family's needs (Walker, 1991). Or surviving family members may choose to participate in rituals specifically related to AIDS, such as the Names Project or AIDS quilt. As family members and friends work together to create a panel honoring the person who died, they begin to reflect on aspects of his or her life not connected to the disease while continuing to acknowledge the enormity of their loss. The Names Project, in particular, is an AIDS ritual that disputes the family's isolation, as when it is assembled, each individual panel becomes one of many thousands (Imber-Black, 1991).

Byng-Hall (1991) commented "A family death teaches individuals not only how to mourn but also how to die" (p. 131). Clinical intervention after an AIDS death can help families develop ways to cope with the loss that will become part of the family's post-AIDS script but not necessarily be limited to AIDS. Coming to terms with the loss of the family member by finding value and significance in his or her life can be expansive and retained by the family to assist with losses they may encounter in the future.

Interventions that facilitate the person with AIDS' self-acceptance, that aid in resolving outstanding family conflicts, and that help the patient achieve a dignified death also will become an integral part of the surviving family's life script (Walker, 1991). Clinicians who are able to help the patient accomplish these goals serve as deliverers of his or her gift to the family members left behind, as the surviving friends and family will have the legacy of the quality of the AIDS patient's death, as well as his or her life, to include in a later death script of their own (Walker, 1991).

## REFERENCES

Bartlett, J.G., & Finkbeiner, A.K. (1991). *The guide to living with HIV infection*. Baltimore: The Johns Hopkins University Press.

Bayer, P.B. (1989, April 2). A life in limbo. *New York Times Magazine*, p. 48, column 1.

Bosk, C.L., & Frader, J.E. (1991). AIDS and its impact on medical work: The culture and politics of the shop floor. In D. Nelkin, D.P. Willis, & S.V. Parris (Eds.), *A disease of society: Cultural and institutional responses to AIDS* (pp. 150–171). Cambridge: Cambridge University Press.

Byng-Hall, J. (1988). Scripts and legends in families and family therapy. *Family process, 27*(2), 167–180.

Byng-Hall, J. (1991). Family scripts and loss. In F. Walsh & M. McGoldrick (Eds.), *Living beyond loss: Death in the family* (pp. 130–143). New York: W.W. Norton.

Cain, R. (1991, June). Relational contexts and information management among gay men. *Families in Society: The Journal of Contemporary Human Services*, 344–352.

Carter, B. (1989). Societal implications of AIDS and HIV infection: HIV antibody testing, health care and AIDS education. In E. Macklin (Ed.), *AIDS and families* (pp. 129–185). New York: Harrington Park Press.

Coleman, S.B. (1991). Intergenerational patterns of traumatic loss: Death and despair in addict families. In F. Walsh & M. McGoldrick (Eds.), *Living beyond loss: Death in the family* (pp. 260–272). New York: W.W. Norton.

Cramer, D., & Roach, A. (1988). Coming out to Mom and Dad: A study of gay males and their relationships with their parents. *Journal of Homosexuality, 15*(3/4), 79–92.

Dane, B.O. (1989). Time of ending: New beginnings for AIDS patients. *Social Casework, 70*, 305–309.

Dane, B.O. (1991, February). Anticipatory mourning of middle-aged parents of adult children with AIDS. *Families in Society: The Journal of Contemporary Human Services*, 108–115.

DiMarzo, D. (1989). Double jeopardy: Hemophilia and HIV disease. In J.W. Dilley, C. Pies, & M. Helquist (Eds.), *Face to face: A guide to AIDS counseling* (pp. 260–266). Berkeley: Celestial Arts.

Drucker, E. (1991). Drug AIDS in the city of New York: A study of dependent children, housing, and drug addiction treatment. In N.F. McKenzie (Ed.), *The AIDS reader: Social, political, ethical issues* (pp. 144–176). New York: Meridian.

Garrett, J.E. (1988, September). The AIDS patient: Helping him and his parents cope. *Nursing, 88,* 50–52.

Gelman, D., Foote, D., Barrett, T., & Talbot, M. (1992). Born or bred? *Newsweek, CXIX*(8), 46–52.

Grief, G.L., & Porembski, E. (1988). Implications for therapy with significant others of persons with AIDS. *Journal of Gay and Lesbian Psychotherapy, 1*(1), 60–66.

Helquist, M. (1989). Too many casualties: HIV disease in gay men. In J.W. Dilley, C. Pies, & M. Helquist (Eds.), *Face to face: A guide to AIDS counseling* (pp. 289–295). Berkeley: Celestial Arts.

Hersch, P. (1991). Secret lives. *The Family Therapy Networker, 15*(1), 36–43.

Holleran, A. (1989). The fear. In J. Preston, (Ed.), *Personal dispatches: Writers confront AIDS* (pp. 38–46). New York: St. Martin's Press.

Imber-Black, E. (1991). Rituals and the healing process. In F. Walsh & M. McGoldrick (Eds.), *Living beyond loss: Death in the family* (pp. 207–223). New York: W.W. Norton.

Kantrowitz, A. (1986, September). Friends gone with the wind. *The Advocate*, 454.

Kelly, J., & Skyes, P. (1989, May). Helping the helpers: A support group for family members of persons with AIDS. *Social Work*, 239–242.

Lamendola, F., & Wells, M. (1991, May). Letting grief out of the closet. *R N*, 23–25.

Land, H., & Harangody, G. (1990, October). A support group for partners of persons with AIDS. *Families in Society: The Journal of Contemporary Human Services*, 471–480.

Levine, C. (1991a). AIDS and changing concepts of family. In D. Nelkin, D. P. Willis, & S.V. Parris (Eds.), *A disease of society: Cultural and institutional responses to AIDS* (pp. 45–70). Cambridge: Cambridge University Press.

Levine, C. (1991b). The special needs of women, children, and adolescents. In N.F. McKenzie (Ed.), *The AIDS reader: Social, political, ethical issues* (pp. 200–214). New York: Meridian.

Lovejoy, N.C. (1990). AIDS: Impact on the gay man's homosexual and heterosexual families. *Marriage & Family Review, 14*(3/4), 285–316.

Macklin, E. (1988). AIDS: Implications for families. *Family Relations, 37*, 141–149.

Maloney, B.D. (1988). The legacy of AIDS: Challenge for the next century. *Journal of Marital and Family Therapy, 14*(2), 143–150.

Monette, P. (1988). *Love alone: Eighteen elegies for Rog.* New York: St. Martin's Press.

Moynihan, R., Christ, G., & Silver, L.G. (1988). AIDS and terminal illness. *Social Casework, 69*, 380–387.

Nungesser, L.G. (1986). *Epidemic of courage: Facing AIDS in America.* New York: St. Martin's Press.

Oerlemans-Bunn, M. (1988, April). On being gay, single, and bereaved. *American Journal of Nursing*, 472–476.

Reiss, D., Gonzalez, S., & Kramer, N. (1986). Family process, chronic illness and death: On the weakness of strong bonds. *Archives of General Psychiatry, 43*, 795–804.

Rolland, J.S. (1989). Chronic illness and the family life cycle. In B. Carter & M. McGoldrick (Eds.), *The changing family life cycle: A framework for family therapy* (pp. 433–456). Needham Heights, MA: Allyn and Bacon.

Round, K.A. (1988, May). AIDS in rural areas: Challenges to providing care. *Social Work*, 257–261.

Savin-Williams, R. (1989). Coming out to parents and self-esteem among gay and lesbian youths. *Journal of Homosexuality, 18*(1/2), 1–35.

Schaper, R.L. (1987, August 12). Pastoral care for persons with AIDS and for their families. *The Christian Century*, 1–4.

Stanton, M.D., & Thomas, T. (1982). *The family therapy of drug abuse and addiction*. New York: Guilford.

Stulberg, I., & Buckingham, S. (1988, June). Parallel issues for AIDS patients, families, and others. *Social Casework, 69*, 355–359.

Tiblier, K. (1987). Intervening with families of young adults with AIDS. In M. Leahey & L.M. Wright (Eds.), *Families and life-threatening illness* (pp. 255–262). Springhouse, PA: Springhouse.

Tiblier, K., Walker, G., & Rolland, J. (1989). Therapeutic issues when working with families of persons with AIDS. In E. Macklin (Ed.), *AIDS and families* (pp. 81–128). New York: Harrington Park Press.

Urwin, C.A. (1988). AIDS in children: A family concern. *Family Relations, 37*, 154–159.

Walker, G. (1991). *In the midst of winter: Systemic therapy with families, couples and individuals with AIDS infection*. New York: W.W. Norton.

Walsh, F., & McGoldrick, M. (1991). *Living beyond loss: Death in the family*. New York: W.W. Norton.

Weiss, A. (1989). The AIDS bereaved: Counseling strategies. In J.W. Dilley, C. Pies & M. Helquist (Eds.), *Face to face: A guide to AIDS counseling* (pp. 267–275). Berkeley, Celestial Arts.

# Chapter 9

# UNSCRUPULOUS SCRIPTS: SCRIPTS FOR FAMILY VIOLENCE

*Joan D. Atwood*
*and*
*Michele Olsen*

Webster defines unscrupulous as, "A disregard for what is considered right or proper; lacking moral integrity" (Webster, 1984).

Who decides what is right or proper? What is moral integrity, and how does one know when it is lacking? What seems to be philosophical is relatively simple. Values, such as morality, integrity, and the rightness or wrongness of an act, are dependent on the consensual recognition of the said act in the context of the society in which it is realized. Although individuals and societies differ as to what they believe to be unscrupulous, the common thread lies is that all behavior is scripted. Scripts are blueprints for behavior that guide our actions and make clear our roles and expectations of ourselves and others (Gagnon & Simon, 1967). Unscrupulous scripts represent those behaviors that, once realized, are deemed wrong and immoral by a given society or a majority of its constituents. In our society, there are many scripts that most would define as unscrupulous but none more heinous and unsettling than domestic violence.

The recognition of domestic violence is relatively new. The attention paid and theories proposed have been traditionally sporadic and fragmented. The one concept that has been a useful predictor and that has sustained over time is the fact that participants in domestic violence come from generations of those using violence in the home. The participants either are involved directly or act as spectators. In other words, the scripts for domestic violence are unscrupulous legacies, passed down from generation to generation.

# NOTION OF SCRIPTS

The concept of scripts has major implications in understanding the causes, consequences, and prevention of domestic violence. This chapter has as its focus the variables that allow scripts for family violence to be played out and perpetuated. The chapter focuses on family violence in the forms of incest and wife beating. It offers socio-historic variables, as well as therapeutic implications and treatment for the prognosis and cessation of domestic violence. To understand the generational transmission of such unscrupulous behavior, one first must ask how such scripts are created and maintained.

According to Berne, (1972), scripts in general come from a preconscious life plan, representing lifelong structures filled with ritual activities that give immediate satisfaction and further the scripts (Berne, 1972). These scripts begin in early childhood and originate in a primitive form called *protocol* (Berne, 1972). Because the young child generally is limited to exposure to family members such as parents and siblings, the roles are played out rigidly, and the child does not learn much flexibility. The scripts for violence are learned and perpetuated even after the child grows and moves away from the rigid family system, because he or she generally seeks out others who will participate in the script. There is strong support in the data that suggest that over 50% of abused children eventually become abusing parents (Denzin, 1984), 47% of battered wives eventually enter a new battering relationship, and more than half of abused children eventually become abusers or become abused in instances of domestic violence (Wetzel & Ross, 1983).

Parents transmit a script as a part of their normal parenting with the purpose of nurturing, protecting, and encouraging their children by showing them how to live (the way in which the parents themselves learned). The child seeks to perpetuate this parentally programmed script because

- it gives a purpose to life,
- it gives an acceptable way to structure time,
- children generally need direction, and
- the child is dependent on the parent for basic needs (Berne, 1972).

Before investigating the specific forms of family violence and their relevance to scripts, it is important to keep certain concepts in mind while reading this chapter. First, scripts require

- parental directives,
- a suitable personality development,
- a childhood decision,
- a real interest in a particular method of success or failure, and
- a convincing attitude (Berne, 1972).

Most importantly, each person decides how he or she will live the rest of his or her life. "The destiny of each human is decided by what goes on inside his skull when he is confronted by what goes on outside his skull" (Berne, 1972).

# SOCIAL CONSTRUCTION OF DEVIANCE

Family violence is considered not only immoral and unscrupulous by a majority of individuals but often is labeled as ***deviant behavior*** because of the violation of social norms and legal system involvement. Family violence is not only a problem in the personal sphere of the family but also one that is both perpetuated by and considered unscrupulous by society.

**What Is Deviance?**

A problem in most research is operationalizing of the concept being investigated. Family violence is no exception. Labeling these behaviors "deviant" complicates matters more because it imposes a value judgment. Value judgments are made by those living in a particular culture or society. Social norms are created and, once established, violators of the social norms are ostracized or punished. Given the history of family violence, it is not difficult to see that social norms have been altered and redefined in light of what can be considered deviant behavior. It is important to state that different cultures and societies have different definitions and scripts around the treatment of family members and what is considered deviant behavior. What is defined as deviant is dependent upon the culture and historical period in which it is being defined (Gagnon & Simon, 1967).

### How Does One Become Deviant?

To speak of deviance is a contradiction. The violators of major social norms are always strangers, either in the literal sense or in the sense that they are products of highly exceptional processes, but few deviants invent their own patterns of deviance (Gagnon & Simon, 1967). The learning of deviant scripts can be understood only with the application of the same conceptual language with which we approach the learning of scripts that suggest conformity. The major criteria of deviant or unscrupulous scripts are not to be found in the behavior as such but rather in its definition as norm-violating behavior. There is no form of behavior that is intrinsically deviant (Gagnon & Simon, 1967). With the exception of incest (a universal taboo), there is a wide variation between cultures as to which specific scripts are defined as unscrupulous or deviant.

Labeling an act or script as deviant in a society requires three elements:

- laws that punish the behavior,
- mores shared and internalized norms of a populace, and
- the actual pattern of behavior exhibited by that population (Gagnon & Simon, 1967).

For an act to be considered deviant, there must be a high correlation between these three elements. This pathological deviance must exist without supportive group structures that serve to recruit the behavior, train the participants, gather participants for its performance, or provide social support for the actor (Gagnon & Simon, 1967).

An act is further deviant if the status and role of the participants depart from the status and role expectations for these persons. For example, the socialization of children requires that parent-child authority relations be maintained. Incest, for instance, is universally tabooed primarily because the status and role expectations for family members cannot be fulfilled when sexual behavior is permitted between members of the same family (Twitch-ell, 1987). While the majority of individuals in our society deems family violence as deviant or unscrupulous, how is it that it is so prevalent? As stated earlier, family violence is not only an individual problem but also one that is perpetuated by society while at the same time frowned upon by society.

It is possible to explore this contradiction by looking at the media. While there seem to be more and more movies and talk shows aimed at educating the public about the prevalence and destructiveness of family violence, other TV channels air typical soap opera scenes in which two lovers resolve their prior violent argument between the sheets. Add to this the flooding of the market with violent video games, and we seem to be a society intent on creating violent individuals. These contradictions and the romanticizing of violent interactions support the beliefs that family violence is an appropriate and constructive way to solve problems and end disputes.

## FEMINIST MOVEMENT

The feminist movement had a great deal to do with the recognizing, publicizing, and fighting against violence and injustices to women and chil-dren. However, there still is a long way to go, primarily because family violence against women and children have a long embedded history. Besides the traditional female role as defined by a patriarchal society, there were other factors that served to reinforce (for better or worse) the position of women and children in our society. One only has to trace the history of the family to see the strides and also the impediments to the cessation of family violence. Of great historic importance is the perpetuation of certain scripts that serve to create, maintain, and perpetuate the beliefs about the treat-ment of family members (Denzin, 1984).

## TRADITIONAL FAMILY

While the social pendulum swings from repressive to permissive social values over time, how people feel about basic issues such as romance, infant life, and family solidarity tends to be a socio-historical constant. Yet the historic transformation of the family has had much to do with the way we view family relationships and family evils. Differences between the contemporary and traditional family may shed some light on the issue of family violence. Elements such as privacy, romantic beliefs, interpersonal relations, and the role of power and control (sex roles) have affected the script of family violence. For example, in the traditional family (16th and 17th centuries), family solidarity and obedience to both family and community scripts were of great importance. The script of the traditional family was established firmly by three sets of ties (Shorter, 1977):

- to kin,
- to the community, and
- to generations, past and future.

An awareness of ancestral traditions and ways of doing things produced scripts about how people led their daily lives. The purpose of life was to prepare coming generations to continue what past ones had done (Shorter, 1977). There were clear rules for shaping family relationships. The traditional family was one that was reproductive and instrumental. Women and children were considered property to be punished or disposed of if they did not meet the needs of the family. There was a strong sense of community solidarity to which the family surrendered its members. The demands of the community were placed above individuals' personal ambitions and desires. Community solidarity had a large impact on scripts and treatment of family members. Community intervention in family life enabled others to compel individual family members to follow collective rules through disciplinary sanctions. The community was not so concerned with the actual offenses against family members as it was with the offenses' consequences on the social order of the community.

Traditional scripts represented a preference for authority over personal choice and custom over spontaneity and creativity. This authority was held by males. There was a strict demarcation of work assignments and sex roles. The male dominated community arranged for private behavior to conform to the public morality. Anyone attempting to break these scripts was ridiculed or punished.

In a society that held as its values absolute sex roles, the de-emphasis of family loyalty and caring, the ownership of women and children, and community reinforcement and often approval of family violence, it is no wonder that women and children in the traditional family suffered such violence and degradation (Walters, Carter, Papp, & Silverstein, 1988).

# CONTEMPORARY FAMILY

The contemporary family (19th and 20th centuries) brought many changes. The contemporary family is one brought together in order to fulfill the socio-emotive needs of its members—mutual love and caring. It is an emotional unit rather than an instrumental unit. Family solidarity has replaced community solidarity and control. This family is a private system in which members feel they have more in common with one another than they do with anyone on the outside. They enjoy a privileged emotional climate that they protect from outside intrusion through privacy and isolation (Shorter, 1977). The dividing line between private and public spheres is clearly drawn. Efforts to blur it are seen as offenses against civil liberty. While these changes have had a positive impact to some degree, these changes have major implications for the families of violence and the perpetuation of this violence through the keeping of family secrets.

At first glance, it appears that the contemporary family has come a long way. On the surface, the contemporary family looks like a stable emotional unit of equality, love, and caring. Research in fact does indicate that most violent families do not contain ogres and monsters as violent families often are depicted as having. Actually, most violent families have loving and caring members who wish to remain together (Blackman, 1989). Even though violence in families goes against the value of the family as being a safe haven, one must keep in mind that if the family can be considered the natural context for healing and growth, it also can be considered the flip side—the natural contest for violence and exploitation (Luepnitz, 1988).

In this chapter, family violence is defined as an unscrupulous script because it goes contrary to the reasons why most come to form a family in the first place—a safe haven, where one has high expectations of love, caring, equality, and fulfillment of needs.

# THE FANTASY

"Once upon a time, there was a family who solved problems through mutual communication and compassion, and had a vested interest in the health and safely of its members. They argued once in a while but always respected each other's rights as individuals. The children in this family grew up, got married, and lived happily ever after."

To violent families, this script is more a fairy tale than reality. The only stable expectations that these actors experience are those of terror and victimization. In some instances, the script unfolds as one of consistent terror. In other instances, the terror is unpredictable and sporadic (Gondolf, 1990). In both cases, the finale is one of disappointment, disillusionment, betrayal, and sometimes even death.

Like any other play, the performance of family violence involves certain elements of production, organization, selection, rehearsal, and, most importantly, script formation. If scripts are well written and the actor's performance well accepted by most viewers, a play enjoys many weeks or even years of success. The scripts of family violence seem to represent a dichotomy. While the script is well prepared and perpetuated, the actor's performance is less than acceptable. With this in mind, how does family violence continue over time?

The successful presentation of a script has much to do with its actors. The actor first must learn the script and have the opportunity to practice or perform it with others who also know the script well. These other cast members are significant in that they have important supporting roles that enable the actor to maintain his or her status and perpetuate the script. Once a cast member attempts to deviate, the script is different. The plot usually remains the same, but the actions are different and generally unsettling to the rest of the cast. In terms of family violence, this applies not only to the perpetrators but to the victims as well.

The script of family violence is much like that of a film star who has a son or daughter to which the "legacy" is passed down. The child observes the parent behind the scenes, learns the business, emulates the style of the parent and eventually gets an agent to further his or her own career. The child is socialized in a world of fantasy and glitz. He or she is sucked in easily. This fantasy lifestyle is perpetuated by significant others who believe and act in the same way. Thus, within this family sphere, there is a consensual recognition that this behavior or lifestyle is appropriate. Even when the child experiences other actors who disapprove of the child's script, the child is reluctant or unable to edit or rewrite the script. This problem (isolation and alienation) is solved by the child by only associating with the actors in his or her own family script.

As stated earlier, the contemporary family is a tightly bound unit mainly responsible for the socio-emotive needs of its members. As social institutions took over more and more of the traditional functions of the family, the family became increasingly more protective of its boundary in terms of the larger social system, thus making it difficult to move in and out of the family unit. Families of violence play to private audiences. They charge no admission, but the cost is high. What keeps the actor in this script is the fear that he or she cannot do or succeed in a different script. Although he or she may not enjoy the role, he or she denies this and obediently plays his or her part. The most powerful way to maintain self-deception is to remain surrounded by those who see things in a similar light (Byng-Hall, 1988).

The family continues to play to a captive audience. Their script is perfected through many years of repetition and rehearsal. Cue cards are no longer needed. Each member of the cast has built a mental representation that predicts sequences of interaction in particular situations (Berne, 1972). These patterns of interaction also serve to define the roles and rules of the relationships between the cast members.

While the best of scripts/plays get much attention, the most horrific scripts either get no attention or a lot of negative publicity. Researchers disagree as to the rise or decline of family violence. What they do agree upon is its consistency across time. Main factors in the degree to which it is recognized are the emotional zeitgeist, its being intertwined in other social issues, the legal status of such events, the amount of social awareness, and the willingness to admit that such things occur.

A major impediment to the above factors and implications for research is the stigma associated with this script. Participants are embarrassed, blame themselves, or feel there are no options (Kantor & Okun, 1989). This fact leads to the belief that statistics on family violence are much lower than reality.

As long as there have been families, there has been family violence. Only a few decades ago, the term family violence meant child abuse, wife beating, and incest, which were understood as family violence but not recognized as serious social problems. Social problems first reflect injustices individually, and then are collectively experienced and publicly acknowledged (Blackman, 1989).

For the purpose of this chapter, family violence will include those acts (physical, emotional, or sexual) that family members engage in or view that hinder human growth and development. In the past, there has been the problem of lumping the different forms of destructive family behaviors under the rubric of family violence. The reason for this may be that the causes and consequences of the different forms have many of the same implications and share many commonalties. While this lumping together of the many forms of destructive family behaviors may simplify research and give a generic understanding, it does not do justice to the unique plights and circumstances of the individuals involved in different forms of violence. The clustering of these different types of abuse doubly victimizes those involved because these individuals are victimized first by their families and then by the victim-blaming public.

If it is society's and therapy's goal to foster the uniqueness and self-esteem of these individuals, it seems necessary to, on one hand, give credence to their unique experience and, on the other hand, help them see that they are not alone.

## "WE OFTEN HURT THE ONES WE LOVE"

This is the family motto in families of violence. We all have heard the cliché, but most of us do not live it to the extent that families of violence do.

In the 1960s and 1970s, there was a reawakening of concern for the abuse of women and children. This was due, in large part, to the multi-issue woman's movement that had attention focused on bringing these personal scripts to public scrutiny. Another factor that brought recognition to these issues was the growing concern for the "crisis of the family," in which family violence was seen as a symptom. Another factor was that America was becoming a culture of self-exposure. "There was a decline in the old etiquette of modesty and privacy in personal life and a new acceptability of a confessional mode" (Shorter, 1977).

The 1960s and 1970s brought much attention to violence between family members. This was sparked by a crusade for the rights of individuals and began with the concern for the welfare of children (Shorter, 1977). This was furthered by the women's movements and expanded from women's individual rights to the rights of women and children in the family. The crusade for the protection of women and children is far from over, but over the years we have seen more research and investigation, more training for mental health professionals, an increase in outside support such as shelters and groups, an increased sympathy from courts and the police, and recognition and protection from legislation (Barker, 1984).

The explanations for family violence shifted back and forth from an explanation of individual pathology to a problem of society and finally to a concept of mutual causality. The actual explanation is perhaps a complex mixture of all factors, mainly because a script does not emerge from a vacuum. Violence in families is not purely spontaneous. It is produced and experienced in situations that have been given, handed down, and tolerated by all (Denzin, 1984).

The explanation of individual pathology is not sufficient on its own. In fact, most abusers are not psychopaths or in any way "mentally ill" (Grizzle & Proctor, 1988). This explanation is too narrow in that it posits a single causal variable and ignores others. Some forms of family violence are more vulnerable to this school of thought. Within the following pages, one can see the traditional influence of thinkers such as Freud on attempting to get at the etiology of family violence at the expense of other family members, especially the mother.

Mutual causality is another theory that not only ignores other factors but also reinforces the victim-blaming mentality, postulating that the victim either provoked or deserved the attack (Margolin & Fernandez, 1987). The recognition and analysis of violence between family members is still in an early stage. Its underdevelopment is due in part to the discontinuity of attention, insights from earlier periods (Freud), and the great social changes of the mid-20th century that define the family in intense social form.

The script of family violence is one that is played out and perpetuated on three levels: (1) the interpersonal, (2) the individual, and (3) the societal. As stated earlier, individuals learn scripts in their families of origin. They then interact with others who fit the script and ignore those who do not (Berne, 1972).

The societal expectation of the family as an emotional unit condones family violence to some extent. The script that society has constructed about the family suggests that whoever you are and whatever you do, you always will have the love of your family members. This gives family members much leeway and is almost a license for any/all kinds of unscrupulous behaviors without repercussion. Individuals frequently discharge violent feelings and impulses in the informal settings of their families, rather than direct the emotionality to where those feelings originated (Barker, 1984).

Individuals in our society inherit different degrees of power depending on their sex, race, class, and age. These differences often are acted out in intimate relationships (Margolin, 1987). The family, in particular, is a social institution that permits and sometimes encourages its members to psychologically or physically hurt each other. People often hurt each other in recognizable patterns that mirror the power (or lack of it) that different members hold in society (Margolin, 1987).

No act of violence is simply the pitting of one individual against another. Each act appears to have deep cultural and psychological meanings. Furthermore, no act of violence is merely a social problem, such as poverty or a male dominant society. Implications for therapy, as well as a general understanding, are served better when family violence is looked at as a personal script, acted out by a unique individual.

**Web of Violence**

The ***web of violence*** is a term used to describe families of violence. "It indicates that family violence spreads from member to member and generation to generation, and it invariably traps every newborn member of long-ensnared families" (Goldenberg & Goldenberg, 1991). Like a spider's web, it traps its victims without killing them right away. No matter how hard the victims try to escape, they remain inextricably trapped for life. In the case of family violence, the head spider is usually male. It is generally a male spider who weaves the violent web that the flies are stuck to. This is the case in 85 out of 100 webs studied (Giles-Sims, 1983).

**A Script of Betrayal**

Although family violence is acted out in different ways, the scripts are basically the same. While the abusers and the abused usually have come from family histories of violence and their scripts are well rehearsed, predictable, and familiar, it does not lessen the uneasiness or betrayal that the abused feel from being attacked by a loved ones. What serves to perpetuate and immobilize these abused individuals is the incorporation of denial into their scripts. This denial is a protective mechanism that serves to legitimize the scripts. Denial rationalizes unscrupulous behaviors in several ways:

- the abused may predict the dangerousness of the situation,
- the abused may feel that they deserved the attack,
- the abused may make excuses for the abuser,
- the abused may incur self-blame for the incident, and
- the abused even may deny that the event occurred at all (Ables & Brandsma, 1988).

The victim even may attempt to normalize the situation. If he or she had grown up in a family who used unscrupulous scripts to express love, rage, or to solve family disputes, the admittance that this is wrong seems foreign to him or her. What is worse is that if he or she is living an unscrupulous script and feels uncomfortable with it, the danger lies in not knowing any other script.

**Evil Takes Many Forms**

Evils in society often go undetected. This is due in part to evil's ability to keep itself secret by taking many forms. Sometimes it goes undetected; people choose to close their eyes and ears, hoping that it just goes away. "Children should be seen but not heard" is a perfect example of family's loyalty demands to their unscrupulous scripts. In a family of violence, the script is acted out in the form of mime. The actors are mute and often invisible. Their script often calls for mechanical, zombie-like performances. For most members, it is better to be zombie-like than to have to ponder about and live in a reality of self-degradation and humiliation. These zombies have no will and only answer to one master, their "script keeper." In over 85% of the cases of family violence, the "script keeper" is the husband or father in charge of keeping the zombies in their roles (Giles-Sims, 1983). In another sense, all family members can be considered "script keepers" due to their conscious or unconscious roles in maintaining the script.

The script of family violence always has the same plot but with different variations. There are many different ways in which family members choose to hurt each other. These ways usually take the forms of physical, emotional, or sexual abuse, or different combinations of the three. A child who has experienced or viewed a particular form of family violence will not necessarily use that particular form of violence in adult life. The probability that he or she will use violence in some form in family interaction is high (62%), but the form it takes is also dependent upon the particular violent script of the other members (Berne, 1972). For example, a physically abused child may not grow to abuse his or her children but instead choose to beat his or her spouse. It is generally the male perpetrating violence upon the female, and this can take the form of wife beating or father-daughter incest. It is only in the cases of child abuse where the female is the perpetrator as often as the male (50%) (Giles-Sims, 1983).

An important and most unfortunate aspect of family violence is that victims of other types of violence may live with fearful and painful memories, but victims of family violence must live with the actual perpetrators!

# INCEST SCRIPT

To the untrained eye, incest appears to be a script built around sexual deviance. This often is not the case. Most incestuous fathers are not pedophiles (1 in 10 is) (Spencer, 1978). Like the rest of the injustices that are discussed in this chapter, incest is a script that stems mainly from issues of power and control. Although the acts involved are sexual, the script is one of domination, submission, and often retribution.

Like most unscrupulous scripts, the incestuous script has many actors. These actors participate either directly or indirectly (Friedman, 1988). The starring roles in incestuous scripts usually are assigned to the father and daughter (94%) (Twitchell, 1987). The adult female (mother) is the perpetrator in 5% of the cases (Lang, Langevin, Van Santen, Billingsley, & Wright, 1990).

## Defining Incest

Incest has been defined in many ways both legally and culturally. Spencer (1978) defined incest as any form of sexually arousing, physical contact between members of a family who are not permitted to marry—it need not involve intercourse. Bradshaw (1988) defined it as overt sexual intercourse occurring between members of a group who are not permitted to marry because of blood ties or legal relatedness. The common elements between the two definitions are those of related actors and the imposition of an overt or covert sexual act. More recently, the definition has been expanded to include relatives or semi-relatives such as the mother's boyfriend (Twitchell, 1987).

## The Incest Taboo

Whatever the definition or form taken, the prohibition against sexual activity between family members is the most universal and strongest taboo in all human societies (Ford & Beach, 1951). There are few societies that have exceptions to this script. Those that do usually differ a great deal on their definition of the family (Belkin & Goodman, 1980). There are many reasons why there is such a universal repulsion to such a script. Most explanations for this stem from the biology of inbreeding (Twitchell, 1987). Other reasons stem from psychological and sociological theories. One such theory postulated by Parsons is that "the taboo is functional for the family and for society" (Belkin & Goodman, 1980). Parsons wrote that erotic drives are seen as potentially disruptive forces within the family.

Theories of the incest taboo explain everything except the striking fact that it is generally always the male who abuses the female. Whether incest is viewed as a biological law that prevents inbreeding, a sociological law that creates exogamy, or a psychological law that promotes viable interpersonal boundaries, the incest taboo should theoretically apply equally to both sexes (Luepnitz, 1988).

"It is believed that men seem to be over represented in this role, because their socialization psychologically prepares them and socially permits them to behave in ways which make this kind of violation plausible to them" (Luepnitz, 1988, p. 223). These male dominant belief systems create belief states that form the male role. This role is played out in a script that is reinforced by society's larger script that is one of male dominance reinforced by a "government of men" (Walters et al., 1988).

This particular script is one that the actors not only play their starring role but also act as understudies for absent or unavailable cast members. Usually, it is the incest victim who holds the script together by aiding the perpetrator in his or her rehearsal of lines and making sure he or she is able to function within the script. This proposes a heavy and unjust burden on the understudy who is forced to learn not only his or her lines but to care for the fragile egos of other cast members. This also produces jealousy on the set. The "leading lady" (mother) may resent the attention given to the understudy. As a result, the leading lady may try to sabotage, blame, or even encourage the understudy to work harder so that the "leading lady" may rest.

Assessment of family interaction and effects are discussed in the following pages, but it is evident that the incestuous script and family is one that contains confused roles, poor intergenerational boundaries, and a problematic relationship between the leading male and female as primary variables (Jacobson & Gurman, 1986). It further involves the individual problems of the family members, the organization and structure of the family, and the interactional aspects of those involved (Friedman, 1988).

The incestuous script is unscrupulous because it fails to meet the basic needs of its members for nurturance, care, and warmth in an appropriate and mature way (Belkin & Goodman, 1980). In the incestuous family, children are responsible for parental roles. While dependency and intimacy may occur in the family (when they involve sexuality), aside from within the marital unit nonsexual dependency and intimacy only occur outside the family unit. This intrafamilial sexual intimacy becomes extremely private and emotionally isolating (Lang et al., 1990). Loyalty to the family comes to mean survival, and outsiders are viewed with distrust (Giles-Sims, 1983).

There are many variables that serve to keep the incestuous script closed to the public. The fact that incest is taboo makes it all the more shameful. Incest is believed to be the most shaming of any form of violence (Blackman, 1989). This is due in part to the victimization and betrayal by a loved one, self-blame because of submission, fear of repercussion inside and outside the family, and a feeling of loyalty to the perpetrator (Belkin & Goodman, 1980). These factors participate in the victim's immobilization and fear around divulging the secret. This fact is evidence that "sex offenses against children are barely noticed except in the most violent and sensational instances" (Kantor & Okun, 1989). Most are never revealed. The average duration of an incestuous relationship is 3.1 years (Luepnitz, 1988) or until the victim gets married, moves out, or runs away. This silent script creates a nonchanging, closed system in which each member plays his or her role(s). Built into this is what is called the "open secret." This is the vital lie that keeps the family frozen. Everyone knows yet everyone pretends not to know (Bradshaw, 1988). To keep the secret, the incestuous script turns into a myth or fairy tale. Family members try to look on the bright side in order to turn the nightmare into a love story. Reframing the hurt, anger, and distress acts to distract the family from what is really going on (Bradshaw, 1988). In essence, it is a conscious rewrite.

The drama of incest is a violation of the child's sexuality. It is played out on the stage of an innocent child's naive trust. It is fueled further by the child's natural desire to be respectful and to please. For the child, the incestuous script becomes a horror movie, a love story, and a mystery all at once. The child vacillates between emotions and is left confused, violated, and sometimes even cherished because of the extra attention (Gagnon & Simon, 1974). Very often the child feels that the occurrences are his or her fault. At first, the extra attention can be flattering, even pleasurable. As the "night visits" progress to stages of intercourse, the first emotions called for in the script are that of raw fear and terror (Spencer, 1978). These feelings then turn to anger, embarrassment, hurt, abandonment, shame, and sometimes denial. For anyone called upon to play so many roles, there is bound to be confusion. The child first turns the anger inward (Spencer, 1978). The child cannot believe what is happening; the child does not/cannot believe that his or her parent is bad. Furthermore, the child needs his or her parent in order to survive. For the sake of survival, the child attempts to internalize his or her parents at their worst (Bradshaw, 1988). When the parent is acting in a way that is most threatening to the child's survival, the child records this vividly. The child adapts to the threat and internalizes it to survive (Bradshaw, 1988). Further confusion is caused by the fact that the parent wears two masks: lover and father/mother. The child never knows what mask the parent will wear at any given time. The child's sibling relations also are affected because of the special attention the child is getting.

Until the recent influence of feminism, Freud's work was the only basic scholarly analysis of incest. Freud's work stated that there is childhood sexual desire for the parent. In light of this, many accusations by children were dismissed as pure fantasy (Twitchell, 1987). The traditional literature also points to the ***collusive mom***. This is a mother who was frigid, has a lack of sexual interest in the husband, is away from home a lot, or either actively or passively participates in the abuse (Lang et al., 1990). The traditional theory also states that the husband feels no other recourse then to turn usually to his only or older daughter. Unfortunately, the traditional explanation scapegoats females by painting the mother as failing to protect daughter and failing as a wife. It even goes to the extent to suggest that the child's seductiveness is the problem. Most traditional therapies focused on the intrapsychic components of the offender. While this is an important step, it is overshadowed by other goals aimed at keeping the family at a level of interaction.

Just as controversial as traditional therapies is the use of a family systems perspective pertaining to family violence. This perspective postulates that the family is diseased, not the individual (Jacobson & Gurman, 1986). This perspective believes that everyone is responsible, but no one is to blame.

Contemporary theorists now point to a different script and assess at levels of individual, spousal, and parental. The concept of responsibility belonging to the father (or other abuser) is neither ignored nor minimized.

## Therapeutic Implications

In therapy, it is not only important to understand the family dynamics and interactions but also to understand how and where the belief systems that formed the scripts originated. Since this script has been played out for many generations, it is important to first intervene at the level of the belief system. This social constructionist theory espouses the importance of joining in an attempt to create a new reality (Atwood, 1993). This concept underlies all work with families of violence and is discussed in summary. Therapy with incestuous families is unique. It must be careful in its application because of the boundary violations involved (Jacobson & Gurman, 1986). More important is to keep in mind certain family myths, dynamics, and a realization of a social reality called the poisonous pedagogy (Bradshaw, 1988).

## Poisonous Pedagogy

The ***poisonous pedagogy*** sets up the roles and scripts that are played out in families of violence. It espouses inequality of power, denial of feelings, and the ownership of children (Bradshaw, 1988). It is a form of violence that violates the child's bodily rights and is passed down to the child's own children. Children are considered obedient and good when they behave as they were taught.

Important pre-conditions are generally in place by the time the incest begins. Pre-conditions consist of the following:

- adults are the masters,
- adults determine right from wrong,
- children are responsible for the anger of adults,
- parents always must be shielded,
- children's wills must be broken at any early age,
- a feeling of duty produces love,
- parents deserve respect,
- severity is a good preparation for life, and
- strong feelings are harmful (Bradshaw, 1988).

Most of these "conditions of the family contract" are carried unconsciously and are activated during stress or crisis. Parents do not even have
a choice about these beliefs until they have worked through and edited their
scripts with their own parents (Bradshaw, 1988). The poisonous pedagogy
plays a major role in the script of incest. It implicitly gives permission for
sexual abuse by promoting a kind of ownership of children (Bradshaw,
1988). If the child must honor and obey the parent at any cost, the parent
implicitly has the right over the child's body.

Before embarking on any form of treatment, the therapist must keep
in mind the degree of immediate danger to the child (remove or keep child
in home), reporting laws, legal implications, and certain unique family
dynamics. When the "secret" becomes "public knowledge," the crisis that
it presents relies heavily on the bond between the mother and daughter (in
the majority of cases, which are of father-daughter abuse). This is important
for two reasons:

- There is much resentment on both sides: The daughter feels that the
  mother did not protect her, and the mother feels jealous or perhaps
  does not believe the daughter.
- The mother must be able to protect the daughter from further violations—in essence, the scene must become a closed set. This is
  often difficult to accomplish because of the already ruptured mother-
  daughter relationship.

Very often the daughter is much more willing to forgive the father than
the mother (Belkin & Goodman, 1980). The father perhaps has made her
feel special. He has visited her. The daughter perhaps also has experienced
power in her position to bargain with the father for what she wants. The
treatment approach is less important than the incorporation of these basic
concepts derived from an understanding of the incestuous family pattern
(Gagnon & Simon, 1974).

Keeping these dynamics in mind, the therapist now must assess as to
the best type of treatment (individual, couple, or family). The ideal situation
would be to explore the belief systems/scripts on all these levels. This is not
always possible. Instances that might deter this are if the father is in jail
(less than 20%) (Spencer, 1978), the mother is unwilling to be in the same
room with the husband, the child's fear of being in the same room with the
offender, or the siblings' disbelief that this situation could ever happen
(Spencer, 1978). Whichever mode is deemed best at the time, it is crucial
to begin counseling right away. This is because the best time to get a com-

mitment from the offender is when he or she is most upset. At the beginning, it is important for family members to have a clear communication about what has happened and its possible consequences (Grizzle & Proctor, 1988).

## Joining

Establishing a relationship with the offender is crucial. This often presents an ethical dilemma for most therapists, who may view this man as an ogre, undeserving of help. As with any client, it is necessary for therapists to discard biases and create a safe environment, and be considerate of where the person came from, where he or she is now, and where he or she wants to go. After a rapport has been established, it is important to help the offender recognize that it is incorrect to blame the child in any way. The offender must "own" his or her behavior and be able to look at how his or her unscrupulous scripts originated.

At the same time, immediate efforts must be made to bolster the offender's broken self-concept. Some offenders have no remorse or do not recognize the wrongness of their actions (Lang et al., 1990), but most feel out of control and truly ashamed. The offender's self-concept can be raised in many cases by arranging for him or her to continue relating to the family in every possible way (Bradshaw, 1988). Considering the circumstances, this is often difficult but becomes easier as family therapy progresses.

If the offender needs much support, the victim needs much more of it! The victim must believe that the therapist is committed to ending the sexual abuse. The victim must be made to feel protected and helped to face what happens to him or her, because he or she is important (Gagnon & Simon, 1974). Important therapist skills are those of listening, reflecting feelings, empathizing, and, above all, conveying to the victim that he or she is cared about and believed. In many instances, the victim's significant others did not believe what was going on. He or she was labeled a liar. Other times, the victim actually was blamed for the events. Above all, therapy is aimed at bolstering the victim's self-esteem so that he or she sees that this was something done *to* him or her, not *by* him or her (Belkin & Goodman, 1980). In session, this is furthered by the offender taking full responsibility and absolving the child fully and sincerely.

Because of the many strong feelings felt by all members, it is important to validate, join, and always create that safe environment. Strong feelings of hate, love, and even ambivalence should not be contained but encouraged. This is necessary because of the lack of communication in incestuous families (Belkin & Goodman, 1980).

In looking at the structure and interactional patterns/scripts of incestuous families, one might agree that some things may appear problematic. Data suggest that incestuous fathers had a negative sexual or exploitive experience during childhood (47%) (Friedman, 1988). While most can feel for such an upbringing, most would agree that this is no excuse. In our society, people feel uncomfortable when they themselves or others are out of control. To be able to control oneself and survive hardships suffered is a feat that is highly valued. It represents strength, endurance, and an upright moral constitution. When people commit crimes and exhibit unscrupulous behavior against others, they more often than not hold rationales that exonerate themselves to others.

Most theorists would agree that much of who we are stems from early childhood experience and ongoing interaction with those in our environments. While scripting theory explains and gives us an understanding of the abusers and the abused, allowing abusers to use their past as an excuse is just as detrimental as the violence itself. Part of creating a new script or reality is being able to bury the past and rewrite the present and future. If we inherit our blueprints for behavior in childhood, then we must take responsibility for those blueprints' rightness or wrongness. The decision to inflict any type of violence is a personal decision.

The issue of family violence touches all of us deeply because each of us is part of a family. At one time or another, we might have encountered a family situation in which we may have anticipated violence or even had a fleeting thought of using violence to vent frustration or impose our will. When family violence involves children, it is even more unsettling. This is because contemporary society views children as valuable and, for the most part, an enhancement to our lives. Their innocence and helplessness oftentimes make them more endearing and can bring out the Santa Claus in even the worst of scrooges. The script for violence against children is one that never should have been written. Unfortunately, it has an extremely long history embedded in both society and families. In order to prevent a cycle of never ending sequels, it is necessary to educate the public, create more support systems and options such as parent effectiveness training, and open more fully our eyes and ears to the cries of children.

Many of us attempt to search for the "child within." When we are having fun or letting loose, our behavior often is described as childlike.

When we are upset, we often regress to childlike behaviors—we want to be parented.

Ponce de Leon searched long and hard for the fountain of youth—an attempt to turn back time to one filled with energy, curiosity, and unconditional love. If you asked an adult survivor of incest if he or she would like to take a drink from the fountain, you more than likely would get an emphatic ''No!''

## Selective Memory

If the survivor of incest is lucky enough to forget, then the script dies for the moment. For most victims, this forgetting is not a reality. There is a theory that postulates that even when a dissociation does occur in the form of forgetting the incident, the body retains the feelings and expresses them in physical manifestations. It is very common for child sexual abuse victims to experience dissociation in the form of multiple personality disorders, flashbacks, chronic depression, and, for some, even suicide. Incest is not only an unscrupulous script, but also one that, if not intervened upon, has a variety of serious implications—none of them good. Whether a victim ''forgets'' or not is of great consequence in light of future implications—we should remember that to forget one's nightmares is to forget one's dreams. The nightmare of incest is about the silence of nights spent holding in screams, holding back tears, holding in one's very self (Bradshaw, 1988).

# WIFE BATTERING SCRIPT

Another equally unsettling form of family violence is that of wife battering. It is just as unscrupulous because it represents the imposition of power of the stronger over that of the weaker. It shares much in common with other forms of family violence in that it is evidence of the subordination of women in our society and families.

Unlike the unscrupulous script of incest in which the parents' script is imposed on the child, wife battering involves the co-creation of two violent scripts coming together and finding each other. Considerable evidence suggests that the chronically abused wife has been socialized for that role. She does not necessarily cause her victimization, but to her it is predictably scripted part of the marital experience (Blackman, 1989).

A woman who continually is abused by her husband tends to come from a family where either both of her parents physically abused her or where her father demonstrated frequent violence against her mother (Blackman, 1989). Most abusing men come from a childhood lacking of warmth or a sense of family love. He too might have been abused or was likely to witness his father physically abusing his mother (Blackman, 1989).

Two things are very evident. First is that each spouse comes from a violent family history in which physical violence was used to express feelings and/or to solve problems (Denzin, 1984). Second, it does not matter whether the spouses experienced the actual abuse or viewed it; the learning still took place, and the script was still handed down. To view abuse is to be abused (Denzin, 1984).

What does appear to make a difference in whether or not the child becomes an abuser or becomes abused is the reaction to the violence in his or her family (Margolin, 1987). If the father is successful in imposing his will and the mother acts in a submissive manner, the child will be likely to identify with the script of the same-sex parent (Belkin & Goodman, 1980). This socialization is fundamentally a process of emulation of the reference group. If the behavior of that group has undesirable characteristics or outcomes, the child makes the decision not to follow the script (Barker, 1984).

Between 26 and 30 million spouses are abused annually (Wetzel & Ross, 1983). Up to 50% of all American wives have been hit or beaten by their husbands, and it is estimated that one third of all married couples will experience violence at some time in their marital relationship. A statistic even more surprising is that one quarter of abuse is husband to wife, one quarter is wife to husband, and one half is mutual (Margolin & Fernandez, 1987). Given these statistics, why is it that more attention and sympathy is given to wives of spouse abuse? In fact, in 50% of the cases, it is the wife that initiates the first blow (Wetzel & Ross, 1983).

An explanation for this is that men are usually of greater size and strength and capable of inflicting more serious injury or even death (Kantor & Okun, 1989). The script of wife beating is nothing new. In our society, a certain amount of violence in marital relations is so common that it is considered normal (Jacobson & Gurman, 1986). In the past, men were expected to physically chastise their wives to reduce wives from their errors.

They were responsible for their wives' behavior and were expected to take whatever measures to keep them under control (Shorter, 1977).

Besides a family of origin script of violence, husband-to-wife violence is legitimized by cultural (sex role) norms. One prominent characteristic of violent men is their belief that to be a man one must be strong, dominant, superior, and successful. Feelings of inadequacy in these areas were devastating to the man's self-esteem. Violence erupts when the man no longer can defend himself from his sense of inadequacy (Blackman, 1989).

What is misleading is that most men who batter are neither psychotic nor are they brutes. What makes them able to solve problems peacefully on the outside and leave manners and morals at the doors of their homes? One explanation is the high expectations and dysfunctional beliefs that people bring to marriages. These scripts include the following:

- If you get too close to someone, you will be controlled or hurt;
- A person is fully responsible for his or her spouse's happiness or unhappiness; and
- You do not have to be polite to your partner as you would a friend or acquaintance or stranger.

These scripts, coupled with high expectations, produce a volatile environment that, upon disappointment and a violent history, will explode.

Usually, the violent script makes its appearance long before the wedding vows are even uttered. The first episode usually occurs in courtship (Margolin, 1987). Women report that they are usually aware before marriage of the violent tendencies of their soon-to-be husbands (Margolin, 1987). Before the violence can become stabilized in the marriage, it first must occur. It may take the form of a slap or an all-out beating. It usually is associated with an oversight on the wife's part, and is defined as insignificant or denied as a form of abuse (Margolin, 1987). Very often, the wife takes responsibility or makes excuses for the husband: "I deserved it," "He had a hard day," "He did not mean it; it was a love tap," or "He was drinking." The reality is that it was not insignificant, accidental, or an appropriate way to vent feelings and frustration. Many women also fool themselves into believing that it was a onetime occurrence (Margolin & Fernandez, 1987). This belief immobilizes the woman from leaving the marriage, seeking help, or even suggesting marital therapy.

This onetime occurrence belief is part of a cycle of violence in which the violence occurs, the woman feels betrayed, the husband acts contrite, remorseful, and loving, and the wife remains in the marriage (Giles-Sims, 1983). Even when the woman comes to see herself as a victim, she usually will fight tooth and nail to prove how helpless she is, as if there was some reward for being powerless. These women usually have low self-esteem and refuse to believe that they have any power to rewrite their scripts on an individual level or in their marriages (Margolin, 1987). In cases where the woman feels uncomfortable enough or confident enough to rewrite the script, the two options are usually: (1) to leave the marriage and find outside support or (2) to suggest marital counseling. Unless the husband feels uncomfortable as well, these two options will meet with resistance. If the woman attempts to distance herself or leave, this activates the husband's sense of a loss of love and endangers his masculinity. His violent script kicks in, and he may threaten his wife with murder or beat her on the spot. Marital counseling also produces a threat to the husband's masculinity. To go for counseling would be to admit that the script he grew up with was defective in some way. For these individuals, defects equal powerlessness. The woman is then put in a script of a dubious nature. There is no safety in leaving and no safety in staying (Margolin & Fernandez, 1987).

What about women who actually do get their husbands into therapy? This is usually accomplished by: (1) the woman actually leaving, not to return until the husband agrees to come to therapy, (2) a court mandate, or (3) a recognition of the problem by the husband. Any of the three ways, this is the first step to a new and healthier script. The agreement to enter therapy or the dissolution of the marriage puts the couple in a state of "limbo." This limbo or crisis leaves them more open to change and success. Although great strides have been made in the prevention and even recognition of wife beating, the training of mental health professionals, intervention of police, and laws creating greater sanctions all leave something to be desired.

The successful cessation of marital violence is attributed first to the couple's reaching out for help, the rising number of women's shelters and support services, and public education and awareness of wife beating as a serious problem (Margolin & Fernandez, 1987). Most success is viewed in couples who choose to leave their scripts at the door and enter marital therapy. It should be noted that anyone practicing marital therapy should include an assessment of the probability of violence, especially in discordant marriages (Giles-Sims, 1983).

What makes most women end the violence is a severe beating requiring hospitalization or outside intervention or the realization over time that the violence is part of a scripted pattern. They stop believing that the violence will never happen again (Giles-Sims, 1983).

As with incest, there is a stigma and the need for secrecy around the issue of wife battering. This is due in part to the victimization of victims. Society reinforces the victims' beliefs that they did something to provoke or deserve the attack (e.g., "One blow to the mouth will quiet a nagging wife for a long while.").

When the violence reaches a crisis level, the couple is more likely to seek therapy. Working at the level of meaning is difficult, especially with the offending men. They view it as a threat to their masculinity. They also may feel that they have been getting what they want through using violent behavior. They may have tried more nonviolent ways that were not as successful (Gondolf, 1990).

**Therapeutic Interventions**

Therapeutic interventions that have met with the most success in recent years have been those taken from behavioral marital therapy. In addition to using these interventions, it is necessary to provide both individual and group counseling to both the abused and the abuser.

In the beginning, therapy is a didactic process. The therapist must convey an absolute abhorrence for any kind of violence and further explain that it is not only destructive to all family members but that it is illegal (Giles-Sims, 1983). Also, no matter what the circumstances, it is an individual decision to use violence in a marriage, and it is a personal decision to stop (Margolin & Fernandez, 1987).

Other concepts and "truths" imparted to the couple are the following:

- The abuser is solely responsible for the violence—the victim cannot cause or eliminate it;
- Violence is a learned behavior from each family of origin—if the husband can learn to be violent, he can learn to be nonviolent;
- Provocation does not equal justification; and
- Once violence has occurred, it is likely to continue unless changes are made (Jacobson & Gurman, 1986).

Once this information has been imparted to the couple, ground rules must be set along with the consequences of breaking them. The most important rule is the immediate cessation of any kind of marital violence. A popular consequence of violation is having the couple separate if the violence continues (Margolin & Fernandez, 1987).

With an understanding of and agreement on the rules, therapy works to produce behavior changes using specific strategies to accomplish the following:

- direct control of the violent behavior and
- resolution of the marital conflicts that set the stage for violent behaviors.

Therapists also can help their clients in identifying cues to violent behavior, time-outs, relaxation, self-talk, and stimulus-control procedures (Ables & Brandsma, 1988). It also is advised that each spouse attend groups in order to be in an environment that serves to empower them and give them the feeling that they are not alone.

Communication and problem-solving work can be done once the crisis is over. Therapists must be very careful and guarded about their prognoses for violent couples. This is because there is usually a "flight to health" or "honeymoon period" in which there is a cessation of violence. This cessation can last for weeks or months but usually leads to another violent occurrence (Jacobson & Gurman, 1986).

In any type of therapy, be it conjoint or individual, the therapist must face certain issues and recognize certain dynamics. Therapist assessment and concern always must be focused on the possibility of immediate danger and the ultimate protection of the abused (Giles-Sims, 1983). The therapist must be prepared with resources such as shelters and hotline numbers, and be on the lookout for the possibility of things such as child abuse. If it is evident that the violence cannot be brought under control, the therapist must abdicate the role of relationship advocate and get the victim the protection she needs (Margolin, 1987).

If the therapist is working toward dissolving the marriage, he or she must keep in mind that if intervention has not been focused on the woman's script, she probably will enter into another relationship that is just as abusive. Most battered women, upon leaving a marriage, almost immediately enter into a new relationship. They enter with the same script and continue to play the role they have since childhood (Jacobson & Gurman, 1986).

Many times, a therapist will see a battered woman alone, because she has either left her marriage or her husband refuses to come because of ignorance or fear of being blamed. In these cases, a therapist must empathize, reflect feelings, rephrase, summarize, prioritize, and clarify (Jacobson & Gurman, 1986).

Rule number one is to believe and validate the horror of the woman's experience. The therapist should not be afraid to reveal his or her own feelings of horror and repugnance. This allows the woman to get in touch with her repressed anger and rage. This is important because many women feel they have no right to be angry (Jacobson & Gurman, 1986). In doing this, the therapist not only joins but shows the woman that she is accepted as a competent person with rights and options.

When working with couples who come from a history of childhood violence (such as most cases of spousal abuse), it is necessary not only to provide the couples with behavioral techniques in the hope of producing attitude change but also to attack the meanings and attitudes directly.

The concepts proposed by social constructionists have given us an understanding as to where are meanings come from and how they are maintained, and, more importantly, give us an idea of how to participate in the co-construction of a new, nonviolent reality for couples.

Attempts at replacing one's script (good or bad) must be approached with caution. This is because a person's script is all he or she has known and lived up to this point. In cases of family violence, though, caution basically must be thrown to the wind and replaced with sometimes brutal honesty.

When an assessment has been made as to the immediate danger no longer existing, one can concentrate more fully and relaxed on helping the couple co-create a new reality. Much of the time, it is advised that the couple do this script rebuilding together. In the instance of wife battering, it is important to have the couple share and understand that their commonality lies in both (more often than not) having had a violent childhood.

By focusing on exceptions to violent incidences, the couple can gain a sense of hope and be more aware of the cues that alert them to impending violence. By further amplifying these exceptions, the couple is helped to enjoy and "deepen the experience of a more positive relationship" and is on the road to constructing a new meaning and script (Atwood, 1993).

There is a common belief among marriage counselors that an indifferent, low-energy couple is one in which the prognosis for saving the marriage is extremely poor. Oftentimes, to see a couple who constantly is engaged in argument can be interpreted as exhibiting a lot of energy and, in a sense, much caring. When couples care enough to fight, they usually care enough period. This is not the case in wife beating. This kind of energy cannot be considered anything but destructive. It is not an expression of caring or love but one of rage, degradation, and humiliation.

Although both participants have known no other script for relating, it does not make it any less uncomfortable each time. The most obvious aspect of this script is the man's recognition that his behavior is inappropriate. This is evidenced by the "kiss-and-make-up" stage in the cycle of violence.

Women as well have the recognition that what is occurring is not right. Fifty-two percent of battered women usually make some attempt, successful or not, to remedy their situations (Margolin & Fernandez, 1987). Why then, if each spouse has one foot out the door of their script, does the other foot remain in cement? One explanation is that contained in a structural definition of family violence are the couple's shared and conflicting scripts toward violence, power and control, and the nature of marriage (Walters et al., 1988). The couple's individual scripts (family of origin), society's stereotype of sex roles, and lack of public recognition all serve to maintain and condone violence between intimates.

## SUMMARY

Incest and wife beating represent only two forms of violence that are inflicted on members in the family. Other forms are child abuse and marital rape. Since the beginning of time, family violence has been a thorn in the side of humanity. The picture of the caveman dragging his woman by the hair is an image with which we are all familiar. With all the attention given by women's groups and, more recently, the media, why has the physical and emotional coercion of women and children in families not seen a marked decline?

The naive acceptance of the home as a safe haven serves to keep us in the dark as to the horrific reality that each of us has the potential to become violent. More at risk are those who grew up in a family whose family script's theme was "it is the strongest that survive." As members of what we hope to be a civilized society, we must focus more not on the strong who use muscle to survive but on those smarter, yet invisible, who hear the brunt of the disappointments and behaviors of the stronger.

# BIBLIOGRAPHY

Gagnon, J., & Simon, W. (1967). *Sexual conduct.* Chicago: Aldine Publishing.

Napier, A. (1988). *The fragile bond.* New York: Harper and Row.

# REFERENCES

Ables, B., & Brandsma, J. (1988). *Therapy for couples.* San Francisco: Jossey-Bass.

Atwood, J. D. (1993). Social constructionist couple therapy. *The Family Journal: Counseling and Therapy for Couples and Families, 1*(2), 116–130.

Barker, R. (1984). *Treating couples in crisis—Fundamentals and practice in marital therapy.* New York: Free Press.

Belkin, G., & Goodman, N. (1980). *Marriage, family, and intimate relationships.* Chicago: Rand McNally.

Berne, E. (1972). *What do you say after you say hello?* New York: Grove Press.

Blackman, J. (1989). *Intimate violence: A study of injustice.* New York: Columbia University Press.

Bradshaw, J. (1988). *Bradshaw on the family: A revolutionary way of self-discovery.* Deerfield Beach, FL: Health Communications.

Byng-Hall, J. (1988). Scripts and legends in families and family therapy. *Family Process, 27*, 167–179.

Denzin, N. (1984). Toward a phenomenology of domestic family violence. *American Journal of Sociology, 90*(3), 483–513.

Ford, C. S., & Beach, F.A. (1951). *Patterns of sexual behaviors.* New York: Harper & Row.

Friedman, S. (1988). A family systems approach to treatment. In L. Walker (Ed.), *Handbook of sexual abuse of children* (pp. 326–349). New York: Springer Publishing Company.

Gagnon, J., & Simon, W. (1967). *Sexual deviance.* New York: Harper & Row.

Gagnon, J.H., & Simon, W. (1974). *Sexual encounters between adults and children. Siecus study guide No. 11: Sex Information and Education Council of United States.* New York: Behavioral Publications.

Giles-Sims, J. (1983). *Wife battering: A systems theory approach.* New York: Guilford Press.

Goldenberg, I., & Goldenberg, H. (1973). *Sexual conduct.* Chicago: Aldine Publishing.

Goldenberg, I., & Goldenberg, H. (1991). *Family therapy: An overview.* Pacific Grove, CA: Brooks/Cole Publishing.

Gondolf, E. (1990). *Psychiatric response to family violence: Identifying and confronting neglected danger.* Lexington, MA: Lexington Books.

Grizzle, A., & Proctor, W. (1988). *Mother love, mother hate: Breaking dependent love patterns in family relationships.* New York: Ballantine Books.

Jacobson, N.S., & Gurman, A.S. (Eds.). (1986). *Clinical handbook of marital therapy.* New York: Guilford Press.

Kantor, D., & Okun, B. (1989). *Intimate environments.* New York: Guilford Press.

Lang, R., Langevin, R., Van Santen, V., Billingsley, D., & Wright, P. (1990). Marital relations in incest offenders. *Journal of Sex and Marital Therapy, 16*(4), 214–229.

Luepnitz, D. (1988). *The family interpreted: Feminist theory in clinical practice*. New York: Basic Books.

Margolin, G. (1987). The multiple forms of aggressiveness between marital partners: How do we identify them? *Journal of Marital and Family Therapy, 13*, 77–84.

Margolin, G., & Fernandez, V. (1987). The spontaneous cessation of marital violence: Three case examples. *Journal of Marital and Family Therapy, 13*(3), 241–250.

Napier, A. (1988). *The fragile bond*. New York: Harper and Row.

Shorter, E. (1977). *The making of the modern family*. New York: Basic Books.

Spencer, J. (1978, November). Father-daughter incest: A clinical review from the corrections field. *Child Welfare*, 581–590.

Twitchell, J. (1987). *Forbidden partners: The incest taboo in modern culture*. New York: Columbia University Press.

Walters, M., Carter, B., Papp, P., & Silverstein, O. (1988). *The invisible web: Gender patterns in family relationships*. New York: Guilford Press.

Webster, D. (1984). *Webster's ninth new collegiate dictionary*. Springfield, MA: Merriam-Webster, Inc.

Wetzel, L., & Ross, M. (1983). Psychological and social ramifications of battering: Observations leading to a counseling methodology for victims of domestic violence. *The Personnel and Guidance Journal, 21*, 423–428.

# Chapter 10

# I THOUGHT IT WAS OUR TURN: THERAPEUTIC CONSIDERATIONS IN MID-LIFE FAMILIES

*Estelle Weinstein*

According to Hagestad and Neugarten (1985), the influence of predictable age systems is that they "develop socially recognized turning points that provide road maps for human lives and outline life-paths" (p. 35). These paths or life scripts are established by a social order of expected or "normative" life events that have "prescriptive" timetables and operate in society as systems of control (Neugarten, Moore, & Lowe, 1965). Societally expected events occurring at their expected time can frame the range of "possible, acceptable, and desirable" future life scripts (Dannefer, 1984; Nurmi, 1992).

Several alterations have occurred within families systems that have implications for mid-life and later life couple living in intergenerational families. These changing health, social, economic, and demographic related factors can produce potentially stressful crises resulting in shifts in family boundaries, meanings, and future life scripts. Oftentimes, past meanings that engender future life scripts are so dissimilar to current contexts that multigenerational families and especially mid-life to later life couples must develop their new scripts with few historically familiar guidelines.

The families we see as clients and the family therapy literature are replete with the problems of primary relationships—parenting young children through adolescence and adulthood. The later life issues tend to be relegated to the gerontological experts (Flori, 1989), who often concern themselves with the problems of negotiating the caretaking of the elderly. Rarely is there a discussion about adaptation problems of families with members in mid- to later life.

Among the major socially influenced changes that interfere with the present and future scripts of mid- to later-life couples are the following: family of origin role models and experiences that are exaggeratedly different from present situations; lifetime economic plans that often change unexpectedly in the present financial arena; the loss or changes in occupational roles that previously defined family members; unexpected illnesses and other disabilities; adult children and their children (single parenthood, divorce) returning to the family setting; the caretaking responsibilities of their aged parents; and the death of one spouse. Future scripts are colored by such factors as gender, socioeconomic status, and level of education (Dannefer, 1984). The increased frequency of later life remarriage, which creates new family systems, and the merging of several cultures and ethnicities also call for unexpected revisions in future life scripts.

Different generations within the family and their experiences with nontraditional role patterns can take many forms. For example, the traditional older couple may be excused, understood, and accepted in the family system more readily than the older couple who has diverged significantly from expected traditional role behaviors (i.e., the older "mom" who works full time may be resented when she is not available for expected grandmotherly activities).

It would be helpful for therapists working with mid-life couples and larger intergenerational family systems to learn about the more frequent family problems that these families experience. The motivation for therapy must be considered. Framo (1981) identified several clinical situations that determine responsiveness or lack of responsiveness to therapy including therapy to settle discord and become closer before the parent's death, therapy to reach one parent that has been unavailable or held distant by the other, therapy to get revenge, and therapy for those overwhelmed with major pathologies or marital crises that interfere with their ability to extrapolate the generational implications. This chapter concerns itself with many issues that face intergenerational families in contemporary society. Implications for therapy then are considered as these families draw their road maps for the remaining stages of their lives.

## MID-LIFE EXPECTATIONS

*The wedding of their youngest son was a special moment. They waited a long time for this experience. Oliver and Joan were approaching their middle 60s and they thought their son, now 30, would never marry, let alone find a very successful job. They spent years paying for college tuition, and now as they drove home from the wedding they were each deep in thought about what it would be like to worry finally only about themselves.*

*Oliver's father had worked until his 80th birthday, never wanting to take a day off. Oliver's mother was a modern woman for her generation. While she maintained the family chores, she also worked part-time. They aged well and needed very little help from their two sons. A year after Oliver's mother's death, his father remarried and lived quite independently until he became ill.*

*Joan remembers growing up in a household with her maternal grand-parents. Her grandfather was a strong patriarchal type who made most of the rules about how things would happen. He was a wealthy man and contributed heartily to the finances of the family. Her grandmother was the "housekeeper." When the grandparents died, Joan's parents retired (in their early 60s). They left Chicago and moved to the south to what they called the "good life." As a result, Joan felt abandoned by them, especially at a time when she needed all the help she could get with her own family of five children. Oliver, on the other hand, thought it was the best thing Joan's parents could have done. All five of Oliver and Joan's children were married, beginning their families, entrenched in their careers, and financially set . . . all except one. Their daughter Lizzie, who has two small children, is recently divorced. While she holds a fairly nice job, she is not able to support herself.*

What is this family's belief system regarding their responsibility for their adult children and their elderly parents? How do the family's notions of residence arrangements and location of kin influence their family's scripts? What are the economic factors that play a role in family interactional patterns? These are among the many questions that influence Oliver and Joan's life's choices.

Nurmi (1992) found that the expectations of the middle aged are related to the final stages of their work, their property or financial status, and their children's lives, whereas later life scripts often are related to health status, retirement, leisure activities, and the losses of a spouse and social network. Such factors as the independence/reliance of the family system and the status of the senior members also affect families.

The continuity of the family experience as studied by (Brubaker, 1985) indicated that interactional patterns in the mid-life to older couple and contentment with their relationship tend to resemble their earlier experiences. Brubaker found that people who were happy in their relationships tended also to be happy later in life. People who were not happy early in their marriages also repeat negative marital interactions later on. For these couples, the dance of distance and closeness was the most frequent complaint and seemed to be maintained in their current lives.

Sociocultural beliefs about the position older family members hold in the family system and in the community also can contribute to the way families design themselves. Lee (1984) found that families that emphasized conformity to parental values and practiced "ancestor worship" placed high values on their mid-life to older members and expected that they would make ongoing contributions to family life. When senior family members are considered "wise" with experience, they are likely to maintain leadership positions where they are respected mentors. Here also the established hierarchies are maintained. In cultures where the experiences of the elderly are defined as outdated, their positions in the family may be threatened. In this situation, mid-life persons often are "sandwiched" between their children who see them as "old fashioned" and their parents who continue to see them as children.

## GENDER ISSUES

Gender differences may have a substantial influence on life scripts and the experience of life cycle transitions. Hagestad and Neugarten (1985) found that men's lives are shaped more by occupational influences and women's lives by family factors. Scripts about social networks and patterns of peer and familial relationships also may differ according to gender. Men whose definition of self and self-esteem are defined closely by their work titles or employment activities may have enmeshed social and employment relationships. Out of work social activities, when they do exist, often may be established and maintained by their spouses. Then, when an unplanned change in the working situation occurs (i.e., downsizing resulting in layoffs and/or bankruptcy), the unfamiliar transactions of daily life outside of work can upset the family balance. Men then often expect to spend their time in the daily activities of their spouses or other family members who have their own established routines. The spouses or other family members may resent having to include the men in their activities or feel guilty when they are unavailable to the men. In the case of death of the spouse, the involuntarily unemployed man, who has no independent social network outside, may feel isolated and depressed.

Women, according to Anderson (1984), especially later life women in traditional families, maintain close relationships with friends and family and can turn more easily to their children in times of crises. Because they tend to maintain this social network outside their spousal relationships, they may be less damaged by retirement. Death of a spouse frequently is associated with severely decreased economic status. The decreased finances may result in dependency upon adult children or the need for a major change in living arrangements. When women's scripts were very heavily vested in maternal roles that are no longer available or in cases of those whose social network and activities outside the home are limited, apprehension about mid-life may develop into depression and immobilization in ways similar to their socially limited male counterparts.

From a historical perspective, women of the 1960s and later probably have more common experiences and values about employment, roles, and family life with their grandmothers of the 1940s than with their own mothers. World War II women pridefully entered the work force in large numbers and raised their families at the same time while their spouses served in the military. The jobs women took were not gender restricted, and employment for these women was considered "patriotic duty" (Moen, 1991, p. 135) for which they received respect and praise. Because of their earlier experiences with dual roles, women of the 1940s held later life expectations that were not tied entirely to their maternal and spousal roles (Adelmann & Antonucci, 1989). As a result, their mid-life scripts tended to be less negative than those that ultimately would be evidenced by their daughters. Yet, while the "war" families had shared employment experiences, men's participation in the armed services maintained their masculine definition of themselves. Hence, the male dominated head of the family role was not really interrupted and when the couple planned their middle and later lives, they were likely to be living in traditional family settings.

The postwar period through the 1950s, known as the time of the "feminine mystique," emerged and femininity became synonymous with "wifely and motherly" activities. This generation, the daughters of World War II women, were expected to look pretty and not brainy. If they entered the work force, they were older and more often took employment not by choice but because of increasing family expenses, divorce, or widowhood (Gove, Grimm, Motx, & Thompson, 1973; Oppenheimer, 1974). Also, having entered the work force late and underprepared, their employment opportunities often were demeaning and beneath their intellect. In these families, the definition of husband/fatherhood as the single-handed breadwinner was challenged and often resulted in conflicting interpersonal problems. Women did not achieve employment success with the expected financial rewards, and their mid-life expectations were likely to be negative as their definitions of self remained tied to their diminishing maternal roles (Adelmann & Antonucci, 1989).

From the 1960s on, the ideology of women as career people has grown; large numbers of women prepare for careers and voluntarily and continuously participate in the work force throughout their lives. Couples delay marriage and childbearing to a later age, and the growth of dual career families continues. Where marriage and child-rearing previously were considered strong predictors of women's likelihood of entering and remaining in the work force, the changes in gender roles, choices, and family systems cause marital and childbearing status to no longer clearly predict employment (Moen, 1991).

While there is evidence of more shared child-rearing couples today, an unprecedented number of 1970s women found themselves in single-parent families (Moen, 1991). They were likely to have some career preparation, worked throughout their lives, or returned to the work force from time to time. The data are not complete, but it is speculated that these "feminist movement" women who are presently entering mid-life are likely to view their future job conditions and financial status more positively (Shank, 1988), resulting in a mid-life experience more positive than their mothers (Adelmann & Antonucci, 1989).

## OTHER FACTORS: A BRIEF OVERVIEW

The social and biological realities of aging, in and of themselves, move parents and their children to a shared status of adulthood. The family's vision about intergenerational adult households or the changes in structure of family businesses, finances, and lifelong roles, can determine beliefs about such factors as the proximity within which intergenerational family members will live, how the chores and responsibilities will be distributed, and how the family will experience such events as divorce, death, remarriage, retirement, and ill health. Several different intergenerational family constellations also define the types of problems that may occur.

Aging parents who no longer envision themselves as parents sometimes reverse roles with their mid-life children when they (the aging parents) are needy. The neediness of adult children in the way of financial and child care assistance sometimes results in the adult children perceiving themselves as dependent children. Mid-lifers are squeezed between the problems of their adult children and the problems of their aging parents, often creating problems for both.

According to Eisenhandler (1992), the ways in which mid-life adults and their parents are involved in each other's daily activities in non-caretaking situations have a powerful influence on the positivity and negativity of intergenerational family dynamics. Eisenhandler (1992) further recognized that this generation is probably the first generation of mid-life families to view the long survival of elderly parents as a matter of course. The attachment of family members and the security that attachment engenders in earlier life cycle phases may provide a context for the experiences of trust, fairness, intimacy, control, etc. within the intergenerational adult family (Bengtson & Mangen, 1988; Bowlby, 1980; Troll, 1988). The personality and interpersonal problems experienced earlier in the life cycle phases of the family are likely to continue or, as Hess and Waring (1978) have described it, "freeze" family relationships and mask unresolved issues (p. 251).

Sometimes, adult children attempt to take charge of parents at the first signs of aging. While these attachment behaviors may be given as expressions of the adult children's love, the mid-life parents, who are not defining themselves as incapable or dependent just yet, may have negative, resentful, and resistant feelings. Yet even when parents are in need of adult children's constant involvement, adjustments to the changes in family dependency patterns may become necessary.

Accessibility to family members who no longer share living quarters is another interesting and sometimes troublesome issue for intergenerational families. When the parental figure, who used to engineer the family gatherings, is no longer interested in doing so, the family get-together patterns must change. If the task is not overtly assigned or accepted by one sibling or another, all sorts of family issues can emerge. Mid-life persons often find themselves crunched again between obliged visits to all of their adult children (who often don't live near one another) and aging parents. If the visits are expected to occur often and are mostly one-way, mid-life persons may become resentful about not being able to live their independent lives, may resent the expenses of such visits, and may be frustrated because they feel unable to language their feelings. This can be especially problematic if their success in coordinating family visits and family functions was contained in a self-definition of "good parents."

# POST-PARENTAL PERIOD: THE EMPTY NEST SYNDROME

The post-parental period of the family life cycle is a somewhat new phenomenon in American society and continues to have new meanings in society as people live longer and children leave home earlier (Borland, 1982; Treas & Bengston, 1982). This phase of life begins when the last child permanently moves from the parental household (Borland, 1982).

The family members' individual scripts about expected relationships, adult children roles, societal factors, etc. influence the meanings the parents give to their "empty nests." Their gender role behaviors and future plans also contribute to how they view this phase, as will the circumstances under which children leave (e.g., married or unmarried). But according to Nichols (1984), adjustment to this period of family change is determined largely by the individual family member's readiness for this "launching time," the individual's "scripts," and how he or she plays them out in the family system.

Before the 1930s, children often remained at home because of financial or work-related reasons (Raup & Myers, 1989). They where expected to leave only when they married. Even today some families expect that their children, especially female children, will live at home until marriage. This often thrusts children into premature marital situations. When children leave sooner than expected and for reasons other than marriage, the family often defines themselves as having a problem. Here the extended family and friends tend to blame one or both of the parents, and oftentimes the parents blame each other. Sometimes the parental couple's financial and chore dependence on their young adult children is enacted as a means of keeping the young adult children at home. Crossed boundaries and triangulated relationships often are established and maintained until children can leave for "appropriate" reasons.

After World War II, things changed. Children who left because of military situations did not always return to live within the family of origin. Today, economic and educational factors contribute to the earlier leaving of adult children, sometimes permanently and sometimes temporarily. These more accepted social changes have allowed for a post-parental period with more options. The new meaning systems can include the viewing adult children's independence and ability to care for themselves as positive expressions of the family's successful launching. In these families, the post-parental scripts may include a vision of the future as a time to "reestablish the marital relationship" (Fox-Lefkowitz, 1984, p. 3616).

Before the availability of better preventive health activities, medical interventions and social security benefits for serious chronic illness (i.e., Medicare, Medicaid), family scripts in mid-life were likely to be centered around preparing for illness and death. Families saved for a "rainy day," and many mid-life couples planed to locate themselves in retirement environments with strong consideration for their health maintenance. If they were lucky, they enjoyed several years before the "rainy day" arrived.

As the average life span increases and the population ages in healthier ways, planning is difficult for an additional 15–20 years between the ages of 60-80 because there are so few historical models. Hence, families may anticipate this time in their lives with great joy and excitement or with anxiety, deep sorrow, and stress. This period often requires a redefinition of roles and responsibilities and sometimes a reassessment of the primary couple relationship.

The empty nest phenomena has been thought to be a more negative and difficult adjustment period for women than for men, especially when the women closely associate their maternal or homemaker roles with their well-being. According to Borland (1982), women who described themselves as having strong "familialistic" notions of themselves were less likely to have been employed throughout their child-rearing years and were more likely to have had their identities and daily transactions associated with their family roles. Yet other researchers have identified a "crossover hypothesis," proposing that satisfaction of the nurturing role during earlier years may result in a woman's desire to meet career and achievement needs at or following the "empty nest" stage (Guttman, 1975; Rossi, 1980). These women are more likely to have a positive expectation of this period of their lives. The current entry of women into the work force throughout their childbearing years in ever growing numbers may confirm these changes in social notions about "empty nests," as might the changes in the social value attached to the maternal and homemaker roles.

Less research is available on men and the empty nest phenomena. While in the past the male carried the primary financial burden for the family, he may have looked forward to the time when things would be easier for him. He could have envisioned a period when he would no longer have to "work overtime," when he and his spouse would be able to live on his base salary. Then, if savings were sufficient, this slowing down time together may be envisioned as a long awaited "honeymoon." In some cases, there may be apprehension about how they will behave together when they have no other distractions. Oftentimes, couples create separate lives throughout their parenting years and sometimes lack shared leisure interests.

The sexual behavior of mid-life to later life couples, while less active, generally resembles their earlier life's patterns (Weinstein & Rosen, 1988). Hence, their scripts for the empty nest phase may include a resurgence of their sexual expression in this more private environment, or it may be envisioned as a return of the earlier problems of unevenness in their sexual needs and desires.

In enmeshed families where there is parental overinvolvement with children, the empty nest period poses a threat to the family's functioning and may be defined by the family members as the "impending end" of the system. As the children reach adulthood, the developmentally expected changes in parent-child relationships may not have occurred, or if one parent was particularly unavailable, one or more of the children may have become paired too closely with the remaining parent and have difficulty letting go. Oftentimes, the children need not only to restructure their relationships with their mid-life parents, but they have to renegotiate relationships with their siblings as well, making leaving possible.

## Effects of Divorce at the Empty Nest Stage

*They divorced when the children were five and seven. Sara had a teaching job in the local school and was home each day in time for the children. Jim married the woman with whom he was having an affair and moved in with her and her children. He contributed very little to his divorced family, and after a while rarely saw his birth children. His children missed him at the beginning, but after a while they "forgot." Sara was always angry that her job and her role as a single parent were so completely encompassing that she could not reestablish her social life. She had remained friendly with some women friends who were married, but she rarely went out with men. As the children grew older, she spent all her time with them, and when they began to find interests outside the home, she felt abandoned. Oftentimes, they would feel guilty as they left for the evening leaving her alone. She secretly planned for the time when they left permanently and she could make a new life for herself, but as that time neared, she became afraid. When the youngest child, Bill, sought a college away from home, many obstacles were presented. Finally, he chose a school close by and continued to live at home, feeling angry with his sister for having gone to an out-of-town college. Sara was both pleased and disappointed.*

Even more complicated may be the problems associated with divorced families or families that have stayed together "for the sake of the children" going through the empty nest period. There is a fair body of literature focused on the effects of divorce on children and also their relationships with both the custodial and noncustodial parent (Cooney & Uhlenberg, 1990). In divorced families where parental relationships and boundaries were maintained and independence was encouraged, children's leaving home tends to be less problematic. When the custodial parent did not create a social or career network of his or her own, the children may have fewer options. For example, the empty nest may be defined as a time when dating and other social activities that had been curtailed during child-rearing are begun, and opportunities to establish new intimate personal relationships are anticipated and sought. In these cases, empty nests can be positively and anxiously awaited, anticipated with excitement, as freedom, and as a new beginning.

In other situations, where the boundaries have not been defined and the children throughout their early adult years played companionship roles to the custodial parent, the empty nest may be envisioned by the parent as a period filled with loneliness and isolation. In these situations, when the that last child readies to leave, resentment and other problems can emerge between the siblings when they are restructuring their transactions with each other and their parent.

The accessibility of parents to children, the continuity of family relationships throughout the earlier life stages, and the timing of the divorce in the development stage of the children have important implications to the definition of the intergenerational family system and the noncustodial parent as well. The determinant of accessibility (e.g., anger at the time of the divorce, court decisions, remarriage and the new spouse's influence, financial status, living places, etc.) may be an important factor in how adult children and their mid-life noncustodial parents re-create their relationships at the empty nest phase.

In most divorce cases, the noncustodial parent is the father and, according to Furstenberg, Nord, Peterson, and Zill (1983), somewhere between one third and one half of noncustodial fathers have less than yearly visits if any with their young children. The effect of absence of contact over time is likely to be emotional distancing that continues into adulthood. Sometimes, contact can be reestablished over kinship needs and available resources. If noncustodial fathers can be and are willing to provide assistance, financial or otherwise, when an adult child is in need of it, new relationships may occur.

While parents consider their adult children important resources as caregivers in later life, little is known about how and under what circumstances adult children are willing to caregive a noncustodial, absent father in his later life. How will the lack of frequent contact affect the noncustodial fathers and the adult children? What events at mid-life or over the life span will condition adult children and their fathers to initiate new relationships.

Research by Seltzer and Bianchi (1988) indicated that better educated men are less likely to be cut off from some contact with their children. This may occur possibly because these fathers conform more to social expectations to maintain close ties and because they are likely to have more resources making continued contact with their children more desirable to maintain. Cooney and Uhlenberg (1990) concluded, in research about divorced men and their adult children, that clear and precise "prediction on the basis of either demographic factors or the marriage and divorce-related events" is extremely complicated. The unique design of the particular divorced family system influences the scripts and meaning systems regarding divorced families and the empty nest.

## Staying Together for the Sake of the Children

*Martha and John have lived together with their five children in an explosive, alcoholic, abusive family system. Martha believes that she tolerated alcoholism and abuse because John maintained financial responsibility for the family throughout most of the marriage. From time to time, Martha would leave with the children, only to return because she could not care for them and earn money at the same time.*

*During the last five years John has maintained sobriety. He believes that he has never had any other value to his wife and family other than his earnings. He uses this to justify his involvement in other sexual relationships from time to time. His membership in AA further divided the couple, as he believes that "if you haven't been there, you will never understand what its like," and she believes that "sobriety is just one more 'dry drunk.'"*

*Their children are now grown and waiting for the time when their parents finally separate and end this cycle of unhappiness. Martha can't leave because there just is not enough money, and the early parental loss in her family of origin has set the stage for her beginning her immobilizing fears of "total abandonment." John stays because "it's too late and [he] just [doesn't] have anywhere to go." And each time the nest is about to be emptied and a separation solution seems to have been found, one of the adult children returns, needing temporary financial help or a temporary place to stay. While the collusion to maintain the unhappy system continues, each member remains angry.*

When the family has "stayed together for the sake of the children," scripts for the empty nest can be covert or overt. Adult children's scripts can include seeing their unhappy parents finally able to separate and leave. Sometimes the children may leave before they are ready. The circumstances under which they design their leaving have implications to the family's continued relationships. When the children leave at an expected time (e.g., marriage, out-of-town employment) and the mid-life couple is in agreement about their own separation, there is likely to be a generalized feeling of relief, oftentimes coupled with sadness. But in some cases, when only one spouse covertly awaited this phase of life, as the last child leaves, the long-term secretive plans to separate are put into operation often without the other spouse's awareness. Now the stage is set for all sorts of possibilities for triangulation that may occur as the mid-life couple fight each other for the adult children's love and attention as confirmation of each parent having been a "better" parent.

Sometimes, the unhappy parental couple have no scripts for what it will be like "after" the children leave. When the time eventually comes, they simply go on in the same distanced ways they had when the family was intact. They construct all kinds of realities about their inability to change things, for example, they "can't afford it," they "have no where to go," they "are too ill," "it's just too late," etc. They often find themselves unable to enact their lifelong threat yet are faced with the reality of being permanently lonely in the undesired relationship. Their children are often angry, confused, and disillusioned. Their anticipated scripts that the many years of long unhappiness would finally come to an end can cause resentment when this does not happen.

## DIVORCE AT MID-LIFE

Divorce at mid-life can be more devastating than at other times in the life cycle because the divorcing couple must give up long-term attachments to the marital roles, routines of daily living, and the common experiences that bonded them in interdependence; at the same time, they are coping with the notion of personal failure to their commitments (Berado, 1982; Hagestad & Smyer, 1982; Wright & Maxwell, 1991). Because of the differing patterns of socialization and development of support networks between men and women, they may experience divorce in mid-life/later life differently from one another. The financial status of mid-life couples at the time of divorce and the previous employment experiences of women may have a more long-term negative effect on women than men who divorce at mid-life. Sometimes women in the life stage just prior to mid-life begin to re-tool through education and employment skills training and prepare for a future divorce. These new education and employment environments can establish new social networks, making a mid-life divorce transition easier.

Oftentimes, as women with no work experience approach mid-life with divorce expectations, they enmesh themselves in the caretaking roles of their grandchildren. This too may act to decrease strong fears of abandonment and provide a safe haven as they maintain their familiar mothering role during mid-life divorce. They may work out payment or living arrangements with their adult children who help the divorcing process. Yet sometimes, mid-life women's weak finances and poor health intervene with their notion of the "right time" to divorce, or they may question their "right" to burden their adult children or aging parents; as a result, they stay married.

Parental patterns of dependency/interdependency in child-rearing sometimes reverse themselves as children perform support behaviors for their parents during the divorcing process. The strength of the earlier interpersonal family history and the family's meaning systems about divorce may shape the kind of support the children are willing to provide. McLanahan, Wedemeyer, and Adelberg (1981) suggested that for those mid-life divorcing persons who are attempting to maintain their existing identities, a close-knit support network is most effective, while more loosely delivered support is more effective for those attempting a new identity. Wright and Maxwell (1991), in research on adult children's roles during mid-life and later life divorce, found that divorcing mothers received more advice, services, and financial and socio-emotional support than divorcing fathers. Furthermore, the researchers found that daughters provided more of the socio-emotional support and sons more of the services and financial support. Divorcing persons seeking a new definition of self may resent their adult children who promote dependence and offer unsolicited advice.

# GRANDPARENTHOOD

*Elsie and Frank were a dual working family when they had their first child, Amy, and they continued to work in the family business throughout their lives. It was a hectic schedule they kept, but they loved every minute of it. The children (Amy and her two brothers) were cared for by a part-time "nanny" and grandma and grandpa, who were retired. Now in their late 40s, Elsie and Frank were to be grandparents for the first time. Amy was having her first child. She and her husband lived about a half hour away, and they too were a dual working family. Their work was in the city, an hour's commute from their home. Money was very tight for them, and they were not sure how they would manage, but they knew they would have to continue working.*

*It was exciting to think about being a grandparent, but neither Elsie nor Frank were sure that he or she was ready. They could not help Amy in the same way that their parents helped them. Their parents were "much older" at the time, much more financially secure, and already retired. Most of the Elsie and Frank's friends were becoming grandparents also, but the women in their social group had not worked, at least not full-time, throughout their lives and had plenty of time to spend with their children and grandchildren. Money was a bit tighter than Elsie and Frank had hoped it would be, and they were saving diligently for that time in the future when they could retire.*

Grandparenthood usually is experienced some time during mid-life. Scripts associated with grandparenthood (and even great-grandparenthood) also are determined largely by such factors as family of origin experiences, ethno-cultural affiliations, age of occurrence, finances, and health. Grandparenting styles also can be influenced by the age of grandchildren, the amount of contact grandparents and grandchildren have with one another, the proximity of their living arrangements, the relationship between the grandparents and the parents as envisioned by the grandchildren, and the marriage status of the parents (divorced, single, etc.).

The timing of grandparenthood is not selected by the person who becomes one, and the transactions that define the relationships within the family shift. Grandparenthood, no matter when it occurs, almost automatically spearheads an individual member into an older generation. If the timing is defined biologically and sociologically as appropriate by the grandparent, then the shift is likely to be easier. On the other hand, if grandparenthood (or great-grandparenthood) arrives before it is expected, or at an early age, people's definitions of self can be conflicted. Hence, grandparenthood brings with it boundary issues and responsibilities that may be sought after or rejected, whether timely or untimely.

Grandparents can represent familial stability and continuity of family rituals (Hagestad & Neugarten, 1985; Troll, 1988). These extended family relationships may exhibit themselves anywhere from emotional support networks to child care and financial assistance (Brubaker, 1983). The mid-life couple may envision grandparenthood as a meaningful time in their lives when they become the "valued" elders (Kivnick, 1982; Kivnick, 1983). Moreover, if recognized as such by adult children, it can be a period characterized by happiness and fulfillment; if unappreciated, in can be characterized by disappointment and disillusionment (Kivnick, 1982).

A couple may have defined the mid-life period as one where they can move in and out of their adult children and grandchildren's lives somewhat freely and without responsibility for day-to-day care. Their scripts may contain a vision of this period as one where they can indulge their grandchildren without uncomfortable consequences, or one where they can "play with them and when we tire, the children go home." Yet increased incidence of divorce among adult children and the need for dual working families and other unexpected caretaking or financial involvements often interfere with mid-life persons' ability to grandparent the way they want. Sometimes children return to live in their mid-life parents' home during transitional periods of time, like divorce or job loss, and call upon the mid-life parents to care for the grandchildren, interrupting the grandparents' plans. Sometimes these caretaking situations maintain the mid-life couple in familiar roles and decrease anxiety about "what comes next." Familiar rules may become reestablished as the family tries to rebalance itself in old ways. Sometimes the rules remain the same but the roles change. For example, grandfathers, who were unavailable for caretaking with their own children, when they retire, may take on primary child care responsibilities in these intergenerational families. The relationships may blend grandparenting and parenting roles. In these cases, later transitions may be problematic, particularly when a single adult child establishes a new relationship and is ready to remarry and leave the family setting again with his or her children.

Grandfathers and grandmothers have been known to have differing scripts about grandparenting and differing definitions of nurturing and expressiveness (Brubaker, 1990). These differences may be observed in the way they language their willingness to be involved, or it may be an outcome of their historical relationship with the particular adult child.

Boundary problems often can become apparent when "living together" arrangements occur. Adult children reentering the single world may find themselves restricted by their parents while they are demoted to "just another child." When their parents are caretaking grandchildren and offering financial assistance, negotiating adult relationships can become a problem.

Mid-life couples' notions of themselves as grandparents may be influenced by their experiences with their own parents and grandparents. When they are sought after for advice, they may feel particularly conflicted as they try to balance themselves between interfering and aloof or uninterested. They may feel in concert with one of their adult children's child-rearing style and not another's. This may complicate the way they grandparent and create new or reestablish old sibling rivals.

The expectations of grandparenthood by the mid-life couple and their adult children may differ considerably and may be a cause of great stress to the intergenerational family. This is complicated by competition between grandparents and in-law grandparents and their differing styles of participation, past experiences, life situations, and scripts about their roles. The complicated extended family issues, especially those of multiple caretaking of grandchildren and aging parents have not been studied effectively; research predominantly represents grandmothers and is limited to three generation families, when today there may be four and more generations in a family system (Brubaker, 1990). The implications of an aging population, interstate families, divorce and remarriage, etc. and their influence on mid-life families' grandparenting styles need to be investigated further. Most importantly, the boundaries of membership in a particular generation, when accepted and appreciated, permit a sense of family belonging that allows for new roles to develop, old loyalty debts to be altered, and new abilities to individuate fostering (Framo, 1981; Whitaker, 1976).

# CAREGIVING

*Lucy and Ari are siblings living at two different ends of the United States, while their parents live somewhere in the middle. They visit frequently, and family reunions are always fun. Then Mom got Alzheimer's Disease and deteriorated very quickly. At first, it seemed reasonable to have a caretaker live with Mom and Dad, and Dad reluctantly agreed to share the role. But the deterioration occurred more quickly than they thought, and while Lucy and Ari traveled back and forth frequently, Dad was wearing thin and feeling very lonely. Ari suggested that they find a nursing care facility for Mom close to Dad's home, but Lucy found it almost unthinkable to "put Mom away." While it was not comfortable to have a caretaker living in their small apartment, Mom and Dad had promised each other that they would do "whatever we have to" for each other until one of them died. Putting Mom in a nursing home was almost unthinkable for both Dad and Lucy. They tried every alternative, including a stay at Lucy's home that was even more difficult because she worked all day, and Dad had no resources or friends in Lucy's town to give him social relief. The cost of home care was more than they could manage, and they began to seriously deplete the family finances. Finally, they got Dad to agree to an inpatient setting.*

There is a vast body of literature that is associated with caregiving and its many dimensions—caregiving of elders, children, spouses, etc. Caregiving these family members may be complicated further by specific care needs (i.e. disability or specific disease). This discussion concerns itself only with caregiving of elder parents and spouses as it affects mid-life couples and their families.

The family's role in caregiving has a long history, and as family members live longer, mid-life families will need to address the caregiving needs of their elderly parents more and more frequently. How mid-life couples and their extended families organize to give care to older parents is not completely understood. This could be because the focus generally has been on crisis situations where coping is difficult or on specific dyads or individuals (daughters versus sons) rather than on family systems (Noelker & Shaffer, 1986; Treas, 1977; Treas, 1979).

Some of the factors that have implications for how families organize to give care are the structure of the family, including the number of members, their ages, genders, etc.; the nature of the ties among them; and their ties to others outside the family of origin (Matthews & Rosner, 1988). Also affecting caregiving styles are the family's stories about caregiving and their definition of themselves as caregivers.

Whether a mid-life family sees caregiving as a natural course of events or as an interruption in their life's plans, the situation may be complicated by elderly parents. When one spouse of an elderly couple becomes ill, the other spouse's response may be as diverse as becoming totally immobilized to taking total charge. The meaning of their very marriage may drive their caregiving and needs. Their long-term commitment and "promised" expectations can influence their caregiving activities. Sometimes these activities take on "martyrdom" type roles, and this can put the well spouse at health risk. Adult children may fear for the health of both parents and want to intervene on behalf of the well spouse. This can result in family conflict or distancing as they struggle with their beliefs about how they each "should be." When elderly well spouses are pressured by children or the medical system to seek inpatient nursing home situations for the sickly spouses when well spouses believe it is their job to care for ill spouses at home, they may become depressed or angry. This conflict of priorities and relationship definitions presents problems for caregiving intergenerational families.

When an elderly parent becomes ill and there is no able or living spouse, the siblings usually determine if they will be active care participants, provide financial resources or other services and/or seek professional caregivers. The mid-life adult sibling's family system and the family's health and other family circumstances are considerations in caregiving families, as is his or her historical role in the family of origin and his or her scripts about the threats of final separation. Where previous dynamics were established (such as in running errands, in establishing visiting routines, or in decision making about medical practices), one might expect that these dynamics are maintained or increased during times of major care needs. The child who is defined by the family as the pseudo-parent, who previously had been the "wise sibling," often will take the same role during health crises. Sometimes there is a sibling who has been designated as the "family doctor" by career affiliation (doctor, nurse, etc.), who may be designated as the person in charge of caregiving. Sometimes other siblings resent self-appointed caregivers or feel guilty for their own lack of participation. Common family of origin responses to caregivers also include caregiving at the convenience of the caregiver and disassociation from family caregiving entirely (Matthews & Rosner, 1988). Old issues about "favorite child" may become reenacted. These dynamics may have lasting effects on the extended family system in later life.

The delivery of caregiving that is necessary may not resemble the ill/ elderly person's view of the caregiving being received. The notion of role reversal in the caregiving family system, discussed earlier in this chapter, may be envisioned by the elderly parent as intrusive and demanding, creating a resistance to assistance, while the adult child views the parent as stubborn and childlike (Moss & Moss, 1992). The balance between dependence and independence can become problematic particularly for the ill person as power declines and control dynamics are played out.

Sometimes families have made preparation for and discussed their future caregiving expectations across generations and, when care needs occur, the routine is expected and planned for. Other times, patterns pre-established from past experiences in caregiving with in-laws or the other parent are resurrected. Because of the myriad of ways in which families react to or plan for caregiving, caregiving issues are important material for family therapy. As the population ages and mid-life couples have longer living parents, the need to address decisions about care, housing arrangements, etc. will increase. What support systems, time constraints, and other extrafamilial ties exist have implications to the family's ability to mobilize (Matthews & Rosner, 1988). Furthermore, the way family systems make adjustments to caregiving activities has important implications for how they will respond to the deaths of their older parents.

**Coresidency**

*Kathrine and Robert were thinking about selling the family home and moving to a smaller place on the lake, closer to where they both work, when Kathrine's dad was diagnosed with cancer. He died within one year. She watched her mom's health decline and depression increase over the next several years as her friends died and her social network began to disappear. Because Kathrine's parents had lived far away in another state, the family decided that it would be best if Mom came to live with Kathrine and Robert, mostly because "Kate" was the closest child and there was room in Kate and Robert's big house. Robert was in agreement though very disappointed at not being able to move. Besides, both of them remembered how it was with their grandparents living close by until they died—Kate's in her mom's house and Robert's in the house down the street.*

*While Kate's mom was able to care for herself during the day, she was lonely at night and made dinner for Kate and Robert each night. Then Kate's mom expected to spend the rest of the evening chatting. On the weekends, Kate felt she should spend some time with her mom, and they often went out shopping or for lunch, leaving Robert at home. Although most of the time Robert was okay with this arrangement, Kate often felt guilty. They rarely invited friends to the house anymore and had little energy for Saturday nights out. Kate's sister, brothers, and their spouses visited when it was convenient but essentially the burden was Kathrine and Robert's. Tension grew in the household as the lack of privacy and lack of "freedom" intervened in their lives. As the arguments grew louder, Kate's mom grew quieter and more depressed. "What have I done by moving here," she thought, and "Where can I go now?"*

The commitments of parent to child have roots in the parent-child history, interactions, and expectations (Rossi & Rossi, 1990). These commitments have implications as to how the parent and child organize themselves around changing residency arrangements. The consistently rising divorce rate, declining economic status of families (especially those with young children), and the longer life span of elder parents has "sandwiched" the mid-life family in coresidency arrangements. It is not uncommon for either half of the sandwich (adult children or elderly parents) and sometimes both halves, to reside together with the mid-life couple or in very close proximity. The rules of the couple's families of origin and present family stories about coresidence, the "in-law" system, and the new expectations each family member has for the other all influence the adjustment to these arrangements. Literature suggests that, while conflicts are expected, most parents and adult children tend to live together harmoniously (Pillemer, 1988). Tensions that may be evidenced at the onset of the coresidency arrangements may decline as all parties learn over time how to decrease conflict and avoid hostile interactions. But, in some cases, where the past relationship was one of negative feelings, resentments, and anger, the close proximity of the co-living arrangement may intensify conflicts (Moss & Moss, 1992).

Moss and Moss (1992), in their research identified three common reasons why families take up coresidency: moving away from inadequate or unsafe housing to what is perceived as a better environment; moving to replace a lost social support system; and moving for immediate caregiving needs or those perceived to be needed in the very near future. As discussed earlier in this chapter, when adult children move into the residence of the mid-life couple and bring their families, alternations in the generational interactions are likely to occur. Grandparenting and parenting roles can become blended, and dependence and interdependence interactions and expectations may change as economic assistance, advice, and other supports are rendered to the younger family members (Brubaker, 1990).

When elderly parents relocate, there is often a sense of final loss and the threat of death of the parent, and feelings of orphanhood for the adult child may surface (Moss & Moss, 1992). In this context, the coresidency arrangement may afford an opportunity to heal past hurts and unresolved conflicts.

While the elderly parent attempts to adjust to the new environment, new social context and loss of their old setting, the mid-life couple deals with the changes in routines and boundaries that existed in their familiar environment (Moss & Moss, 1992). The definition of the family often broadens as new contexts for relationships are developing. While historical knowledge of each other from earlier role configurations return initially, they may not have relevancy in the present, since each family member needs to learn more about the other as independent adults.

The expectations the extended family has about the time each will spend with the other and how this living arrangement will affect other activities also play a part in how problematic the coresidency will be. The complicated transactions of achieving closeness and yet maintaining separate identities is an ongoing challenge (Bleizner & Mancinci, 1988).

Membership in the family of origin sets up a lifetime attachment that is complicated by the distances in living arrangements that often exist between adult children and their parents later in life. These distances may present problems as families prepare for increasing needs for assistance in the daily living of parents as they enter the final life stage. Hence, the need for coresidency has several interwoven themes that families must transact to minimize problems. Different expectations, daily living styles, habits, values, and visions of their roles in coresidency arrangements are best negotiated before the arrangement occurs, and continued dialogue must be maintained as they share everyday interactions (Moss & Moss, 1992). The mid-life scripts that accommodate for the possibility of coresidency or caretaking arrangements may mediate unexpected problems. Those life scripts that do not accommodate may find the family experiencing a revisit of old tensions, guilt, and other conflicts.

# SUMMARY

The discussion about special situations within this chapter in the context of transactions of family of origin, interactional patterns between spouses and other extended family members, and the social systems within which individuals function in their day-to-day activities is aimed at increasing understanding of how these situations contribute to mid-life scripts. The problems that keep families "stuck" in inadequate scripts or de-energize and deplete families can render them vulnerable to future behaviors that could be more dissatisfying. Therapeutic interventions are aimed at mobilizing the family to reinitiate past successful meaning systems. Such factors as political power structures that exist within intergenerational families need to be addressed since they tend to result in intimidation and special privilege or obligation and inhibit members from becoming reacquainted as adults (Williamson, 1981). The problems of children as they negotiate their mid-life relationships have history in the parental marital relationship (Framo, 1981). Family scripts and other family patterns of relating are passed on from one generation to another (Boszormenyi-Nagi & Spark, 1973). The degree of differentiation achieved by family members influences their ability to function autonomously/independently and in turn will influence how they transact mid-life (Bowen, 1978).

The blueprints that drive future life plans are altered by expected or unexpected events like divorce, illness, death, etc. How individuals or families cope with these events and the meaning families will give to these events can influence what families expect will happen at mid-life and then how they will behave. The opportunity for longer, healthier life and the physical distances between extended families are creating gaps in "knowable" scripts. These gaps may provide opportunities for new roles, new meanings, and new realities that expand traditional boundaries and options.

# REFERENCES

Adelmann, P.K., & Antonucci, T.C. (1989). Empty nest, cohort, and employment in the well being of midlife women. *Sex Roles, 20*(3/4), 173–189.

Anderson, T.B. (1984). Widowhood as a life transition: Its impact on kinship ties. *Journal of Marriage and the Family, 46*, 105–114.

Bengtson, V.L., & Mangen, D.J. (1988). Family intergenerational solidarity revisited. In &. D.J. Mangen & V.L. Bengtson (Eds.), *Measurement of intergenerational relations* (pp. 229–238). Minneapolis, MN: University of Minnesota Press.

Berado, D.H. (1982). Divorce and remarriage at middle age and beyond. In F.M. Berado (Ed.), *Middle and late life transitions* (pp. 132–139). Beverly Hills: Sage Publishers.

Bleizner, F., & Mancinci, J.A. (1988). Enduring ties: Older adults' parental role responsibilities. *Family Relations, 36*, 176–180.

Borland, D.C. (1982). A cohort analysis approach to the empty-nest syndrome among three ethnic groups of women: A theoretical position. *Journal of Marriage & Family, 44*, 117–129.

Boszormenyi-Nagi, I., & Spark, G. (1973). *Invisible loyalties: Reciprocity in intergenerational family therapy.* New York: Harper & Row.

Bowen, M. (1978). *Family therapy in clinical practice.* New York: Jason Aronson.

Bowlby, J. (1980). *Attachment and loss.* New York: Basic Books.

Brubaker, T.H. (1983). *Family relationships in later life.* Beverly Hills: Sage Publishers.

Brubaker, T.H. (1985). *Later life families.* Beverly Hills: Sage Publishers.

Brubaker, T.H. (1990). Families in later life: A burgeoning research area. *Journal of Marriage and the Family, 52*, 959–981.

Cooney, T.M., & Uhlenberg, P. (1990, August). The role of divorce in men's relations with their adult children after mid-life. *Journal of Marriage and the Family, 52,* 677–687.

Dannefer, D. (1984). Adult development and social theory: A paradigmatic reappraisal. *American Sociological Review, 49,* 100–116.

Eisenhandler, S.A. (1992). Lifelong roles and cameo appearances: Elderly parents and relationships with adult children. *Journal of Aging Studies, 6*(3), 243–257.

Flori, D.E. (1989). The prevalence of later life family concerns in the marriage and family therapy journal literature (1976–1985): A content analysis. *Journal of Marital and Family Therapy, 15*(3), 289–297.

Fox-Lefkowitz, A.B. (1984). Fathers' perception of the empty nest transition. *Dissertation Abstracts International, 45*(11B), 3616.

Framo, J. (Ed.). (1981). *The integration of marital therapy with sessions with family of origin.* New York: Brunner/Mazel.

Furstenberg, F.F., Nord, C.W., Peterson, L., & Zill, N. (1983). The life course of children of divorce: Marital disruptions and parental contact. *American Sociological Review, 48,* 656–668.

Gove, W.R., Grimm, J.W., Motx, S.C., & Thompson, J.D. (1973). The family life cycle: Internal dynamics and social consequences. *Sociology and Social Research, 57,* 182–195.

Guttman, D.L. (1975). Parenthood: A key to the comparative study of the life-cycle? In N.D. &. L. Ginsberg (Eds.), *Life-span developmental psychology: Normative life crises* (pp. 167–184). New York: Academic Press.

Hagestad, G.O., & Neugarten, B.L. (1985). Age and the life course. In R.H.B. & E. Shanas (Eds.), *Handbook of aging and the social sciences* (pp. 153–176). New York: Nostrand Reinhold.

Hagestad, G.O., & Smyer, M.A. (Eds.). (1982). *Dissolving long-term relationships: Patterns of divorcing in middle age.* San Diego: Academic Press.

Hess, B.B., & Waring, J.M. (1978). Parent child in later life: Rethinking the relationship. In R.M. Lerner & G.B. Spanier (Eds.), *Child influences on marital and family interactions* (pp. 241–273). New York: Academic Press.

Kivnick, H.Q. (1982). Grandparenthood: An overview of meaning and mental health. *Gerontologist, 22*, 59–66.

Kivnick, H.Q. (1983). Dimensions of grandparenthood: Deductive conceptualization and empirical derivation. *Journal of Personality and Social Psychology, 44*, 1056–1068.

Lee, G.R. (1984). Status of the elderly: Economic and familial antecedents. *Journal of Marriage & Family, 46*, 267–275.

Matthews, S.H., & Rosner, T.T. (1988, February). Shared filial responsibility: The family as the primary caregiver. *Journal of Marriage and the Family, 50*, 185–195.

McLanahan, S.S., Wedemeyer, N.V., & Adelberg, T. (1981). Network structure, social support and psychological well-being in the single-parent family. *Journal of Marriage and the Family, 43*, 601–612.

Moen, P. (1991, February). Transitions in mid-life: Women's work and family roles in the 1970s. *Journal of Marriage and Family, 53*, 135–150.

Moss, M.S., & Moss, S.Z. (1992). Themes in parent-child relationships when elderly parents move nearby. *Journal of Aging Studies, 6*(3), 259–271.

Neugarten, B.L., Moore, J.W., & Lowe, J.C. (1965). Age norms, age constraints, and adult socialization. *American Journal of Sociology, 70*, 710–717.

Nichols, M. (1984). *Family therapy: Concepts and methods*. New York: Gardner Press.

Noelker, L.A., & Shaffer, G. (1986). Care networks: How they form and change. *Generations, 10*, 62–64.

Nurmi, J. (1992). Age differences in adult life goals, concerns, and their temporal extension: A life course approach to future-oriented motivation. *Journal of Behavioral development, 15*(4), 487–508.

Oppenheimer, V.K. (1974). The life-cycle squeeze: The ineraction of men's occupational and family life cycles. *Demography, 11*, 227–245.

Pillemer, K. (1988, November). Explaining intergenerational conflict when adult children and elderly parents live together. *Journal of Marriage and the Family, 50*, 1037–1047.

Raup, J.L., & Myers, J.E. (1989). The empty nest syndrome: Myth or reality? *Journal of Counseling & Development, 68*, 180–183.

Rossi, A. (1980). Life-span theories and women's lives. *Signs, 6*, 4–32.

Rossi, A.S., & Rossi, P.H. (1990). *Of human bonding: Parent-child relations across the life course.* New York: Aldine de Gruyter.

Seltzer, J.S., & Bianchi, S.M. (1988). Children's contact with absent parents. *Journal of Marriage and Family, 50*, 663–677.

Treas, J. (1977). Family support systems for the aged: Some social and demographic considerations. *Gerontologist, 17*, 486–491.

Treas, J. (1979). Intergenerational families and social change. In P. Ragan (Ed.), *Aging parents* (pp. 58–65). Los Angeles: USC Press.

Treas, J., & Bengston, V. (1982). The demography of mid- and late life transitions. In F.M. Berardo (Ed.), *The annals of the American Academy of Political and Social Science: Middle and late life transitions* (pp. 11–22). Beverly Hills: Sage Publishers.

Troll, L.E. (1988). Rituals and reunions. *American Behavioral Scientist, 31*, 621–631.

Weinstein, E., & Rosen, E. (1988). Sexual attitudes, interests and activities for senior adults. *International Journal of Aging and Human Development, 27*(4), 261–270.

Whitaker, C. (Ed.). (1976). *A family is a four dimensional relationship.* New York: Gardner Press.

Williamson, D. (1981). Personal authority via termination of the intergenerational hierarchical boundary: A "new" stage in the family life cycle. *Journal of Marriage & Family Therapy, 1*, 441–452.

Wright, C.L., & Maxwell, J.W. (1991). Social support during adjustment to later-life divorce: How adult children help parents. *Journal of Divorce & Remarriage, 15*(3/4), 21–49.

# Chapter 11

# THE FINAL SCRIPT: A DEVELOPMENTAL CRISIS—DEATH

*Frank Genovese*

"Death," wrote Rabbi Lamm (1969), "is a night—a night that lies between two days." The Rabbi's words mean different things to different persons. To some, the second day might be interpreted as the mourner's coming alive again through the process of bereavement. To others, Rabbi Lamm is affirming and assuring the existence of an afterlife. To the latter, death does not mean that the lost one is gone forever; his or her soul or ghost, in some form or another, lives on in another place. The place where the soul resides and the form it takes vary across cultures. In one, it may be Heaven or Hell, while in others it may be in Valhalla or Nirvana.

Why the numerous meanings concerning a very simple reality—that we all shall die? Social constructionist theory and the theory of scripts provide one possible avenue of inquiry. The model suggests that the manner in which an individual makes sense of his or her world is a process that can be understood only in the context of culture. The rules of one's sociocultural environment, the idiosyncratic restatement of these rules within one's family of origin, and the impact of significant childhood others combine, via the process of socialization, to construct an individual's meaning system (Atwood & Genovese, 1993).

**299**

Gagnon (1990) suggested that scripts flow from a person's socially constructed meaning system. A script directs behavior and makes it congruent with the meaning system. Each person has a number of scripts. Many of these involve the various social roles people play: age scripts; child, adolescent, and adult child scripts; parental and grandparental scripts; worker scripts; lover scripts; etc. Scripts write the dialogue and direct the play. Scripts limit and define what is permissible, justifying what is in agreement with them and challenging what is not. Scripts also may include scenarios for their own expansion; the dialogue of those scripts contain certain passages that direct behavior, cognition, and affect to seek out new "realities," new meanings.

Scripts play out in one's relationships with others, at the level of conscious awareness, and at the intrapsychic level as well. Most importantly for the purposes of this discussion, scripts derive from meaning systems that originally are created and maintained by interactions with significant others (Atwood & Genovese, 1993).

Central to constructionist thinking is that the stories persons construct with others about the meanings of their lives are not representations of a true reality. Our scripts often disallow the perception of other truth. White and Epston (1990) wrote the following:

> The structuring of a narrative requires recourse to a selective
> process in which we prune, from our experience, those events
> that do not fit with the dominant evolving stories that we and
> others have about us. Thus, over time and of necessity, much
> of our stock of lived experiences goes unstoried and is never
> "told" or expressed. (pp. 11–12)

The work of constructionist therapists consists of a journey to find parts of reality that have been "pruned" by dominant scripts. Whether it is White and Epston (1991) looking for unique outcomes or deShazer (1991) searching for exceptions to scripts, the rewriting of narratives is the goal. Winderman (1989) quoted Harlene Anderson on the nature of the therapeutic work:

> It is not just the therapist trying to understand the client,
> collecting information and data and placing it on some kind of
> cognitive map in a unilateral way. Rather, it is the natural
> search in which client and therapist puzzle together in search
> for understanding, to develop a story that has not been told
> before. (p. 11)

The vast majority of persons and systems of persons who undergo second-order change and who rewrite their scripts do not do so with the help of a therapist. Restoring is done in the context of repeated performances of the dominant script by persons in relationship until the limitations of the story become obvious. White and Epston (1990) made this point clearly:

> Stories are full of gaps which persons must fill in order for the story to be performed. These gaps recruit the lived experience and imagination of persons. With every performance, persons are reauthoring their lives . . . every telling and retelling of a story, through its performance, is a new telling that encapsulates, and expands upon the previous telling. (p. 13)

What happens, though, to meaning systems and their scripts when one of the principal players is permanently lost through death?

In previous works, this author has considered how different people behave following the death of a loved one (Krupp, Genovese, & Krupp, 1986; Krupp, Genovese, & Krupp, 1988; Genovese, 1992; Atwood & Genovese, 1993). In these works, sometimes implied and sometimes stated, an arbitrary dichotomy between "normal" and "incomplete or pathological" mourning was made. This dichotomy was predicated on the premise that bereavement is a developmental process (Bowlby, 1980; Parkes & Weiss, 1983; Sanders, 1989). "Normal" mourners were thought to have progressed through the entire process from the point of the initial loss through identity reconstruction. Incomplete mourners were seen as people who, for myriad reasons, were stuck somewhere in the process. Such a dichotomy may be more congruent with the author's meaning system than to those who are grieving.

## DEVELOPMENTAL CRISES: DEMANDS FOR CHANGES IN SCRIPTS

Both individuals and families go through a series of predictable developmental changes that irrevocably transform them. As Erikson said, "The child may be the parent of the adult," but the adult is by no means the same individual who was the child. The child's dependency on his or her parents that is appropriate for a young child is inappropriate and devastating to the age-appropriate psychological growth of an adolescent. As another example, the sorts of interactions—scripts—that may make for a very happy couple will have to be altered as the couple becomes parents.

In a sense, the transformations demanded of individuals and families at times of developmental transition may be understood as calls for a change in scripts. The demand is that the individual's personal script be reasonably congruent with society's dominant script concerning a particular phase of development. If a 14-year-old boy persists in a script that is more congruent with society's script for a 14-year-old girl, for example, he is likely to be labelled as abnormal. But abnormal—away from the norm—from what? If his script flows from his meaning system, then his behaviors, cognitions, and affect seem perfectly consistent to him with the way things "ought to be." The real inconsistency is to be found between his script and that which is expected from him by others. To be sure, the confrontation between the boy's meaning system and the expectations of others may produce a perturbation that might impact upon, and possibly alter, his meaning system eventually. However, the original anxiety is to be found in others, and not in the boy himself.

That such perturbations can impact upon scripts is evident in cases in which an individual feels completely removed from the content of an earlier script. Previous modes of acting, thinking, and feeling seem ego-alien. Consider a hypothetical young person who pridefully reflects on her ability to be successful in her career, marriage, and parenthood. It is difficult for her to believe that there was a time when she needed her mother's guidance in the most trivial of matters. It is as if she were a different person then. The script she followed at the earlier point in her life was wholly consistent with her meaning system at that time. Her current script reflects her current meanings, and the old one is as alien to her as is the too-tight shell discarded and abandoned by a growing lobster.

The "new" person is a product of discontinuous (Hoffman, 1981) and second-order change (Watzlawick, 1978, 1984). Discontinuous change is not incremental. It does not come about by doing either more or less of the "same old things." One's entire way of being, thinking, and feeling are altered. Hoffman (1981) described the process of discontinuous change in relationships:

> First, the patterns that have kept the system in a steady state relative to its environment begin to work badly. New conditions arise for which these patterns were not designed. Ad hoc solutions are tried and sometimes work, but usually have to be

abandoned. Irritation grows over small but persisting difficulties. The accumulation of difficulties eventually forces the entire system over an edge, into a state of crisis. . . . The end
point [of the process] . . . is that the system breaks down, or
creates a new way to monitor the same homeostasis, or spon-
taneously leaps to an integration that will deal better with the
changed field. (pp. 159–160)

Watzlawick (1978, 1984) referred to incremental change as first order,
while second-order change alters the entire frame itself. The "new" person
has undergone discontinuous, second-order change.

The death of a loved one can be conceived of both as a permanent
change in external reality and also as a demand for a second-order script
rewriting change in internal reality. The unexpected demise of a 35-year-old
father of one child provides an example. In a split second, his wife's external
reality was altered permanently—a partner is gone, economic status is
changed, and fewer hands are available to complete requisite tasks. Relationships with in-laws, with family, and with coupled and single friends are
all made different to the degree to which they were predicated upon the
presence of the now-dead person.

Legally and socially, the woman's external definition was changed in-
stantaneously from wife and mother to widow and single parent. Internal,
subjectively held self-definitions, however, take much more time to change
than do legal ones (Atwood & Genovese, 1993).

Both external, societal pressures and internal, developmental ones impinge upon bereaved persons and demand alterations in their scripts. The
meaning system must be redefined based on an altered external reality.
However, because of the gap between the time when legal versus psychological self-definitions change, the bereaved will in some circumstances
think, feel, and behave as if he or she were still in relationship with the
deceased, while at other times the bereaved person's cognitive, affective,
and behavioral responses will reflect the permanence of the loss. To the
external observer who is aware of constructionist theory, the vacillation of
the mourner may be understood in terms of attempts at script revision. To
the person who has suffered loss, the vacillation is at the heart of the
bereavement work.

# TRADITIONAL APPROACHES

While constructionist theory may well represent a paradigmatic shift in family therapy theory (Atwood & Genovese, 1993), a vast amount of bereavement literature predates it. For many years, a few classic works such as those of Freud (1917) and Lindemann (1944) dominated theoretical speculation concerning the nature of grief (Krupp et al., 1986).

The impact of *Mourning and Melancholia* (Freud, 1917) insured that theoreticians would consider bereavement from an individual perspective for many decades. The subject of inquiry was limited to those internal mechanisms activated within a mourner when faced with the death of a loved one. Denial, identification, and projective identification were seen as attempts by the unconscious to deny the permanence of the loss: We never willingly give up those we love (Freud, 1917). The refusal on the part of the mourner to give up the fantasy of reversing the loss is central to nearly all traditional theories of incomplete mourning.

Freud (1917) understood resolution as the result of the ego's decision to remain with the living rather than with the dead:

> Reality passes its verdict—that the object no longer exists—upon each single one of the memories and hopes through which the libido was attached to the lost object and the ego, confronted as it were, over a decision whether it will share the fate, is persuaded by the sum of the narcissistic satisfactions in being alive, to sever its detachment to the non-existent object. (p. 65)

A careful rereading of this last citation allows for the ego's decision to be understood as a "spontaneous leap to an integration that will deal better with the changed field" (Hoffman, 1981, p. 160). In his own way, Freud seemed to understand successful bereavement in terms of the modern concept of second-order change. So, also, do more contemporary writers. Parkes and Weiss (1983) believed that recovery from loss is different from other recoveries in that mourners do not return to a previous place. Mourners must recognize and accept that their lives are altered forever.

Unlike Freud, the conclusions of Parkes and Weiss (1983) and those of Bowlby (1980) derived from empirical research. Bowlby's theoretical position also is reminiscent of discontinuous, second-order change. Recovery involves the decision to live with one's new reality. The mourner redefines the self and finally begins to live with the knowledge that the loss is permanent.

Freud, Bowlby, and Parkes and Weiss were not schooled in what Hoffman (1981) and Watzlawick (1984) referred to as discontinuous and second-order change. Family systems theorists, however, are. Yet it is only in the very recent past that systems thinkers have addressed the question of bereavement.

Walsh and McGoldrick (1991) suggested that the past-orientation of bereavement work was not a good fit for systems theory for that extended period of time during which systems thinking was limited to considerations of the here and now. Reactions to the death of loved ones were conceived of as being "content" saturated, and not "process" in nature; as owning an individual rather than with a systems frame; and as being associated with more reductionistic models of psychotherapy than those derived from systemic theory.

That the continuing development of systemic thinking now allows for the consideration of grief issues is indicated by the publication of Walsh and McGoldrick's (1991) volume that is dedicated to a discussion of those issues from a family perspective. Here, too, "recovery" from bereavement does not imply a return to previous "healthy" state from a current "pathological" one. These writers also seemed to view bereavement as an example of a second-order change:

> Based on research and clinical experience, we can identify two major family tasks that tend to promote immediate and long term adaption for family members and to strengthen the family as a functional unit: 1) shared acknowledgement of the reality of death and shared experience of loss; 2) reorganization of the family system and reinvestment in other relationships and life pursuits. (p. 8)

The foregoing discussion has provided a number of theoretical descriptions of successful bereavement. A fundamental question, however, remains. Could Freud's mourners' egos choose the "narcissistic joys" of life, or Bowlby's mourners "finally relinquish all hope that the lost person can be recovered," or Parkes and Weiss' mourners "examine how their basic assumptions about themselves and their world must be changed," or Walsh and McGoldrick's families "reinvest in other relationships and life pursuits" if each of their cognitions, affects, and behaviors were directed by scripts that still assumed that the lost loved one were alive?

The answer is obviously no. Successful mourners have changed their scripts, and the re-scripting reflects a change in the meaning system.

## RE-SCRIPTING ATTACHMENT THEORY

Of all the traditional approaches to an understanding of the bereavement process, attachment theory (Bowlby, 1980) is the most thoroughly articulated. Rooted in a biological frame and empirically researched in social settings, attachment theory presents a developmental course for mourning that is accepted widely by many theoreticians and therapists.

The assumption of a Bowlbian stance, however, is uncomfortable for constructionists. Although Bowlby and others who have taken a developmental view of mourning (e.g., Parkes & Weiss, 1983; Sanders, 1989) warn that the proposed stages are only outlines of a general process, it appears as if these writers know a "truth" that is unavailable to others.

The uncomfortability felt by a constructionist therapist should he or she take a developmental tact is that he or she assumes the traditional role of expert. Rando's (1984) caveat to therapists that, "Each person's grief will be idiosyncratic, determined by a unique combination of physiological, social and psychological factors," does little to ease the felt role confusion on the part of the constructionist therapist. As suggested by Nichols and Schwartz (1991), constructionist therapists shun the role of expert when they take on the notion that their knowledge is arbitrary. If reality is unknowable, nothing can be asserted about it. Hoffman (1988) operationalized the dilemma: An expert who no longer is an expert no longer *knows* how to do therapy.

For the purposes of this chapter, the author has adopted a solution, an accommodation at best, offered by Nichols and Schwartz: ". . . we can know *approximations* [author's emphasis] of reality, but we must remain humble about them because of our awareness that they are distorted and incomplete . . ." (1991, p. 147). So, what follows is a humble exposition of attachment theory.

Byng-Hall (1991) directly addressed the question of individual and family bereavement scripts. His assumption was that these scripts are no different from any other in that they are created from past experience, are enacted in the present, and serve to direct behavior in the future:

> [Scripts] inform one, from experience, what to do next, and the ensuing interaction provides a model for him to behave when similar circumstances occur in the future. . . . Family members inherit from previous bereavement experiences their rules about what should be repeated and what should be avoided. (Byng-Hall, 1991, pp. 130–131)

Persons and families who repeat previous death-oriented feelings, thoughts, behaviors, and interactional patterns are following replicative scripts, according to Byng-Hall. The author also suggested that at times individuals and systems of individuals may opt to avoid previously painful experiences and adopt corrective scripts. This sort of script leads to affects, cognitives, behaviors, and ways of being together that are opposite from, and in reaction to, what was played out in the past.

The power and pervasiveness of scripts is illustrated by a client who was, among other things, puzzled by his reaction to the death of his mother. Throughout the wake and funeral he was stoic and took the role of seeing to the myriad details that surround a death. At home at night, he grieved deeply and openly. Why was he so cold in public and so emotional in private?

Several weeks into group therapy, the client recalled his paternal grandmother's death. One day, when he was six years of age, the phone rang. The boy picked up an extension and heard his father inform his mother, in a monotone and unemotional voice, "Well, Jean, my mother has died." Family history informed the boy that his father and grandmother had enjoyed a close and loving relationship. The father was a private, not public mourner. The client had adopted a replicative script.

Byng-Hall (1991) acknowledged the debt that his work owes to that of Bowlby (1980). Bowlby's influence is obvious as Byng-Hall enumerates ways in which bereaved family members "cushion the impact of the death by altering the script in a number of ways" (p. 131). The author outlines four such alterations in script.

In the first, there is an emotional numbing through which some or all of the affect associated with the loss is disconnected from the cognitive knowledge that the loss has occurred. In the second variation, the reality of the loss is denied, and the mourner continues in a dyadic relationship with the departed's ghost. A third possibility is the selection of one individual by the rest of the family to serve as a replacement for the lost one. The dead person is thus kept "alive" in the replacement person. The fourth is an identification process by which the mourner adopts the role of one of the important players in the death scenario.

The first two of these "cushions" against the impact of a loved one in a manner parallel to Bowlby's (1980) first two stages of grief. For Bowlby, the formation of attachment bonds is a human behavior that has been selected over evolutionary time. The offspring of mates who bond with their young are much more likely to survive to sexual maturity than the children of mates who do not bond. Hence, each new generation will be richer than the last in the genetic information that leads to bonding behavior. Bowlby's attachment theory posits that the tendency to form attachment bonds is greatest among human parents and their children, and between paired human mates.

Threats to the bond lead to biological anxiety and anger. The little girl who suddenly realizes that she is lost is filled with separation anxiety. Her parents are filled with anxiety also, and all are propelled by the separation to initiate action that will remove the threat to the bond. They search wildly for one another.

Upon being reunited, each member of the family has an immediate reduction of anxiety. The threat to the bond has been removed. A new affect replaces the anxiety quickly, however. Anger, usually expressed openly by the parents and covertly by the child, serves to protect future threats to the bond. The message that is conveyed is clear, "Don't you dare ever do that again!"

As the anxiety-anger response to threats to attachment bonds is rooted in biology, it cannot be brought easily, if at all, under cognitive control. That a mourner understands that death cannot be undone, and that this particular severed bond cannot be restored, does not short-circuit the response. The evolution of the separation anxiety-anger response to a bond that cannot be restored is, to Bowlby, the process of mourning. The brain knows that the loved one is dead. The body does not. The person follows the body's script.

Bowlby's (1980) thinking with respect to the course of mourning includes four stages: numbing, yearning and searching, disorganization and despair, and recovery.

## Numbing

*Numbing*, as described by Bowlby, is similar to Byng-Hall's first script alteration. Viewing it as a defensive variation on information processing, Bowlby suggested that the mourner, who is cognitively aware of the loss, does not respond affectively or behaviorally. It is as if the body needs time to prepare for the onslaught of the mourning process, a process that will, among other things, impact negatively on the body's immune system.

## Yearning and Searching

Denial of the loss, described by Byng-Hall as a script revision, is an expected turn of events in the stage described by Bowlby as *yearning and searching*. During this phase, the mourner is in conflict. At times he or she accepts the reality and finality of the loss, and behaves, feels, and thinks accordingly. At other times, however, the mourner is under the sway of the fantasy of eventual reunion or of having suffered no loss. It is at this point where ego, as defined by Freud (1917), refuses to abandon its libidinal position, and it is here where other theorists suggest the battle between internal and external reality is waged.

Mourners going through the yearning and searching stage typically are filled with both anxiety and anger, the classic emotional responses to threats to an attachment bond. The anger may be targeted at God, at persons thought to have caused the loss, at the mourner for having failed to rescue the loved one, at the loved one for having gone away, or even at well-intentioned persons who remind the mourner of the loss.

As the ebb and flow of the conflict between internal and external reality plays out, the mourner appears to alternate between two scripts. The first, in a sense a replicative one, directs the mourner to think, feel, and behave as if he or she were still in relationship with the dead. The second, a corrective script, alters the field and directs the mourner toward a life without the lost loved one.

People tend to follow the logic of their internal scripts and to ignore the dominant societal one. Sixteen-year-old Tommy provides an example. The boy was referred to the school psychologist by his father. The presenting complaint was defiant, angry behavior directed toward the father and his second wife.

Tommy had come to live with his father after the death of Tommy's mother who had succumbed to lung cancer. From the time of the divorce and throughout their time living together, Tommy and his mother had constructed a script that cast the father/ex-husband as the villain in the piece. The mother's death did nothing to alter the script, and perhaps it intensified it. Tommy felt justified in his anger towards the father as well as in feeling proud of his loyalty to his mother and their co-constructed script. His logic: If the father had been a good man, he would not have divorced the mother; if there had been no divorce, the mother would not have been upset; had the mother not been upset, she would not have smoked; had she not smoked, she would not have died. But he was not, she was, she did, she died; the father must be punished.

That Tommy found himself referred to the psychologist is not an unexpected event. Often, in following the logic of their own internal scripts, people are labelled as abnormal by others who follow society's dominant one. It appears to be a nearly universal co-constructed societal script: Follow the demands of external reality; ignore those of internal "truth."

Consider the case of a 50-year-old woman whose college-age daughter had died six months earlier in an automobile accident. The mother apparently was following a "reunion" script one day as she was working in her garden. Looking up from her work, she noticed a young woman driving the same sort of car that had been her daughter's. Convinced that this was her lost child, the mother jumped into her car and followed the young woman— a wholly "sane" response for one who wishes to remove a threat to an attachment bond. To the rest of the observing world, however, the woman was acting "crazy."

The rest of the world, including many in the psychotherapeutic community, also would label those who employ the last two of Byng-Hall's script alterations as pathological. Theorists who work from both an individual (Krupp, 1965) or from a systems perspective (Walsh & McGoldrick, 1991) agree that an overreliance of identification processes leads to less than maximal adjustment to the death of a loved one.

Traditional and family object-relations theories understand that the many variations of identification processes are preceded by introjection. Introjection is an unconscious process through which memory traces of the self and others are stored, assimilated, and organized. As it is an unconscious process, introjection cannot be observed directly.

If one or more introjects is activated, the identification process may begin. Identification has occurred when an introject alters a personality and directs the personality to take on the characteristics of the internalized object (Krupp et al., 1986).

From a psychodynamic perspective, Krupp (1965) suggested that identification on the part of the mourner may take the from of assuming the personality characteristics or the physical symptoms of the deceased. Krupp believed this to be a common phenomenon following the death of a person with whom the mourner had shared a highly ambivalent and conflictual relationship.

At the level of the unconscious, the mourner cannot bury the dead until some sort of resolution around the relationship is attained. Krupp understands identification with the deceased as a method of keeping the dead alive within the mourner. The denial of the reality and permanence of the loss induces the mourner to invest his or her energies on the conflicted past relationship and to ignore relationships in the here and now.

Walsh and McGoldrick (1991) described a family projection process whereby the object of the deceased is, through the process of projective identification, placed onto some family member who is to serve as the "replacement person" for the deceased. Often, the replacement person will take on the role in the service of the family's needs. Eventually, however, the family fails to thrive as they struggle to deny their loss and to relate to the replacement as if he or she were someone else.

While there can be little doubt that persons and families who overuse the processes of identification will be out of step with the culture's dominant bereavement script, their behaviors, thoughts, and feelings are congruent with their own meaning system: He or she must not be allowed to die.

John and his family supply an example. Before becoming known to this author, 61-year-old John had been in psychoanalytic treatment for more than 15 years with a number of professionals for help with what he described as his "anger and melancholy" (Krupp et al., 1986). He viewed himself as incompetent and weak, and lived in fear of "collapsing psychologically" in the face of everyday stress. John related to this internal reality despite the fact that to the external, "rational" world he was a powerfully built person who was highly successful in business and who was loved by his family.

John had introjected an angry, unpredictably punitive object of his father, as well as a weak and incompetent object of himself. These objects, and the scripts that would be needed to express them, lay dormant until the unexpected and untimely death of the father. In some way, the anxiety around the loss elevated the introjects into identification. Obviously, John did not always follow the "incompetent who is doomed to be punished at any time" script. The success of his family and business indicated that he had at least one other constructed meaning about who he was. Yet, the "can do" script seemed artificial, ego-alien, and simply a role that John could at times assume. John felt "at home," ego syntonic, with the "incompetent" script, however.

John had introjected two other self-objects of note. The first was a needy person who needed to be nurtured continually, and the second was a compulsive caregiver. John projected the introject of the needy object onto his daughter, and oftentimes identified himself with the caregiver introject. As predicted by family systems theory (Kerr & Bowen, 1988), the daughter was not a passive screen onto which John projected the object. Over time, she came to be so in need of the father's nurturing that she felt, unconsciously, unable to assume a fully adult role. It was not until her decision to marry that her negative view of herself became overt. So fearful was she of her inability to function in the adult roles of wife and mother, she became prone to severe anxiety attacks and anorexia.

Had John chosen to keep his father alive within himself via a script that was more congruent with the culture's dominant scripts, neither he nor his daughter would have been considered pathological. There would have been no need for psychotherapeutic intervention had John, for example, understood his father to be burning eternally in the fires of hell and co-constructed a script congruent with that meaning with the others in his family.

## Disorganization and Despair

Bowlby's (1980) third stage, *disorganization and despair*, indicates that for some people there may be a time lag between the time that one script is discarded and a replacement constructed. In Bowlby's terms, mourners become disorganized and depressed during that period of time when they no longer define themselves in terms of the relationship with the deceased but have yet to redefine themselves in other terms. In Byng-Hall's paradigm, this is analogous to an attempt at an improvisational play, an attempt that fails badly. Without a script to direct feelings, thoughts, and behaviors, the mourner feels alone and confused. There is no meaning system around the fundamental question of "who am I?"

Therapists who work with bereaved clients know well the markers that indicate that this "between scripts" phase either has or has not yet begun. From a meaning system-scripting perspective, there is a world of difference between clients in different stages of mourning.

A 37-year-old woman who had been widowed unexpectedly five years prior to entering treatment exemplifies the tenacity of old scripts. Among her concerns were her extreme reactions to any romantic attentions from men. She was confused at her sense of guilt when a male colleague asked her to join him for a cup of coffee after work. After much work she finally understood her reaction: "I still feel married to Jim. I would never get involved in an extramarital affair!" Although five years had passed since the death of her husband, this client was actively following the "married person" script that she and her husband had co-constructed during their time together. Of course dating was out of the question. She was a married woman.

Difficult for the therapist is that part of bereavement work that involves helping the mourner with the obsessive review (Parkes & Weiss, 1983). This is a process that allows the mourner to bring up painful memories, to think and talk about each and every one of them, to experience the pain of the memories, and finally, to erase them as lines in the script. If the specific memories and assumptions of the old script dredged up during the obsessive review change over time, the therapist understands that the script is in the process of being rewritten. If the same lines from the old script continue to be considered, the mourner is not in the process of altering the old script or of reconstructing a new one.

Much different than that of the young widow is the case of the 63-year-old widower. Up until the time of his wife's death, he and she had written a script that starred two active and productive persons who were both lovers and friends to one another. Currently, he was acting out a script that had him depressed and immobilized. Not only could he not enjoy doing the things he once loved doing, he could not even think of anything that he might enjoy doing now, or had enjoyed in the past, or might enjoy in the future.

This man was not clinging to an old internal script that was at variance with external reality. He was between scripts. Without a script, he had nothing to direct the course of his life.

## Recovery

From a traditional perspective, **recovery** from bereavement does not imply a return to a previous state, but the creation of a new state in which the mourner's internal truth generally matches external reality, and in which the person can function well and enjoy life (Genovese, 1992).

That scripts have been created to direct the lives of mourners following the loss of loved ones is indicated along three axes.

The first of these involves the construction of an intellectual acceptance. For many mourners, rewriting scripts that include intimacy with others is frightful. Until the mourner has accepted a story—written a script—that "explains" why the previous loss has occurred, he or she will be loathe to be placed in danger of losing a new attachment. Recovery is predicated on the scripting of "Why it happened, and I understand," and not on the "truth" of the script. Failures to construct the explanatory script, and the absence of behaviors that indicate the following of an "It is safe to love" script are contraindicators of growth.

An emotional acceptance script also is needed. Such a script directs the mourner's belief system in the direction of being in control over the grief, pain, and remorse that dominated prior to script revision. Indicative of this sort of script construction is a gradual change in the content of the previously described obsessive review.

Finally, an identity script is called for. This script allows the mourner to answer the fundamental "Who am I?" question without reference to the deceased. It directs the mourner's actions, thoughts, feelings, and interactions with others to a life that is satisfying and fulfilling. It is a script that has buried the lost loved one, who may now exist only as a pleasant memory of bygone love. A sweet memory, yes. An active player in the newly constructed script, no.

## SUMMARY

This chapter claims neither a traditional nor a constructionist point of view. It attempts to break with tradition by depathologizing certain bereavement reactions. The dichotomy of importance is not the normal/abnormal one, but rather that of internal and external reality.

## REFERENCES

Atwood, J.D., & Genovese, F. (1993). *Counseling single parents.* Alexandria, VA: American Counseling Association.

Bowlby, J. (1980). *Attachment and loss, vol. 3: Loss.* New York: Basic Books.

Byng-Hall, J. (1991). Loss and the family: A systemic perspective. In F. Walsh & M. McGoldrick (Eds.), *Living beyond loss: Death in the family* (pp. 130–143). New York: W.W. Norton.

deShazer, S. (1991). *Putting difference to work.* New York: W.W. Norton.

Freud, S. (1917). In W. Gaylin (Ed.), *Psychodynamic understanding of depression* (1983) (pp. 50–69). New York/London: Jason Aronson.

Gagnon, J.H. (1990). Scripting in sex research. *Annual Review of Sex Research, 1,* 1–39.

Genovese, F. (1992). Family therapy and bereavement counseling. In J. Atwood (Ed.), *Family therapy: A systemic-behavioral approach* (pp. 91–104). Chicago: Nelson-Hall.

Hoffman, L. (1981). *Foundations of family therapy: A conceptual framework for change.* New York: Basic Books.

Hoffman, L. (1988). A constructivist position for family therapy. The Irish *Journal of Psychology, 9*(1), 110–129.

Kerr, M.E., & Bowen, M. (1988). *Family evaluation*. New York: W.W. Norton.

Krupp, G. (1965). Identification as a defense against anxiety in coping with loss. *International Journal of Psychoanalysis, 46.*

Krupp, G., Genovese, F., & Krupp, T.(1986). To have and have not: Multiple identifications in pathological bereavement. *Journal of the American Academy of Psychoanalysis, 14*(3), 337–348.

Krupp, G., Genovese, F., & Krupp, T. (1988). Role of identification in pathological bereavement: Individual and multiple. In E. Chieger (Ed.), *Grief and bereavement in contemporary society* (pp. 97–112). London: Freund.

Lamm, M. (1969). *The Jewish way in death and mourning*. New York: Jonathan David.

Lindemann, E. (1944). Symptoms and management of acute grief. *American Journal of Psychiatry*, 101.

Nichols, M.P., & Schwartz, R.C. (1991). *Family therapy: Concepts and methods* (2nd ed.). Boston: Allyn and Bacon.

Parkes, C.M., & Weiss, R.S. (1983). *Recovery from bereavement*. New York: Basic Books.

Rando, T.A. (1984). *Grief, dying, and death: Clinical interventions for caregivers*. Champaign, IL: Research Press.

Sanders, (1989). *Grief: The mourning after*. New York: John Wiley and Sons.

Walsh, F., & McGoldrick, M. (1991). Loss and the family: A systemic perspective. In F. Walsh and M. McGoldrick (Eds.), *Living beyond loss: Death in the family* (pp. 1–29). New York: W.W. Norton.

Watzlawick, P. (1978). *The language of change: Elements of therapeutic conversation*. New York: Basic Books.

Watzlawick, P. (1984). *The invented reality*. New York: W.W. Norton.

White, M., & Epston, D. (1990). *Narrative means to therapeutic ends*. New York: W.W. Norton.

Winderman, L. (1989). Generation of human meaning key to Galveston Paradigm: An interview with Harlene Anderson and Harold Goolishan. *Family Therapy News, 20*(6), 11–12.

# Index

# CONTRIBUTORS

Nancy Cohan, M.A., is the supervising social worker of the Family Mediation Project at Children's House in Mineola, Long Island, New York.

Susan Dershowitz, M.A., is a family therapist and the Assistant Dean of Students at Hofstra University, Hempstead, New York.

Audrey Freshman, C.S.W., CAC, is the Clinical Program Director at TEMPO Group, Inc., an outpatient substance abuse treatment program located in Woodmere, New York. She is also an adjunct professor of marriage and family therapy at Hofstra University, Hempstead, New York.

Frank Genovese, Ph.D., is a school psychologist at Xaverian High School and an adjunct professor of marriage and family therapy at Hofstra University. He is a Clinical Member of the American Association for Marriage and Family Therapists and is an Approved Supervisor in the same organization. He has written extensively in the area of bereavement.

John Mince, Ph.D., is a school counselor at Three Village High School in Setauket, New York, and adjunct professor of marriage and family therapy at Hofstra University. He is a Clinical Member of the American Association for Marriage and Family Therapy and is an Approved Supervisor in the same organization.

Michele Olsen, M.A., M.S.W., is a family therapist, currently interning at Schneider's Children's Hospital, a division of Long Island Jewish, Great Neck, New York.

Joan Ruiz, M.A., is a family therapist in private practice in Long Island, New York.

Ann Marie Sturniolo, M.A., P.D., is a family therapist and child development specialist at Hicksville Counseling Center, a division of Family Service Association of Nassau County, Long Island, New York.

Estelle Weinstein, Ph.D., is the Coordinator of the Graduate Programs in Health, Hofstra University, Hempstead, New York. She has published extensively on adolescent sexuality, is a clinical member of the American Association for Marriage and Family Therapy, and is certified by the American Association of Sex Educators, Counselors, and Therapists (AASECT) as a sex educator and counselor.

# ABOUT THE EDITOR

**_Joan D. Atwood, Ph.D., C.S.W.,_** is a social psychologist and the co-ordinator of the graduate program in marriage and family therapy at Hofstra University, Hempstead, New York. She is a certified sex counselor and social worker and has a private practice in Rockville Centre, New York. She has done extensive research in the areas of couple and family therapy and human sexuality, has published numerous articles, and has made professional presentations on subjects in these fields.